PLEASURE BOUND

PLEASURE BOUND

VICTORIAN SEX REBELS AND THE NEW EROTICISM

Deborah Lutz

W. W. NORTON & COMPANY  New York • London

Printed in the United States of America
First Edition

For information about special discounts for bulk purchases, please contact
W. W. Norton Special Sales at specialsales@wwnorton.com or 800-233-4830

Manufacturing by Courier Westford
Book design by JAM Design
Production manager: Devon Zahn

Library of Congress Cataloging-in-Publication Data

Lutz, Deborah.
Pleasure bound : Victorian sex rebels and the
new eroticism / Deborah Lutz. — 1st ed.
p. cm.
Includes bibliographical references and index.
ISBN 978-0-393-06832-0 (hardcover)
1. Sex customs—Great Britain—History—19th century.
2. Artists—Great Britain—Sexual behavior. 3. Great Britain—
Social life and customs—19th century. I. Title.

HQ18.G7L88 2011
306.770942'09034—dc22

2010027029

W. W. Norton & Company, Inc.
500 Fifth Avenue, New York, N.Y. 10110
www.wwnorton.com

W. W. Norton & Company Ltd.
Castle House, 75/76 Wells Street, London W1T 3QT

1 2 3 4 5 6 7 8 9 0

For P.J.L.

Contents

Acknowledgments

WANT TO BEGIN by expressing my gratitude to my sister, Pamela Lutz, whose tenderness provides a backdrop to all my best work. I owe Maggie Nelson a great debt for being a brilliant and enthusiastic reader of this book and for helping me to understand more about pleasure. Benjamin Friedman has my gratitude for his unwavering attention to the minute and for his special ability to locate clusters. And for his willingness to share rooms, cities, and architecture with me. I am grateful to Kristofer Widholm for those countless hours we spent in that sunny kitchen, sharing the same workspace. Thanks to my mother for her pride in me. Wayne Koestenbaum taught me about pornography and the erotics of collaboration. Jean Mills shows me how to push through and gives me her fire in the woods. Thanks to Elaine Freedgood for her unflagging encouragement and for telling me about materiality. Melissa Dunn demonstrated the value of stepping outside of academia. Talia Schaffer I thank for her many words of support and for telling me about women's crafts and their collaborative sharing. Conversations about sexuality with Duc Dau and Will Fisher provided me with ideas, early and late. The kindness, wit, and enthusiasm of my colleagues at Long Island University helped me clear space to write; James Bednarz, Rachel Szekely, Tom Fahy, Katherine Hill-Miller, and John Lutz remain especially in my mind. I am grateful to my agent, Renee Zuckerbrot, for her astute professionalism and her cheerful persistence. At W. W. Norton, Amy Cherry enriched this book with her wise and sensitive editing. And thanks to Deborah Rubin, who persuades me to find pleasure, even in what seems most impossible.

I wish to thank Long Island University for two grants that made the pictures possible.

Introduction

"DID I TELL you that I saw Powell when he was here and that he carried off a little picture of mine that I painted in Rome? I have had it photographed and I write a line under it from 'Hermaphroditus' 'Love turned himself and would not enter in,'" penned the painter Simeon Solomon to his intimate friend Algernon Charles Swinburne in the first cool days of autumn in 1869.[1] This little painting depicted Swinburne's poem about the erotic attractions of a fellow who is neither a woman nor a man. Swinburne and Solomon were groping their way toward a new view of the sexual body, at a time when the artists and writers of their set were testing, in their work and lives, the boundaries of sexual propriety. If one was neither female nor male, then might all gender rules get thrown out the window? A month earlier, in a momentous break from tradition, Girton, the first college for women at Cambridge, was established. Respectable gentlemen prowled the night streets of London for young grenadiers to bend them over in a public toilet.

Solomon and Swinburne joined, in 1860s London, two loosely overlapping groups of men who were more than usually involved in questions of erotic freedom and expression. Not only did many of them navigate the fringes of sexual deviance with their bodies—frequenting flagellation brothels, sleeping with a best friend's wife, cruising for male-male anonymous sex—but they carried the pleasures of the body into their work. Rather astonishingly, out of these two clans—the Cannibal Club and the Aesthetes—sprang most of the sexually themed writing and painting (including out-and-out pornography) of the latter half of the nineteenth century. Much of what they dipped their hands into feels strangely modern to us today. Dante Gabriel Rossetti painted sickness and death with sensual longing. Cropping up are memoirs penned solely to recount sexual exploits, failures, and torment. Richard Burton brought out how-to manuals on sex positions, like a Victorian Dr. Ruth. Littered throughout their work are glimmerings of what feels like the future: the femme fatale, S-M implements, Christian symbolism turned homoerotic.

Yet all the while these fellows remained deeply dyed in Victorian thinking and being—steeped, even in their acts of rebellion, in their contemporary scene. Forming the Pre-Raphaelite Brotherhood in 1848, the young artists Dante Gabriel Rossetti, John Everett Millais, and William Holman Hunt made a gesture of defiance against the establishment's adoration of painters before Raphael—the master of three-dimensional, Renaissance perspective. Rossetti and his "brothers" (which also included his sister Christina) called themselves "pre-Raphael" because they imitated the flat, one-dimensional perspective of the quattrocento (fifteenth-century Italy) artists, including painters like Fra Angelico whose style seemed splendidly primitive alongside the floridity of Raphael. The Brotherhood had largely broken up by 1853, but in the early 1860s another set, this one more sensually attuned and politically radical, began to pool around Rossetti.

With a darkly languid, elusively symbolic sophistication, and with new members such as the painters Edward Burne-Jones, William Morris, James McNeill Whistler, Simeon Solomon, and the poets Christina Rossetti and Swinburne, this group turned aesthetic or, as some scholars term it, entered their "Aesthetic Pre-Raphaelite" period. By the time Swinburne imported the term "art for art's sake" (first rule for budding aesthetes) to the English public from France (*l'art pour l'art*) in 1868, their poems, paintings, and designs had begun unsettling critics and startling the public with their strange, enigmatic inwardness. Had they brought these works home from some alien land? Had they emerged from diseased minds? Foreign as they appeared, much of the scandal and absorption that developed around Rossetti and his clan arose not so much from these works' unfamiliarity but rather because they called up an uncomfortable familiarity, exposing troubles that ran beneath the surface of the larger social fabric: the just-stirring struggle for women's emancipation, the dissolution of traditional religions into more personal expressions of faith, the pressing need to expand definitions of accepted forms of sexual expression.

When Swinburne and young Solomon couldn't be found making a drunken, gleeful ruckus at Rossetti's bohemian soirees at Tudor House, they were likely to be found eating out with the Cannibal Club. A radical dining club and an offshoot of the Anthropological Society formed in 1863 by the explorer Richard Burton, this group brought together men of letters and scientists to analyze "deviant" sexual practices and encourage one another in personal and artistic investigations into the outer reaches of sexual behavior. Inhabiting a new liberal looseness that pervaded the salons and dinner parties of educated London, the members Richard Monckton Milnes, James Campbell Reddie, Edward Sellon, George Augustus Sala, and Burton himself wrote and collected most of the erotica and pornography of the 1860s and 1870s, as well as many works of serious scientific and cultural enquiry on sexuality. The prominent atheists Thomas Bendyshe and Charles Bradlaugh found support here for their work against evangelical purity campaigns. Cannibals, not so different from the Aesthetes, reveled in using their iconoclastic, maverick selves to shock their contemporaries out of a certain smug complacency, one that tended toward restraint, silence, and conservatism, especially in matters of sexuality and gender.

I WAS DRAWN to these two groups because I found in them something so rare today among artists and writers: a will to collaborate. Conviviality sparked inspiration for their work; shared rooms in houses and studios kept a seriousness of creative intent circulating. Poets, deeply inspired through looking, wrote verse limning the paintings of their friends. Painters took as themes for their pictures the poems of their friends. Pornography was scribbled by being passed from hand to hand, yielding a text written by six or more fellows. They read aloud to each other; sometimes they had sex with each other. Collaboration involved tenderness, often caresses, and sometimes fierce competition. The fact that so much influential work on sex was done in this wise—as gestures of love—seems to me a useful discovery. I felt close to something almost alive when turning over the letters and memoirs of these men: I was watching a modern approach to sexuality get hammered out through acts of intimacy. Illuminating these collaborative networks became a way for me to think about why and how we, today, have mostly lost this means of doing creative work and of approaching erotic art.

In telling the stories of these radicals, I also wanted to steadily question certain assumptions we have today about the Victorians. We have the tendency to think of them as being at an earlier stage, sexually speaking, than we are at today, as if history were merely a progression from prudery to openness and tolerance. Of course, it's true that, today, certain ways of being sexual are protected by laws that didn't exist in the Victorian period, but it's also the case—as the French philosopher and historian Michel Foucault has taught us—that we find a self-congratulatory pleasure in proving how repressed those Victorians were and how much we've fixed things. With this book, I took a somewhat divergent stance, one attuned to this past culture as not so much "more repressed" than ours, but rather as profoundly *different* from it. Instead of less progressive versions of us, I wanted to understand the Victorians as having their own kinds of blindnesses, pockets of prudery, and openings of freedom. I treat as equal all sexual interests and sensual ways of using the body, without, as much as possible, activating twenty-first-century political attitudes. Could I, I asked myself, place myself and my readers in these drawing rooms, public urinals, and studios and see them without the layers of cultural accretion that veil our eyes today? Could I shake off, temporarily, all the modern "isms"—feminism, postcolonialism, post-Marxism—and step back into this time, studying these men with an unembellished attention and curiosity? Probably not. Still, my task in this book has been to look back with a kind of relaxed gaze, one that *takes in* without making judgments, without trying to squeeze the life I arrest into modern boxes.

And within this sweeping gaze I also relished thinking about *place*. How did these particular spaces of Victorian England—Bertolini's restaurant, the Cremorne Gardens, the Argyll, William Morris's Red House—shape the work and the sex that happened in them? How does the dusky, fog-ridden London park provide a fit backdrop for particular kinds of sexual experimentation and art? How might Victorian locales be thought of as places to do passionate things in? Placing these writers and artists in their settings—in the rooms and streets where they worked and played—became a crucial means for me to tell their stories, to imagine how time-bound places molded men and their art.

The chapters of this book are each structured around a theme, and the book as a whole follows a rough chronology. With each of these themes I created a dual movement. One stroke of this movement: How did the works of these fellows spring out of a very particular historical moment? What do we need to know in order to find ourselves *there*, with them? And the second stroke: How did these groups clear the ground—or even muddy the waters—for later artists and writers to make even bolder statements, to discover even greater sexual freedom? This latter type of historical influence is not easily traceable, and I generally don't make hard arguments about who begat whom. Rather, I wanted to trace little networks of inspiration, small threads that tied movement to movement—from Aestheticism to Decadence to Modernism to twentieth-century sexual identity politics, for instance—or blocks of work by various men that serve to wedge open, to question effectively, to push toward new fields of sexual openness.

Yet the most pressing impetus for this book remains: If we could be young sexual innovators and deviants out for action in Victorian London, *how might that feel*?

PLEASURES TAKEN

CHAPTER ONE

Erotic Melancholia

Darkling I listen; and, for many a time
 I have been half in love with easeful Death,
Call'd him soft names in many a mused rhyme,
 To take into the air my quiet breath;
Now more than ever seems it rich to die,
 To cease upon the midnight with no pain . . . .

—KEATS,
"Ode to a Nightingale"

EBRUARY 10, 1862: Intense fog set in and a deep freeze spread across England, snapping the telegraph wires up north, on the Malton and Thirsk Railway line. At around ten in the evening, feeling the world pressing in, the young artist Lizzie Siddal deliberately swallowed a massive overdose of laudanum and, floating off in an opium trance, stretched herself out on her bed to die. Her husband, Dante Gabriel Rossetti, had gone out around nine to the Working Men's College, where he taught art classes. Returning at eleven-thirty to their house in Blackfriars—a structure jutting right up from the dark currents of the Thames—he found his thirty-two-year-old wife sunk into an unnatural unconsciousness, the empty laudanum bottle next to her. Rossetti frantically called a nearby doctor, who came immediately and, unable to rouse her, began pumping her stomach. Other doctors were summoned. But it was soon clear that all effort was too late. She died in the early morning hours of Tuesday, February 11. As she lay in her simple box, Rossetti, in a passionate act of contrition and grief, added to the coffin a manuscript of his poems. "I have often been writing at these poems when Lizzie was ill and suffering, and I might have been attending her, and now they shall go," Rossetti reasoned to his fellow Pre-Raphaelite painter Ford Madox Brown.[1] A true sacrifice for a poet: the publication of the poems had already been announced, and he consigned his only copy to the tomb. The added loss of the poems would signal, Rossetti felt, his undying love, his desire never to forget. His inspiration for writing would be walled into darkness with her, his grief told him. Still, this wasn't fully true. After a time, the loss of his poems came to haunt him, as did the absence of Lizzie, except she was gone forever. Had the notebook begun to decompose, deeply buried in the arms of a corpse? Were worms eating his verses? There underground, on the other side of death, were his words still legible? Lizzie's leave-taking remained irrevocable. But his poems, could they be revived?

Seven and a half years after his wife's interment, Rossetti decided he wanted his poems back. Not willing to undertake the gruesome task himself, he enlisted one of his less scrupulous friends to recover the book, bound in rough gray calfskin. "I feel disposed, if practicable," he wrote to Charles Augustus Howell, "by your friendly aid, to go in for the recovery of my poems if possible, as you proposed some time ago. Only I

Dante Gabriel Rossetti, around 1863, when he began working on *Beata Beatrix*, after Lizzie's death. Photographed by C. L. Dodgson, who wrote under the pseudonym Lewis Carroll. *Hulton Archive, Getty*.

should have to beg *absolute* secrecy to *every one*, as the matter ought really not to be talked about."[2] He applied successfully to the home secretary, who happened to be an old friend, for an exhumation license. In October of 1869, Lizzie Siddal's grave in Highgate Cemetery was dug up, her coffin pried open. Howell led the grisly expedition, with the help of some gravediggers, a lawyer (to make sure no secret wills or legal documents that might have been buried with her were destroyed or taken), and a doctor (to be certain no disease would cling to the manuscript and infect those who touched it). The ghoulish scene is easy to imagine—the group of men pressing around the dark hole, the notebook raided from the rotten tomb, the long-dead body of the lovely woman bereft of its artistic significance. The manuscript emerged in bad shape. "Soaked through and through," with a terrible smell of decomposition clinging to it, the book could hardly be opened.[3] Leaves adhered together, and the poem Rossetti wanted most had "a great wormhole right through every page of it."[4] Still, his poems had been exhumed, emerging from the grave: revivified, back from the dead.

Howell recounted that, when the lid was wrenched open, "all in the coffin was found quite perfect."[5] His words have gone down in legend—although they are actually quite ambiguous—to signify that Lizzie's body was preserved by all the opium she took; her pale visage intact; her red hair holding its shimmer. She has been imagined as being as captivating in death as she was in life, a continuation of all the painted images of her. Although it's impossible to tell whether this was true, and in fact it's quite unlikely, still, over these many years she has indeed been preserved. Whereas in life she was just another virtually unknown female artist, whiling away her time like so many other working-class women who had no power and little voice, only to vanish utterly upon her death, today her face is famous. Ghost-like, Lizzie stares out at us from paintings hung in the most illustrious galleries around the world; people who will never know her name have her countenance etched in their memories. Lizzie's trace remains, an outline of her cheek, a turn of her neck caught in oils, struck forever in a momentary expression.

LATER GENERATIONS HAVE not forgiven Rossetti for disturbing his wife's rest in the service of his own fame. Yet there is a strange logic to these events. Imaginatively, it seems right that his poems should have passed through the grave, with the miasma of decay still clinging to them. Well before his wife's death, even before he met her, Rossetti's writing and paintings carried a rich load of themes that brought death, revivification, sensuality, and inspiration together. In some sense, all art that persists has a relation to death, since it outlasts the demise of its creator and the disappearance of the society from which it developed. Art museums house little bits of life plucked out of the tide of relentless time, giving voice to the death that is behind, ahead, and all around us. But the Aesthetes, and indeed the Victorians, made the relationship between art and death more concrete—their art often depicted death. The elaborate mourning culture of the Victorians—represented famously by Queen Victoria and her lugubrious, public grieving for her husband, Prince Albert—included drawing, sculpting, or photographing the just-dead body. Aesthetes studied, in their work, this lingering over the dead body. With their art they began to consider the sensuous, erotic implications of mourning: the one who grieves excessively covets the body. Taking as their subject the tinge of melancholy that ran through the period, they drew out its inherent sexuality.

JUST BEFORE CHRISTMAS in 1861, Rossetti was making a delicate pencil sketch of an unwell, unhappy Lizzie. Light strokes score the paper: in a seated pose, her head upturns on a long, stemlike neck, throat almost exposed. Large eyes hidden under heavy lids, lips opening, she seems entranced, possibly filled with overwhelming pleasure. Rossetti sketched her as Beatrice—the beloved muse of the poet Dante—as he had done many times before. Rossetti learned to revere Dante early on, especially Dante's unrequited love for Beatrice, and the yearning, inspiration, and pain Dante drew from it. His father, Gabriele Rossetti, a distinguished Dante scholar, named his son after the Florentine poet. Gabriele focused his research on the monumental *Divine Comedy*, but his son began his work on *La Vita Nuova* (*The New Life*), autobiographical poems, with commentary, about Dante's own spiritual, ethereal love for Beatrice, a passion never touched by the sensuous gratifications of the earth. Dante held her up as an impossible ideal: she was the vehicle for the pure goodness of the world, the divine. Her death at the age of twenty-four only increased Dante's ardor, inspiring him to draw poetry out of grief. After Beatrice's death Dante imagined, in heartbreakingly moving passages from the *Paradiso* section of the *Divine Comedy*, finally meeting her celestial form in heaven. Drawing Lizzie as Beatrice, just a few months before her suicide, seems tragically prophetic. She would soon become another woman to be desired without hope of satiation. And by December 1861, it must have been easy to conceive of Lizzie on the other side of death; she was so morosely depressed and ailing, so clearly slipping away.

Rossetti always felt himself drawn to the ill. The sickly can have a gravitas; life appears both weightier for them and more transparent, lighter. Part of the attraction for Rossetti came from his generous, benevolent nature. When confronted with a passive, infirm creature, he felt a tenderness come over him, a need to care for and nurture. Lizzie Siddal was a sorrowful, dependent woman; at least this is how Rossetti liked to see her. As a working-class girl—her father had an ironmongery business and she had jobs in dressmaking and millinery—Rossetti and his middle-class, intellectual family were separated from her by great gulfs of difference in status. Lizzie wanted to become an artist herself, and one of the few ways women could move closer to this dream was working as an artist's model. Walter Deverell, Rossetti's friend who first discovered Lizzie making bonnets in a Leicester Square shop in 1850, described her as "stupendously beautiful . . . magnificently tall, with a lovely figure, a stately neck, and a face of the most delicate and finished modelling . . . exactly like the carving of a Pheidean goddess."[6] The Pre-Raphaelites snapped her up because she was a "stunner"; her gleaming coils of riotous red hair, translucent skin, and hooded dreamy eyes were their ideal of female beauty—wild, a bit sickly, with a remote gaze. As radical, avant-garde artists, they fell in love with extremes, with the mad, the strange, the shocking. The Pre-Raphaelite painter Ford Madox Brown noted her oft-ill appearance with admiration, "looking thinner and more deathlike and more beautiful and more ragged than ever."[7] She had a "look" that the Romantic poets, particularly Lord Byron, made attractive among "bohemian" writers and artists: blooming good health was for the materialistic bourgeoisie. Self-defined outsiders suffered glamorously, misanthropically, for their art, in defiance of conventions. Waif-thin, they implied by their pallid demeanor that they were perpetually wounded by the emptiness of the world, always ready to leave it in all its worthlessness. Such beauty needed salvation: Rossetti thought of himself as the prince who would swoop down and carry off the poor girl, caught up in the drab life of health-crippling work, or of unspecific sickness and weariness, or deep depression and black humors (all of which Lizzie did suffer, at one time or another).

It took nine years for Rossetti to step up to the mark and finally marry Lizzie—they met in 1851, married in 1860. Many were convinced she would become just another mistress from the lower orders, a popular practice among the group (Madox Brown and James McNeill Whistler, for instance, both had working-class mistresses). Middle-class gentlemen like Rossetti didn't marry girls from Lizzie's station. She was very sick when Rossetti finally succumbed, an event that had been, in his own words, "deferred almost beyond possibility."[8] Her health "constantly failing," she appeared "ready to die daily and more than once a day."[9] It was almost as if he had begun to find her irresistible as death pulled her away. She became a kind of buried treasure, just out of reach, with deep stores of potential value. Life was more intense as it was just leaving.

What was wrong with Lizzie? The medical profession in the nineteenth century was appallingly ill informed. Was it just that she worked too much at her drawing and painting (as one doctor thought—unwell from "mental power long pent up and overtaxed"—following a prevailing opinion that women were constitutionally "delicate" and that mental and creative labor was unhealthy for them)?[10] Did a curvature of the spine cause all this trouble? Or perhaps that romantic, wasting disease—consumption? Opinions abounded, and there doesn't seem reason enough to lend any of them credence. Doctors agreed, however, that giving her laudanum—tincture of opium—to cure her troubles was a good idea. A Victorian magical cure-all, laudanum was used for any kind of pain, sleeplessness, or mental torpor; it was even added to some baby formulas. Lizzie quickly settled into serious addiction, so easily done with opium (and its modern form, heroin) with its dark moods and nightmarish withdrawals, adding substantially to her other bodily and mental woes.

Ill-fated almost from the start, their marriage was struck by disaster a mere year in. On May 2, 1861, Lizzie gave birth to a full-term, stillborn baby. Succumbing immediately to a combination of grief, postpartum depression, and a bad dream of opiate doses, she never truly recovered. When the painter Edward Burne-Jones (still Edward Jones at this date and not to become Burne-Jones until the 1880s) and his wife, Georgie, dropped by for a visit, they discovered Lizzie rocking an empty cradle, cautioning silence so as not to wake the child. That was Lizzie's state when Gabriel drew her in December; by February she had taken her fatal overdose. Rossetti and his friends covered up the suicide, calling it an accidental overdose, worried as they were about the immoral stigma of suicide. But it later came out that she left a note, either pinned to her nightgown or on the bedside table, asking Gabriel to take care of her youngest brother.

"BEATRICE IS GONE up into high Heaven, / The kingdom where the angels are at peace," Dante wrote. When death becomes aestheticized—is imagined in an artwork or as an idea—it comes to represent the poignancy of fleeting life: even the young, the most beautiful are destined to disappear utterly. In death, all of the pathos of Lizzie's illness, all the pain of yearning for her, was crystallized and frozen in time. The wound would always bleed; the affliction would forever spark inspiration. Lizzie became Rossetti's Beatrice, the unchangeable muse, always youthful and lovely.

Late in 1863, Gabriel took up the sketch of Lizzie as Beatrice, put it down again, and then, in 1865, began to turn it into a full-scale oil. It was to become his signature painting, considered by many art critics to be his greatest. He worked on *Beata Beatrix*—Blessed Beatrice—off and on until 1870, finding it difficult to call it finished. As he slowly added layers of paint, then rubbed parts out, mused on its meaning, and finally put down more color, the composition came to represent a process of mourning, the kind of perpetual yearning that Freud was to call "melancholia" in his classic essay of 1917, "Mourning and Melancholia." The painting makes manifest the pull Rossetti felt from the dead, the call he continued to hear. When in a state of melancholia, according to Freud, the lost person is so fully internalized that the whole world comes to take on the tone of that loss. From youth, Rossetti's open, easy temperament could often tip into depressive, irritable moods, which he called the "blue devils" or the "shadowed valley." "The black visitant" was another term he used, imaginatively linking his states of mind to gothic, demonic stories. After Lizzie's death, his dark side grew more pronounced. He became a laudanum and chloral hydrate abuser, taken primarily for insomnia, but also for depression, delusions, and paranoia. Around the time Rossetti returned to *Beata Beatrix*, his friend John Marshall reported, "For two years he *saw* her ghost every night!"[11]

While painting her was a means to try to hold on to a connection with her, Rossetti also tried more obvious methods to keep in touch. In December 1864, he attended his first séance, arranged by the Davenport brothers, traveling spiritualists who claimed to be able to converse with the dead. Spiritualism was in vogue in the 1850s and 1860s, and even many quite respectable and rational people believed that messages from the departed could be rapped out from tables (a rap on table or floor was a standard indication of a spirit's presence) or spoken through mediums in a trance. The queen herself was to conduct séances in an attempt to converse with the spirit of her husband, Prince Albert, after his premature death in 1861. At his rambling, labyrinthine Cheyne Walk mansion, Tudor House,

Rossetti began to hold his own spiritualist gatherings, where he believed Lizzie spoke to him. "It seems Gabriel's wife is constantly appearing (that is, rapping out things) at the séances at Cheyne Walk—William affirms that the things communicated are such as only she could know," wrote one skeptical friend.[12] In 1869, just around the time he exhumed his poems, Rossetti found himself obsessed with suicide (which he would attempt, in 1872, by taking an overdose of laudanum, like Lizzie). Contemplating throwing himself off a cliff into a whirlpool—called the "Devil's Punch Bowl"—when staying in Penkill, Scotland, he saw strange signs of doom everywhere he looked. While he was out on a walk, a chaffinch flew up and perched on his hand. He became convinced it was Lizzie's spirit, warning him of impending disaster.

Beata Beatrix speaks of these haunted thoughts, departing greatly from his other work of this period. The woman depicted isn't the stylized Rossetti type—pouty, lush, with great waves of heavy, frizzy hair that exude a buzzing sexuality, all done in thickly laid, vibrant color (for instance, *Helen of Troy* [1863] and *Lady Lilith* [1868]). These paintings more clearly earn the label of "erotica," awash with sexual connotations. The spectator wants to walk into the decorative world of surfaces, with their carnal beauty worn on their sleeve. It's a leisurely ravishment; the viewer can take what she wants and leave uncomplicatedly. But *Beata Beatrix* works its magic in a more nuanced way. It troubles, mesmerizes. The picture glows, but in a misty film, as if the moody light will soon be extinguished. Lizzie as Beatrice doesn't have the radiant, hot skin tones of Rossetti's beauties; but rather, there is a heaviness, even a grayness, about her face. Her eyes are closed; her hands lie passively in front of her, palms turned up. Spectral figures pause in the background. Rossetti catches the moment when Beatrice gains divinity—in other words, when she dies. Rossetti describes this instant as her spirit "suddenly rapt from Earth to Heaven."[13] This is a beautiful death, a direct passage from ecstasy to transcendence, seemingly without pain or regret, except for the ones left behind.

The text for *Beata Beatrix* comes from Dante's *Lamentations* (Rossetti usually added a quotation to his paintings): "How doth the city sit solitary, that was so full of people! How is she become as a widow!" In a letter to the purchaser of the painting, Rossetti explains its context: "You will remember how much Dante dwells on the desolation of the city in connection with the incident of her death, and for this reason I have introduced it, as my background, and made the figure of Dante and love passing through the street and gazing ominously on one another, conscious of the event . . . whilst the bird, a messenger of death, drops a poppy between the hands of Beatrice. She sees through her shut lids, is conscious of a new world . . . ."[14] He paints Beatrice and medieval Florence, but he also depicts Lizzie and mid-nineteenth-century London. London mourns Rossetti's lost wife. It becomes haunted by her absence. Perhaps the poppy symbolizes opium? And the bridge in the background, might it be Blackfriars Bridge, which spanned the Thames just behind the house they lived in when married? Possibly it was a comfort for Rossetti to envision the death of his wife this way, as ecstatic and without torment, erotic even, in the way that so much religious art of the past can be, like Gian Lorenzo Bernini's sculpture *The Ecstasy of Saint Theresa* (1652), where spiritual ecstasy appears no different from orgasm. The painting holds Lizzie eternally, wrapped in the amber of the image, always dying and perpetually to be yearned for.

MELANCHOLY BECAME ALMOST a national means of expression for the Victorians, a major subject for art, literature, and design. Queen Victoria's unending grief after the death of her husband continued the melancholy tone for a nation whose most loved poet, Alfred Tennyson—given the poet laureateship in 1850—had taken the elegiac as his dominant theme and tone almost from the beginning. Still today, Tennyson remains the master poet of melancholy. As a young man forming his poetic voice he, too, had suffered a grievous loss. Tennyson's best friend and the love of his life, the brilliant young scholar and poet Arthur Hallam, died of a stroke when visiting Vienna, at the age of twenty-two. This death opened a wound in Tennyson's consciousness that never closed and profoundly affected his poetic vision, bringing to it a bittersweet sorrow. Tennyson's fame came from a miraculous poem, as long as a novel, begun on the very day he heard of Arthur's death, and eventually titled *In Memoriam A.H.H.* (in memory of Arthur Henry Hallam) and published in 1850. One long struggle to cope with Hallam's death, to eulogize him, to keep his memory alive, *In Memoriam*, written off and on over seventeen years, also works as a record of Tennyson's thoughts on many themes that crowd in: immortality, evolution, geology, religious doubt and faith, his own emergence as an individual and poet. It is a rambling work full of trance, dreams, speculation, love. Tennyson finds a sweetness in savoring grief, as any true melancholic person would. Such relish can be found in "Tears, Idle Tears," which ends thus:

Dear as remembered kisses after death,
And sweet as those by hopeless fancy feign'd
On lips that are for others; deep as love,
Deep as first love, and wild with all regret;
O Death in Life, the days that are no more!

These kisses have an odd texture and temporality. They are dear because no longer possible, even dearer when never possible in the first place, when "by hopeless fancy feigned." Death is likened to first love; both have the depth of intensity, of wildness, of regret. To be in love with death, the poem seems to say, is to feel the deepest love possible. Death, as much as love or the erotic, lingering kiss, is a revelation, a spur, the center of being. A friend described Tennyson as "a man always discontented with the Present till it has become the Past, and then yearns toward it, and worships it, and not only worships it, but is discontented because it is past."[15] Hallam became Tennyson's dead muse, just as Dante had his Beatrice, Rossetti his Lizzie. Rossetti, Burne-Jones, Millais, Holman Hunt, and Swinburne all cherished *In Memoriam* (Rossetti read the entire poem aloud, after midnight, to a large party in 1850), became friends with Tennyson, and created paintings based on his poetry. Not surprisingly, many of the Aesthetes wove Tennyson's melancholy temperament—with its dreamy love of the past and what's gone forever—into the fabric of their thinking.

This thinking always of the dead can be partially explained by the spreading religious doubt of the time, brought on by various strands of modern reasoning and scientific discovery (especially Darwin's 1859 *Origin of Species*). Christians can feel the comfort, when a beloved dies, of imagining him or her in a happier place, still existing, even if in a different form. Such a death need not be lamented, since it is only a passage from one state to another, and a pleasant one at that. Better yet, the beloved would be waiting in the celestial sphere, to be joined eventually by those still on earth. As Christianity lost its hold on the imagination, this solace might disappear. What if people were truly wiped out by death, never to appear again? Actual absence loomed; death brought the despair of the irrevocable. Deep and long mourning could perhaps stave off this permanent annihilation. The dear one had to be grieved endlessly, kept alive in memory, poetry, and painting. The Victorians thus teetered on the edge of modernity, caught in the tension between Christian faith and the nihilism that accepts death as a finality.

Along with new forms of atheism and agnosticism, modernity brought with it an unfamiliar world. The need to hollow out a place within themselves, and their culture, for the dead, for a settled melancholy, came from the Victorians' deep anxiety in the face of change. Industrialization, starting in earnest around 1800 and sweeping across Britain before other parts of the West, stripped much of the familiar from the world the Victorians knew, with startling rapidity. The population of London exploded as country folk streamed in for jobs in factories, offices, and banks, if they were lucky, or, as happened with so many, for a day-by-day struggle on the streets—as prostitutes, crossing sweepers, scavengers of all sorts. Unplanned pestilential slums sprang up, full of ramshackle buildings, while at the same time other neighborhoods reaped the new influx of wealth, becoming glamorous, gated, and guarded. With the industrial revolution came the burdens of newness: railroads, photography, moving images, factories, iron ships, industrial pollution, printing presses, telegraphs, machine guns, and mass manufacturing. Dr. Thomas Arnold, father of the poet Matthew

Arnold, lamented early in the century, "We have been living, as it were, the life of three hundred years in thirty."[16] This pace continued: in 1863 the first underground line opened; in 1878 the first electric street lights lit up the foggy byways. Everything sped up, transformed in a dizzying propulsion forward (or backward, as some thought). Some greeted it with enthusiasm; for others it caused an existential angst that flowered into nostalgia and a deep-set melancholia. With seemingly all around them passing away, as it felt to some, the need to revere the just departed tended to create a culture focused on looking back, on holding on to what couldn't, in the final analysis, be held on to.

ON BREAK FROM Oxford in 1855, Edward Burne-Jones, a shy, loyal, tall, and gawky fellow, with a tendency toward gloominess, rummaged through used bookstalls in his hometown of Birmingham. Even though he was only a twenty-two-year-old student, he already had those mournful, dreamy eyes seen in almost every photo. His best friend was William Morris. The two were a study in opposites. Morris was a blustery, strong-willed man who was to become the founder of the Arts and Crafts design movement, as well as of the first socialist political party in England. The year before, the two had absorbed the already renowned art critic John Ruskin's Edinburgh lectures, which praised the work of the Pre-Raphaelite Brotherhood. Later they stumbled upon an issue of the short-lived journal the *Germ*, which the Brotherhood had produced, and read Rossetti's poem about a just-dead "stunner," gone up to heaven, "Blessed Damozel," and his short story "Hand and Soul," about a youth who devotes himself to art that speaks of his soul. These writings sank deep into their consciousness, and after seeing such Pre-Raphaelite Christian paintings as Millais's *The Return of the Dove to the Ark* and Holman Hunt's *Light of the World*, they felt confirmed in their ambitions to become artists and designers. They would make art with an intensely spiritual tone, but a darkly secret, personal spirituality. It would hark back to earlier types of art, consciously breaking with the popular Victorian style, with its fussy Greek classicism and Renaissance perspective. In those musty tomes in Birmingham, Burne-Jones found what was to be the most important tale of his life: Sir Thomas Malory's *Mort d'Arthur* (1485)—the classic tale of King Arthur and his knights of the Round Table, of Lancelot's perfidy with the gorgeous Queen Guinevere. This strange dreamland of sacrifice, doomed love, a holy, intangible quest was to become Burne-Jones's sacred text, and many of his paintings were to illustrate its fantastic tales.

Burne-Jones and Morris learned their love of the medieval, which was to take center stage in almost all of the work of their lives, first from the Pre-Raphaelites. The group as a whole most often took its inspiration from Italian painting from the 1400s (pre-Raphael), also called the late medieval, early Renaissance period. And Dante was, of course, *the* medieval writer, along with Chaucer, another favorite with Burne-Jones and Morris. Attracted to this distant period's mysteriousness, its inaccessibility, they could fill it with all their own ideals. They imagined it as a more humane time, before industrialization turned people into parts of a materialist machine, before the land had been darkened by factory smoke and divided by railways. Objects made with care and by hand held the mark of the individual workman and were thus more organically alive. Humanity took in stride the sexual and the bawdy, not bottling it up like their contemporaries. All of their dissatisfactions with their own time seemed cured when they imagined themselves in such an idealized medieval setting. What moved Burne-Jones about the King Arthur cycle, however, was the quest for something so sacred that it must not be found. The unfulfilled quest had much in common with another medieval ideal: courtly love. The knight or troubadour turned his worshipping eyes to the good and pure lady, loving her chastely. He based all his noble actions on a desire to please her. Wars were fought for ravishing women, the only reward being the women's favor. A spiritual love, akin to the Christian love of Christ, courtly love glorified constant deferral, desires raging but not released.

Burne-Jones felt something like this obsessive and unconsummated love for Rossetti, whom he worshipped and wanted to emulate. "Clinging tight to Gabriel whom I loved, and would have been chopped up for,"[17] he remarked with macabre relish. In his first years as an artist in London, without work and near to starving, he searched out Rossetti's studio. Much like Lizzie Siddal, he was a working-class kid—his father had a framing shop in Birmingham—and his health was poor. Ned, as Rossetti renamed him, of course needed saving. Rossetti promptly did so, teaching him how to paint and finding patrons for him, even when he could use more himself. "This man could lead armies and destroy empires if he liked," Ned wrote of Gabriel, "how good it is to be with him."[18] One idea Rossetti passed on to him was to paint always his inner vision, ignoring outside pressures. Of all the Aesthetes, Ned was to take this most to heart.

WORSHIPPING FROM AFAR, like the knight's gaze on his liege lady in the courtly love tableau, explains the atmosphere of many Pre-Raphaelite and Aesthetic paintings. The signature women of the school had distant, inward-turned eyes. Such dreamy eyes stare out of the canvases of Rossetti, Burne-Jones, and early John Everett Millais. Silent, still, and wholly unavailable to the viewer, this gaze shows contemplation, broodiness; it expresses either a rich interior life or a kind of emptiness. One of the most famous and haunting of these looks can be found in Burne-Jones's *King Cophetua and the Beggar Maid* (early attempts in 1861–62; others in 1875; completed 1883–84). It caused a sensation at the Grosvenor spring show in 1884: one critic asserted that it "assured finally the painter's claim to the highest place in English art."[19] The story comes from an Elizabethan ballad, taken up by Tennyson in one of his poems of 1842, "The Beggar Maid." The king looks up at the maid (she sits above him in a strange room, crowded and awkward in that flattened Pre-Raphaelite way) in a reverent attitude; she is the true love he has searched for, the world over. He is ready to offer his jeweled crown to her, and all his riches, but his attitude has a sense of defeat to it. This is because the maiden, whose pale skin glows as the main source of light in this blue-and-gray painting full of gloom, appears frozen in a timeless reverie. She is of another world. Her eyes, set in dark, sunken sockets, will never belong to anyone. Although the painting is steeped in an unbearable romanticism, it's also washed in melancholy. Why can't the two ever come together? Some argue that the painting proves Burne-Jones's disapproval of running after wealth: riches have no worth to the beggar. While there may be some truth to this—Burne-Jones did have some socialist leanings; on the death of John Cardinal Newman he exclaimed, "In an age of sofas and cushions he taught me to be indifferent to comfort, and in an age of materialism to venture all on the unseen"—the painting is also about being fascinated by what we can't have, like children who always want the toy the other child plays with, not the one they hold in their lap.[20] The king finds himself entranced by the unattainable woman, and the viewer of the painting becomes the king: yearning, too, but standing even farther outside.

When someone draws away, she or he often seems more desirable, just as a smooth stone appears like a jewel at the bottom of a stream. Death magnifies the desire, turning the loved one into a paradise lost. Freud and his disciple Jacques Lacan had a lot to say about unending desire, but Rossetti, Burne-Jones, and Millais were already at work painting and writing the raw yearning for the lost paradise fifty and more years earlier. Such desire can be taken to the extreme of desiring desire itself—the condition of melancholy. Studying Burne-Jones's painting tells the viewer a good deal about the anatomy of melancholy: here pining forever becomes a state of being, a quality of stillness.

IN EARLY JULY 1851, reeling from the abuse of the critics who called his paintings "monstrously perverse," "decadent," "morbid," "offensive," the most ambitious Pre-Raphaelite, Millais, painted in the countryside near Ewell. Braving biting flies and a hard wind threatening to blow his canvas into the water, he was practicing another Pre-Raphaelite maxim: ultrarealism. Sitting somewhat uneasily amid other aims of the Pre-Raphaelites—the medieval lack of three-dimensionality, which included impossibly crowded spaces and elongated or foreshortened figures—was a need to return to nature and represent it as faithfully as possible. Painting a sparkling stream, Millais labored to represent accurately, in infinite detail, *everything* he saw there. He needed to get down the exact color of underwater mosses in their upwelling toward the surface, the arch of branches bending into the stream, the gray-green of bladelike reeds surrounded by clear current. He was following the advice of John Ruskin, whose *Modern Painters* (volume one published in 1843) was like the gospel to the young Pre-Raphaelites. Artists "should go to Nature in all singleness of heart," Ruskin propounded, "and walk with her laboriously and trustingly, having no other thoughts but how best to penetrate her meaning."[21] This stream painted with such faithfulness to nature was to be the background of the death of Ophelia. Possibly in response to the nastiness of a critic in the *Morning Post* who vituperated, "As long as Messrs Hunt and Millais confine themselves to missal and medicinal subjects, we can bear the infliction, but we must protest against either of them meddling with Shakespeare," Millais chose to illustrate a passage from *Hamlet*.[22] The lovely Ophelia, whose sanity unravels when her father dies, falls into a river while decorating a willow with flowers. Rather than saving herself, she floats downstream, surrounded by flowers, singing while she drowns. Hamlet's mother, Gertrude, describes the scene.

> There is a willow grows askant the brook, . . .
> Therewith fantastic garlands did she make
> Of crowflowers, nettles, daisies, and long purples . . . .
> There on the pendent boughs her crownet weeds
> Clamb'ring to hang, an envious sliver broke,
> When down her weedy trophies and herself
> Fell in the weeping brook. Her clothes spread wide,
> And mermaidlike awhile they bore her up,
> . . . like a creature native and endued
> Unto that element.

Millais's task lay in marking the moment, through color both intense and translucent, when Ophelia's body dissolves into the glittering water that surrounds her. Woman becomes nature in an epiphanic transformation.

How to express the tragedy, along with the fragility and stillness of the primal strike of death? After spending more than two months on the background, Millais needed to paint in Ophelia. In another uncanny prefiguring, Lizzie Siddal was to be the model. He began by having her lie down and drawing her in pencil, with her head back and mouth opened slightly. Needing to simulate the stream, he had her get into a tin bathtub in his studio, while wearing an antique dress embroidered with silver. Now February, the studio was frigid, and Millais set up candles under the tub, to keep the water warm. When the candles went out, Millais was so absorbed in his painting that he didn't notice. Lizzie became numb in the water and found she couldn't move. Luckily, Millais got her out of the water in time, but the possibility that she could have drowned was frighteningly real, and the chill sent her to bed for days.

Millais's painting envisions Ophelia's last moment as an entrancing array of sensual color, a languorous climax with rich flowers and underwater greenery intensely joining the trance of the lustrous woman dying. Her heavy gown spreads, picked up by the fingers of the current. Hair fanning out like the tendrils of water plants underneath, she begins to sink. With her hands and wrists held above the water in a kind of passive supplication, her parted lips and tilted head show a willingness to be ravished. Death appears as the ultimate ecstasy, its climax reaching a similar intensity as the sexual orgasm.

A few key Aesthetic paintings of eroticized death fed Victorian interest in the theme and forever associated Aestheticism and Pre-Raphaelitism with the sexually macabre. In addition to Rossetti's *Beata Beatrix* and Millais's *Ophelia*, the minor Pre-Raphaelite painter Henry Wallis made a splash at the Royal Academy in 1856 with *The Death of Chatterton*. Chatterton, a struggling poet with the classical features of a Greek god, swallowed arsenic in despair over his failing career. Wallis depicts his idyllic body, draped seductively on a small bed in an attic garret, dead but also perhaps ravished or waiting to be ravished. Rossetti and Swinburne, along with Keats, Shelley, and Wordsworth, took up Chatterton as a tragic emblem of the artist in a world of philistines.

In one of his early poems, well before *Beata Beatrix*, Rossetti began to think about the romantic implications of the death of the young and beautiful. In "The Blessed Damozel" (1848), a young woman has passed away so recently that "the wonder was not yet quite gone / From that still look of hers." Her "eyes were deeper than the depth / Of waters stilled at even," her hair "Was yellow like ripe corn." She is described as being still alive, in heaven, and pining to see and touch her lover. To see him below on the earth,

> . . . she bowed herself and stooped . . .
> Until her bosom must have made
> The bar she leaned on warm.

In death, this damsel ("damozel" is an archaic rendering of "damsel") retains all the shimmering beauty and glow of the living earth. The author describes her as being in a state of erotic yearning and even more desirable after death. He has her envision a mystical consummation with her lover, when he dies:

I'll take his hand and go with him
To the deep wells of light . . . .
We two will lie i' the shadow of
That living mystic tree . . . .

Their bodies will come together in death, and the suffused light of heaven as well as its darkness symbolize orgasm. Sex and death become linked moments. The luminous woman, once she has died, transforms into the muse of the living artist, and mourning for her comes to be an erotic yearning.

Victorian artists came from a long tradition of twinning these two moments of intensity. During the Elizabethan period a slang phrase for orgasm was "to die," and it was in the nineteenth century that the French began to call orgasm *la petite mort*—the little death—perhaps on the heels of Charles Baudelaire's book of necrophiliac poetry, *Les Fleurs du Mal (Flowers of Evil*, 1857*)*. The poetry of John Keats, read avidly by Rossetti, Holman Hunt, Millais, and Burne-Jones, described the moment of death as a climactic swoon, an unbearable "sweet unrest."

What is erotic about death? This question could be asked today of popular television shows such as *CSI: Crime Scene Investigation* (and all its many offshoots, ancestors, and imitations), where beautiful corpses proliferate in glamorous cities, and equally gorgeous professionals piece together the dramatic deaths. Or the goth style minted in the 1980s could be interrogated: why the corpse-pale visage and the reverence for all that is macabre? Or, as many have asked, why those models that fall in and out of fashion, with their skeletal thinness and heroin-induced pasty-green complexions? Sexual climax can have all the emotional finality and drama of death, or at least an imagined death. Orgasm and death are both moments when we lose control of our bodies—when we experience pure being, without the intervention of personality and consciousness. As Georges Bataille writes, eroticism is "assenting to life up to the point of death."[23]

Death is terrifying, but for many Victorian men and women sex was, too. Prevalent evangelical thinking dictated that sex outside of marriage, masturbation, and sodomy all held the taint of sin and corruption, and would lead to everlasting torment in hell. For believers, to dive into this sinful state was reckless, akin in feeling to throwing oneself off a cliff. Those who didn't adhere to such Christian morality had medical opinion to deal with. Most doctors throughout this period, including those who wrote popular books on the topic, claimed that masturbation, also called self-abuse, led to indolence, ruined lives, and possibly madness. It was widely believed that when men expended too much semen, they would suffer from "spermatorrhoea"—"a state of enervation produced, at least primarily, by the loss of semen."[24] Other symptoms might develop: debility, loss of sight, and confusion of ideas. When semen left the body, the thinking went, it took a quantity of life force from a limited pool with it. Thus the "little death" of orgasm. For women, sex could lead to pregnancy, and often enough did, since most forms of birth control carried a stigma. Pregnancy was dangerous in an age when medical knowledge was limited: it was all too easy to die in childbirth. And this is not to mention the burdens, mental and physical, of a large, perhaps unwanted, brood of children.

Diseases picked up through sexual contact could strike the fear of God into even the most severe of atheists. Condoms were rarely used, even when having sex with strangers, and syphilis and gonorrhea were easy to contract. Exact statistics are hard to come by, but an example of its pervasiveness is that in 1864 it was estimated that one-third of the men in the British army were admitted to the hospital for the treatment of gonorrhea or syphilis (and these were just the ones who sought treatment). Gonorrhea was barely recognized as a disease, and the regimen for syphilis was almost worse than the disease itself: regular doses of mercury, which led to cases of poisoning. The terrifying effects of syphilis—the last stages include paralysis, insanity, and death, and the disease could be passed on to future generations—were thought to be deserved punishment for sin, and most believed that it could be caught only by those who sank themselves into the deepest pit of depravity.

SWINBURNE KNEW THE attractions of sexual danger. This was one of the reasons he fell so hard for Richard Burton. And he certainly wasn't the only one. At the heart of the formation of the Cannibal Club was a crazy stag love for Burton—he called the meetings his "orgies." A powerful, athletic man, he cut a forbidding, ultramasculine figure—the sexually experienced world traveler. A scar running the length of his cheek, made by a javelin thrust into his face during an attack by Somalis, gave his handsome face a dark twist. One of Burton's drinking buddies recalled, "He reminded me . . . of a black leopard, caged but unforgiving . . . a countenance the most sinister I have ever seen, dark, cruel, treacherous, with eyes like a wild beast's."[25] The poet Arthur Symons felt "he was gypsy in his terrible, magnetic eyes—the sullen eyes of a stinging serpent."[26] His cousin Elizabeth Sisted remarked that "women fell in love with him by the score, often careless whether their affection was returned or not."[27] Swinburne's love for Burton had in it a desire to be overpowered, mastered—to be subsumed in another.

Swinburne, so often an autobiographical writer (Ezra Pound put it succinctly: "his biography is perfectly well-written in his work"), carried themes of sexual dissolution into his poetry, playing with the traditional gender roles that mark the feminine as the most ready to submit.[28] His gender mobility, in both his personal life and his writing, made him more modern than his cohorts. In their artworks, Rossetti, Burne-Jones, and Millais all projected their sense of death as sensual onto the figures of women, whether it was Beatrice, the beggar maid, Ophelia, or the blessed damozel. These feelings—a rapturous loss of agency and power—were difficult for them to own for themselves, openly, in their need to fit a masculine ideal of bodily and emotional control. Edgar Allan Poe, one of Rossetti's favorite authors, remarked in 1846 that "the death of a beautiful woman is, unquestionably, the most poetical topic in the world."[29] It's doubtful that the beautiful woman found her death poetical. But Swinburne, who affirmed that "great poets are bisexual; male and female at once," littered his stanzas with the erotic deaths of male figures, with an openness to admitting his own desire for an ecstatic loss of self.[30] His figuration of the sex/death coupling makes him the father of a new erotica: artists turning the gaze back on themselves, imagining their own sickly, pale, mortal flesh as worthy of desire. Taking charge of the erotic appeal of their bodies, twentieth-century artists such as Egon Schiele and Frida Kahlo drew their naked selves viscerally marked by mortality—distortions of time and sickness painted with reverent self-love.

Swinburne's verse holds some of this confessional sensuality:

men often fall victim to *la petite mort*. Women might succumb, but their aggressors are either muscular women (the idea of lesbianism enthralled Swinburne) or, perhaps even more subversively, androgynous figures. In his poem "Fragoletta," included in the 1866 *Poems and Ballads* and probably written the year before, the narrator falls into a reverie about an encounter with the eponymous hermaphrodite.

> I dreamed of strange lips yesterday
> And cheeks wherein the ambiguous blood
> Was like a rose's—yea,
> A rose's when it lay
> Within the bud.

He asks where this "mysterious flower" could have come from, and what types of "groves" concealed it. A superficial reading leads to these lips being strange and the blood "ambiguous" because the genitals themselves have a dreamy quality in their indeterminacy. An oral approach occurs, or perhaps the dream of one:

> I dare not kiss it, lest my lip
> Press harder than an indrawn breath,
> And all the sweet life slip
> Forth, and the sweet leaves drip,
> Bloodlike, in death.

Is this a description of cunnilingus or fellatio? Is the "mysterious flower," in its "groves," a penis or a clitoris? Below this initial layer of the poem can be found another one: perhaps it no longer matters, when "the sweet life slip / Forth"? The true strangeness lies not in how the fleshy parts are configured but in the mystery of the sex act itself. Two separate identities come together and, in an emotional overflow that may have a certain violence to it, dissolve into each other. With the orgasm comes the "death" of separateness, bringing a unity:

> Thy mouth is made of fire and wine,
> Thy barren bosom takes my kiss
> And turns my soul to thine
> And turns thy lip to mine,
> And mine it is.

From the intensity of intimacy, full of secret sights, comes the figure of death—a delightful disappearance.

CHAPTER TWO

Erotic Faith

Remember me when I am gone away,
Gone far away into the silent land;
When you can no more hold me by the hand,
Nor I half turn to go yet turning stay.

—CHRISTINA ROSSETTI,
"Remember"

AUTUMN 1858: ONE evening Dante Gabriel Rossetti headed to the Royal Surrey pleasure gardens. Visitors to the popular gardens had the delight of stepping out of the clanging city into the sighing darkness of trees punctuated by the tinkling of a band from the distant music hall. Winding their way past the ornamental fountains, Londoners found that the pathways led to gas-lit garden bars, flickering out of the leafy gloom. At one of these bars Rossetti caught the attention of another drinker. A bold, pretty prostitute with thick, wavy hair the color of corn—what Rossetti and his set would call a stunner—pouted at him from across the room. She cracked nuts and threw the shells in his direction, giggling. Gabriel got up to speak with her, leading to an invitation back to his studio. Rossetti, with his grave, dark, Italian eyes, unruly hair hanging down past his collar, plum-colored frock coat with books stuffed in its capacious pockets, and lounging ways, found it easy to draw others to him, particularly young men who wanted to emulate his charmed "bohemianism" (an idea imported from Paris in the 1840s). It was Rossetti's easy, languid eccentricity that made this pose popular among progressive artists in midcentury London. He naturalized it so that to be a radical artist meant being a kind of "gypsy" outsider who proclaimed independence from the moneygrubbing "philistine" public with their blindness to the beautiful life, their drab suits, and strict appointments in the City.

But Rossetti developed this seductively defiant identity over time. Up until the late 1850s, he had led a fairly chaste, even restrained life. He had just broken off his courtship of Lizzie Siddal (they would reconcile later), and there's no evidence they had yet had a sexual relationship. Rossetti and his siblings were raised staunchly High Anglican, leaning heavily toward Catholicism, in a household of Italian expatriates—his father, a member of the secret revolutionary party of the Carbonari, had been forced to flee after the failed uprising under General Pepe against King Ferdinand I. But his mother was half English, and the four children (Maria, the eldest, then Gabriel Dante—who later reversed his two names—William Michael, and Christina) were brought up in the shadow of the Church of England.

Some of this piousness clung to Gabriel until the late 1850s, when London itself was shaking off a certain puritanism. Not only was religious doubt softening moral rules among progressives in the big city, but the Crimean War led to a loss of respect for the old order among the general public, a result of scathing newspaper reports about aristocratic ineptitude. Nights in the West End relaxed into glamorous revelry. Pleasure seekers crowded the numerous entertainments, with a license to be extravagant in their spending, dancing, drinking, and general dalliance. Places to stage such dissipation proliferated: supper rooms, theaters of all kinds, gin shops, night gardens in the summer. The first music halls had just opened up. Gentlemen could retire to smoking rooms and cigar divans, which often maintained rooms for casual sexual encounters. Gabriel, infected by a new attitude of sexual experimentation, began haunting such places, trying on a new decadent self. He would often dine with a friend "at the Old Cock or at Dick's or at John of Groat's in Rupert Street." After dinner they might head to Leicester Square for the Victorian version of the striptease, the *poses plastiques* where women would re-create classical "scenes" wearing tight, flesh-colored body stockings that made them appear nude. Some of these women were "fast," and Gabriel would buy them negus in exchange for a "pose." As the evening wore on, he and his friend repaired to Piccadilly Salon, which only opened at two in the morning, "where ladies and gentlemen wildly and, I regret to say, generally tipsily, danced to the music of an old piano and fiddle," as one of his drinking buddies, the painter Val Prinsep, recorded.[1]

Contrast this behavior with Rossetti's of 1849. In Paris with Holman Hunt, they found themselves appalled by the cancan at Valentino's, where the dancing women wore no underwear. Gabriel penned some obnoxiously prudish lines about this, addressed to his brother:

> I confess, William, and avow to thee,
>   (Soft in thine ear!), that such sweet female whims

> As nasty backsides out and wriggled limbs
> Are not a passion of mine naturally;
> Nor bitch-squeaks, nor the smell of heated quims.[2]

Rossetti was much more at ease with his sexuality, indeed his whole expansive selfhood, by the late 1850s. The prostitute he picked up from the Surrey gardens became a fixture in his life for many years to come: an artist's model, live-in lover, and friend. Called Fanny Cornforth, her "art name," she was born Sarah Cox, a working-class girl from Sussex. Fanny is the pretty (in a somewhat coarse way) woman, with her flushed face and her slightly thick neck, to be seen in many of Rossetti's paintings of the 1860s: *Regina Cordium*, *Fair Rosamund*, *The Blue Bower*. Fanny's advent in Rossetti's life and her appearance in his paintings mark a key turn in his aesthetic development. By 1860 Rossetti had given up the stoicism, the monkish chastity, of his Pre-Raphaelite phase and had entered the epicureanism of his emerging Aestheticism. The paintings he hung at the 1860 Hogarth Club exhibition boldly state his new interest in beauty for beauty's sake (with no didacticism and a dash of the amoral): the notoriously wicked Lucrezia Borgia (*Borgia*) and the dreamily overripe Renaissance woman from Boccaccio's *The Decameron*, who, because of her promiscuity, has a mouth that has been kissed by many men (*Bocca Baciata*).

GIVEN HIS LATER reputation for libertinism, it is easy to forget that Rossetti started his career as a painter of sacred subjects. When he founded the Pre-Raphaelite Brotherhood in 1848 with Millais and Holman Hunt, their radicalism had only a slight dash of sexuality about it. They were aesthetic and political rebels, at a time when much of Europe was in the throes of bloody revolution. Karl Marx, who was becoming too hot to handle for continental Europe and would be permanently exiled to London in a year, had just put into print, with Friedrich Engels (already living in England), the *Communist Manifesto*. London, relatively peaceful compared with the rest of Europe, saw a mass demonstration of workers in April under the first labor unionists, the Chartists, a protest heavily suppressed, in a state of high fear, by thousands of armed troops.

Still in their twenties and drawn together initially by a shared thinking of themselves as the brightest young stars in painting (an idea the public would soon take up), Rossetti and Hunt posted a manifesto on their Cleveland Street studio wall for their friends to sign. The manifesto created their own subversive hierarchy, based not on any religious or political creed but on a belief only in "man's own genius or heroism." It included a list of "Immortals," which began, rather conventionally, with Jesus Christ and continued with such figures as George Washington, Joan of Arc, Elizabeth Barrett Browning, and over forty others. They affirmed a break with the "British School of Painting," which was "wishy washy to the last degree," as Rossetti's brother William wrote in his history of the group, "nothing imagined finely, nor descried keenly, nor executed puissantly."[3] Thus a secret, collaborative brotherhood was born, the identity of its members cryptically conferred by the "PRB" they worked into the signatures on their paintings.

The secret got out quickly enough, with a row in the press over their "pictorial blasphemy," as a screed in the *Athenaeum* protested.[4] Referring to Rossetti's second major painting—a work with a deliberately primitive spatial cramping that depicted the angel Gabriel announcing to Mary her pregnancy (Rossetti's first major oil was also biblical: *The Girlhood*

The Rossetti family, 1863, photographed by C. L. Dodgson (Lewis Carroll) in the garden at Tudor House, Cheyne Walk. From left: Christina, Maria, Frances (their mother), and Dante Gabriel. *Goblin Market and Other Poems* had been published about a year before this photograph was taken. *Hulton Archive, Getty.*

of Mary Virgin)—and Millais's *Christ in the Carpenter Shop*, the *Illustrated London News* revealed the initials to belong to the "Prae-Raffaelite Brotherhood," "ingenious gentlemen who profess themselves practitioners of 'Early Christian Art'" and "devote their energies to the reproduction of saints squeezed out perfectly flat."[5] Abuse fell especially on Millais's work, which eschewed the stylized idealism of Christ images for physical and historical accuracy: Christ's family as carpenters, with bodies based on living, breathing working men and women, marked by toil and hard living. (Dickens wrote of this painting, in his family magazine *Household Words*, as dealing in "the lowest depths of what is mean, odious, repulsive and revolting. . . . Such men as these carpenters might be undressed in any hospital where dirty drunkards in a high state of varicose veins are received.")[6]

The Pre-Raphaelites sought to see, and show, the old stories with fresh eyes, done up in the excitement of the new egalitarianism: a lowly workman might also represent the savior. In Rossetti's annunciation scene, which he called *Ecce Ancilla Domini!* (Mary's words referring to herself: behold the handmaid of the lord), Mary has just been stirred awake in her bed, her eyes bleary and melancholy (or is she still asleep and having a mystical but somewhat oppressive dream?). She is a tense, sensitive girl—nobody's icon—who sees only trouble ahead. For this Mary and the one in *The Girlhood*, Rossetti used his sister Christina as a model (contrast this with his later use of prostitutes and mistresses), and they work as striking portraits of her in her youth. Thus, in these paintings, Mary appears as a young poet, her countenance complicated by intelligence, character, and a kind of awkward unhappiness. In what is clearly a bedroom scene, the angel Gabriel, hovering close on feet winged with fire, holds a phallic lily, pointed suggestively toward Mary's lap. They are both in states of visible undress, with the angel's long flank exposed, and the viewer feels the erotic charge of the message he delivers to her. Does she want to shoulder the burden of giving birth to the son of God? She doesn't appear to.

These early paintings show Rossetti caught up in a struggle to digest and refashion the faith pressed on him as a child, to make it an expression of his own movement through life. His compulsive need to break with traditions of all sorts, which would lead him in the late 1850s to give up sacred subjects altogether, brought him to take his still active spiritual belief and couch it in the everyday, modern world of his immediate experience. The waning of religious conviction around him cleared an opening for him to localize. The sacred Virgin Mary becomes a surprised girl, uneasy with her body and the role it must play in history. *Ecce Ancilla* manages the most difficult feat of being a biblical picture that has no moral or message. The painting does not say: look at the nurturing peace to be found in Mary's saintly forbearance. It doesn't compel, push, or persuade one to worship, strike a pose of reverence, or feel awed by majesty. Rather, it's about one particular, unhappy girl.

When he started the painting, Rossetti wanted it to be "almost entirely white," as he explained to his brother, William.[7] He was already mulling over the idea that one might not even need to "read" a painting at all, as symbolic (dove, halo, lily), narrative (the story of the annunciation), or personal (a portrait of Christina's budding, strange sexuality? Rossetti's own sexual unease?). It could work simply as a nonabstract formal study of color. Purity of color became Rossetti's watchword as he developed as an artist, achieved through the novel practice of laying down a white background and applying intense color thinly over it. Presaging Whistler's *Symphony in White* of 1862 (both a Rossetti admirer and influencer, Whistler became part of this set when he moved to London from Paris, setting up shop down the street from Rossetti's Cheyne Walk mansion), Rossetti's annunciation signals the beginning of a major shift in thinking. In the late 1840s and early 1850s, he relied heavily on traditional biblical narrative to advance his belief in the mystery of some higher power, something transcendental that we cannot know but that gives life ultimate meaning. Mystical elements in the painting express this idea—the floating angel, the dove—but already Rossetti is moving toward a celebration of such mystery through the beauties of this world rather than the next. *Ecce Ancilla* transforms conventional Christian belief into a love of pure color. The white of the painting beats against the vision as a revelation: "color for color's sake first of all." Rossetti's startling discovery: the great unknowns of existence can be revered through the most elemental of sensuous joys.

Even when Rossetti entered his Aesthetic phase with the 1860 Hogarth Club exhibition, his paintings obsessively revolving around depictions of "beautiful women with floral adjuncts" (as his brother, William, called them), he never lost his faith in a spirituality that art could express. Never going as far as the two doubters closest to him—William and Swinburne—in their unbelief (despite their immense friendship, he found Swinburne's blasphemous poems too abrasive and nihilistic), still Rossetti's religion took an elastic, romantic form, with sometimes a dash of satanism and superstition intermixed. Slowly, Christian (mostly Catholic) symbols became merely a means, rather than an end. They no longer expressed a heavenly order that was above or beyond us, only to be experienced when we die. These things of beauty (color, light, paint) embodied what could solely be found here: redemption through earthly miracles, through such everyday impossibilities as love.

It was Rossetti's feeling, matured in the 1860s and 1870s, that only love could redeem a fallen world that made him such a force for later writers like D. H. Lawrence—who felt sexual love was the only possible salvation in a world bereft of God—and the many authors of twentieth- and twenty-first-century romance novels (of the Harlequin variety) who followed on the heels of *Lady Chatterley's Lover* to discover the "holiness of the heart's affection" (in Keats's famous words). And it was in his love sonnets, especially his sonnet sequence *House of Life* (published in part in 1870 and in a much expanded edition in 1881), that Rossetti finally found the exquisite balance of the sexual and the spiritual. In these sonnets, desire for another takes on the intonations and coloring of prayer. Love begins always with a capital *L* and is personified as a saint, angel, or Christ-like character. The body of the beloved creates a stilled center, a temple through which the mysterious forces of the world are worshipped. The lover's breath is "the inmost incense of his sanctuary" (the "his" referring not to God but to Love). She has a face that is an altar his eyes use to find "that Love through thee made known." This last line is from "Lovesight" (sonnet IV), a jewel of a poem that equates the loss of the sight of the eyes and face of the loved one with "Life's darkening slope." The octave opens with the question "When do I see thee most, beloved one?" and ends with a possible answer:

> Or when in the dusk hours, (we two alone,)
>   Close-kissed and eloquent of still replies
>   Thy twilight-hidden glimmering visage lies?
> And my soul only sees thy soul its own?

Such meetings, which Rossetti expresses throughout the sweep of the sonnet sequence, might represent the only divine transcendence that can be reached, if life here on earth is all there is. Unlike his atheist friends, Rossetti kept open the possibility of an enchanted unknown, a final rich meaning. And if it was there, art and poetry remained the best means of uncovering it, of taking its full measure.

CHRISTINA ROSSETTI'S GOOD news came to her on a nipping October day in 1861, the unusually harsh winter to come foreshadowed by the biting breeze. Rossetti received the letter in the midst of a crowded stream of duties. Reading the Bible aloud, moving among her charges as they diligently sewed and mended, watching over them at night to curtail any sexual irregularities, Christina labored in her nunlike role, her slim figure hidden in a black muslin dress and white veil. She had been immured for two weeks behind the walls of the St. Magdalene Penitentiary in Highgate, and the missive from her brother Gabriel worked like a fresh breeze from the outside world, carrying the seductive whisperings of ambition—fame, even. Magdalene was a religious home (not an actual prison) for young prostitutes willing to be "rescued" from their errant ways through Christian discipline and prayer, and Rossetti was there as a volunteer "Associate Sister," doing the kind of charitable work middle-class, evangelically leaning young women of her time threw themselves into. Or rather, it was the kind of work *daring* young women did, who were willing to risk the social censure that could come when a buttoned-up, respectable woman, unmarried, in her early twenties and something of a beauty (with a wan, long-eyed mien, abstracted and sorrowful, giving her a modern type of brooding look), befriended girls who made their living selling sex. Well brought-up ladies like Rossetti were not even supposed to know of the existence of the boisterous London sex trade. Polite conversation veiled prostitution's gritty realities behind euphemistic language: "the great social evil" drew in "unfortunates," who became "wretched sisters." Helping these "fallen" sisters came as a duty, a keystone of Rossetti's High Church devotion, yet it also worked as research for her true vocation. She was a poet, and, if she needed proof, here it was: the golden news laid out in the letter was that Macmillan would publish her first volume of verse.

The title poem of the book, *Goblin Market* (which would be her masterpiece and speedily pull her into being one of the most influential poets of her time), took as a central theme girls who have had a moral fall. Rossetti had a keen interest in fallenness. Her God worked in dark ways, his hand lying heavily on her own wayward (as she saw it) path. So many pleasures felt sinful and needed to be tamped down. Like George Eliot's Dorothea, the heroine of *Middlemarch*, with her "strain of Puritan energy," Rossetti worried when her joys came "in a pagan sensuous way," and she "always looked forward to renouncing" them. Not only should Christians follow the narrow path of self-denial, but women, according to certain ideals of Victorian femininity, were especially suited for submission and renunciation. Rossetti listened attentively to such talk, some mysterious guilt working in her, keeping close check on her brimming-over desires. She gave up men (there were at least two potential husbands), a radical move in light of the celebratory Victorian attitude to motherhood. Then came the theater and, later, chess. Her great effort to restrain the will attests to the strength of imploded passions. But it also expresses a fear of the dark wave of religious doubt and unbelief that lapped around her (both of her brothers were freethinkers who had shed most of the traditional trappings of faith), leading her to clasp fervently a self-fashioned type of worship, lest she lose it altogether. Rossetti fell into the throes of doubt—black valleys of the soul—at least twice in her life. Correction came through redoubled restraint and repression. Biographers have made much of the deprived quality of Rossetti's life. (Virginia Woolf later observed that "the pressure of a tremendous faith circles and clamps together these little songs. . . . [Y]our God was a harsh God, your heavenly crown was set with thorns. No sooner have you feasted on beauty with your eyes than your mind tells you that beauty is vain and beauty passes.")[8] Living always with her family (mother, sister Maria until she took a nun's vows, brother William, sometimes aunts), she moved through the common rounds of the spinster: hands busy over needlework, calm visits with acquaintances exchanged at the proper hour, long chattering letters written daily, church devotion at least twice a week, the occasional extended stay at the kind friend's country house. She was "a fountain sealed," William felt, and her verse is full of such images of keeping-in and closing-off.[9]

Yet developing the winnowing instinct makes good training for poets. Discipline (not only mad acts, the wild life) can lead to genius. Rossetti's poetry does away with so much as it comes into being that the eye must be sharp to catch the core of its complexity. As Virginia Woolf explained, "Yet for all its symmetry, yours was a complex song. When you struck your harp many strings sounded together."[10] Stripped down, her life and work can appear pared to the bone. But like those of her reclusive American contemporary Emily Dickinson (who found what she called a "finite infinity" in her room, with its key—locking everyone out of her little space—representing freedom), Rossetti's acts of renunciation had their own aesthetic, inspirational worth. She hewed so closely to the careful boundaries of Victorian propriety, enclosed herself so strictly in the walled-in spaces of domesticity and sober evangelicalism, that her inwardness became a pleasure held in her mind for herself only, "telling of the hidden life / That breaks forth underneath."[11] (An article in *Fraser's* in 1864 recognized this "mask of a mood of deeper feelings which she can not afford to disclose.")[12] Glimmering behind many lines of her verse is the sensuous joy of holding back secrets. "I tell my secret? No indeed, not I."[13] Like the sonnet form, a little box whose rigid grid works as a tool for endless invention, Rossetti's sublime restraint opened an interior cathedral, full of dappled light.

GOBLIN MARKET HAS the simplicity of a tale for children. Charles Dodgson (who was to publish under the pen name Lewis Carroll) found inspiration for his Alice adventures in Rossetti's girls and goblins and felt it an honor to photograph her. "*Goblin Market* seems to me a work of real *genius*. If only the Queen would consult *me* as to whom to make Poet-Laureate!"[14] Rather unchildlike, though, is the fact that it was Rossetti's work with prostitutes that gave her the idea for the poem. And then its richly layered sensuality, found even on the microlevel of single words (so succulent they make the mouth pronouncing them feel carnal), led *Playboy*, in 1973, to publish *Goblin Market* in its pages with graphic illustrations. How did such a devout woman write this voluptuous piece?

Goblin Market is a verse tale about two "gleaming" young sisters saved from disaster by their deeply intimate tenderness for each other. "Golden" Lizzie and "glossy" Laura, rushing home but caught out in the dangerously magical dusk, meet with grimacing little goblin men. These leeringly "queer" creatures tempt the girls with soft-fleshed fruit, ripe with juices: "plump unpecked cherries," "figs to fill your mouth," "peaches with a

Algernon Charles Swinbume, photographed around 1865, when he began frequenting flagellation brothels. *Hulton Archive, Getty.*

velvet nap." Laura, with her sweet tooth, gives in to the goblin cry, purchasing some of these little chunks of bodily bliss with a "precious golden lock" of her hair. Falling on them with an insatiable lustiness, she

> Then sucked their fruit globes fair or red;
> Sweeter than honey from the rock
> Stronger than man-rejoicing wine,

> Clearer than water flowed that juice . . .
> She sucked until her lips were sore.

The young child pulling greedily on luscious candy comes to mind here (not to mention Eve and the apple snatched from the tree of knowledge), but so does drug and alcohol abuse, fellatio, and, perhaps, cunnilingus. While it's unlikely Rossetti would have known anything about these latter two sexual acts (and most Victorian readers would not have thought of anything so sexual), clearly this sucking and the sore lips that result come from ecstatic desires of the flesh. Laura's dissolving into orgasmic pleasure, despite coming through the Goblin *men*, is purely personal, even masturbatory. The self-pleasure that runs through *Goblin Market*, essential to the Rossetti aesthetic, is of a particularly feminine type: rounded, clear-juiced, honey-tipped. Later, during the very different climate of World War I, T. S. Eliot would write of J. Alfred Prufrock, who could not risk such self-loss, such all-out letting loose: "Shall I part my hair behind? Do I dare to eat a peach?" The answer, apparently, was no.

Laura, having partaken of the "evil gifts," begins to dwindle "and burn / Her fire away." In her pining need, she ceases participating in the simple acts of housekeeping the sisters used to enjoy together. No more of those quieter sensualities, productive of other types of oral and tactile gratification: kneading cakes, churning butter, whipping cream. The only person who can save her from this frantic addiction, undomesticated and so wild that it tears through her body and brings her to the edge of death, is clear-eyed Lizzie, who must risk sacrificing her own body and sanity to do it. What Lizzie does to save Laura opens a little window into the lives of Victorian spinsters, the kind of life Christina herself eventually fashioned. Mixed up in the idealized image of women of the time was the belief in their warmhearted, physically affectionate natures. Of course, this could be practiced with men only to a very limited extent, given the stiff rules of middle-class "respectability," unless they were husbands or fathers. But with other women, the playing field opened up. They slept curled up together—Lizzie and Laura spend their nights "folded in each other's wings . . . cheek to cheek and breast to breast / Locked together in one nest." Friends kissed each other on the lips, strolling through parks with arms circled around each other's waists. Setting up permanent house together and calling each other "wife" were normal intimacies, encouraged rather than dissuaded.

It was just such a rich and varied love that Christina shared with her life partners: her sister, Maria, and her mother. In her decision to make these two relationships her fulcrum and scaffolding, she certainly sacrificed much. She felt keenly her childless state. Not marrying involved giving up certain freedoms: the wife or widow had freer rein to socialize than the spinster, a larger world in which to move with the protection of a husband in the background. Did Christina find ample recompense in the companionship of her sister and mother, individuals on whom she doted? We can never know. Still, little telling moments gleam out. Maria is "made beautiful by mind; / Lighted up with dark eyes." A valentine she wrote for her seventy-five-year-old mother gallantly calls her "fairer than younger beauties, more beloved / Than many a wife."

Intimacy between two sisters provides the only saving grace in *Goblin Market*. Lizzie can't watch her sister die, so she goes to buy the charmed fruit to suckle her sister, knowing she risks becoming an addict, too. The goblins cooingly coax her to eat.

When she won't, they wax angry and violent. The scene grows dangerous. Using force, they "squeezed their fruits / Against her mouth to make her eat." But Lizzie is a Christ-like martyr whose innocence works as a shield. Standing strong, a kind of bastion of lilylike power, she bravely holds her mouth clenched down. It's difficult not to read this scene as an attempted rape and to feel jubilation when she not only withstands their attempts but thrills to feel her face, and indeed her whole body, covered in syrupy, sinful juice. Running home, the girl calls out in joy for her starving sister to come and embrace her: "Hug me, kiss me, suck my juices . . . Eat me, drink me, love me; / Laura make much of me." Laura's caressing consumption of the drug dripping off Lizzie's body works as an antidote, first bringing a frenzied ecstasy, so violent she barely holds on to life. But the fabric is repaired: Laura's redemption comes through her sister's clever and courageous act. Saved, she returns to her dutiful ways. The didactic tale closes with its central message: "For there is no friend like a sister."

Despite modern interpretations, barely avoidable, of the poem, Christina Rossetti was not a lesbian and certainly was not advocating incest. Rather, she was writing a common Christian morality tale: the tumble from grace, with redemption through atonement. Yet Rossetti could use such carnal language, and relate the message through breathing, loving (sucking!) bodies, *because* of the poem's moral underpinnings. Victorian critics and readers did not doubt its essentially virtuous meaning (even though *Playboy* might), and its edifying frame made its erotic cadences acceptable (even laudable). A strict moral code governed literature of this period, and women especially had to follow aesthetic rules if they wanted to be published (let alone popular). Sentimental, didactic, melancholy: these were the proper literary purlieus for women to haunt. The key to Rossetti's success was to make the strict rules themselves, the godly confinement, the spiritual self-postponement, vibrate with eroticism as they clamped into place. From Rossetti we learn the ecstatic pleasures of submitting the body to the greater moral good of the loved one. The genius of *Goblin Market* is in making Christian self-sacrifice as lusciously delightful as the sinful fall itself.

Rossetti's own commitment to altruistic good works formed around supporting and loving other women, even when she found their actions morally suspect (as with the home for fallen women). While her brother Gabriel was at the center of his set of like-minded freethinkers, Christina joined the loose association of radical feminists around Langham Place (not, however, agreeing with all its tenets, especially having women actively involved in politics, which took them too much into the public sphere). What attracted her to this group was their championing of women's creative work: poetry, painting, typography, bookbinding, and more. With the artist Barbara Leigh Bodichon as its leader, the Langham Place circle consisted of early fighters for women's equality, with a journal, a scientific association, a reading room, an employment bureau, a press, and other means of action and support. Christina sent her poems to the Portfolio Society, another Langham Place satellite, many of which ended up in their *English Woman's Journal*. She became close friends with Bodichon. In fact, Christina organized much of her working life around enriching and enlarging a female literary tradition, with a smattering of feminist poems, her active support for younger female poets, and her paeans to earlier masters of the art like Elizabeth Barrett Browning. Thus, it is less surprising than it might otherwise have been, given Rossetti's demure Christianity, that she became something of an icon to lesbian writers of the 1890s and later. The collaborative couple Katherine Bradley and Edith Cooper, an aunt and niece who became lifelong lovers and wrote erotic poems under the pseudonym Michael Field, penned her an ode of love and admiration (and perhaps a bit of criticism for her austerity). Published in 1896, a couple of years after her death, "To Christina Rossetti" beholds her "moving bright" amid the "cool shadows" of the night trees. They give her permission, at long last, "to slip into the universe."

IN AUGUST 1861, a few months before Christina Rossetti found out that *Goblin Market* would be published, Algernon Charles Swinburne wiled away the sticky days in the cedar-paneled library at Fryston. Because of its stone-flagged floor and heavily draped windows, the library was the coolest room in the cavernous mansion in Yorkshire, which belonged to Richard Monckton Milnes (made Lord Houghton in 1863), a well-connected member of Parliament. Fryston Hall, known for its collection of books so numerous they spilled out into the hallways, bedrooms, and every hidden cupboard on the premises, would eventually become notorious for a subset of this library: its huge stash of rare and illegal erotica, which earned the whole house the nickname Aphrodisiopolis. Many years and a good deal of cunning went into this collection, as the passing of the Obscene Publications Act in 1857 (opposed stridently in Parliament by Milnes himself) made an already prudish book culture downright dangerous. Most of Milnes's erotic volumes came via a looser Paris, with the libertine expatriate Englishman Frederick Hankey acting as go-between. Hankey, so well-known among European men of letters for his cruel sexual tastes that he was the model for the stereotype of the English sadist in novels of the period, smuggled pornography into England in British embassy diplomatic bags, addressed to a friend of his in the Foreign Office, or in the small of Augustus Harris's back (manager of Covent Garden), which had such a pronounced curve that large books and even statuary could be concealed underneath his clothing.

The twenty-four-year-old Swinburne, already a budding sexual radical, soaked up these bawdy books, filling out his sexual education and providing colorful themes for his poems in progress. In the 1860s Swinburne developed the kind of vivid public persona, full of a high-strung cleverness and a conversational brilliance (pitched at times toward the hysterical), that would make his character an integral part of his art in the minds of his readership, a mixing of the aesthetic and personal that Oscar Wilde would emulate thirty years later. (Guy de Maupassant, then a young French writer, called Swinburne "the most extravagantly artistic person alive in the world today.")[15] The American intellectual Henry Adams, visiting Fryston in 1861, found Swinburne like "a tropical bird, high-crested, long-beaked, quick-moving, with rapid utterance and screams of humour." The company "all sat till far into the night, listening to the rush of Swinburne's talk. In a long experience, before or after, no one ever approached it."[16] Part of Swinburne's genius involved a temperamental need to make art and to embody that art in his own person, which shocked the highly decorous and rule-bound society in which he lived. Swinburne had an allergy to most moral dictums, to the double lives many Victorians led (following sober rules of propriety for appearance' sake, even castigating others for their peccadilloes, but then transgressing these very rules in secret). Reveling in exposing what went on behind closed doors, Swinburne became notorious for such shockers as loud conversations at the Arts Club in Hanover Street about sodomy and lesbianism, sessions fueled by alcohol and the extravagance of a friend, the gay painter Simeon Solomon (all of which eventually led to Swinburne's losing his membership, despite the intervention of another friend, the painter James McNeill Whistler). His willingness to risk arrest under the Obscene Publications Act for publishing verse on hermaphrodites, bisexuals, sadists, and incestuous lovers made him (in his friend the artist Seymour Kirkup's estimation) "our champion against tyranny, temporal and spiritual."[17] Swinburne was in many ways the opposite of the stereotypical Victorian hypocrite. As Oscar Wilde remarked, Swinburne was "a braggart in the matter of vice, who had done everything he could to convince his fellow citizens of his homosexuality and bestiality, without being in the slightest degree a homosexual or a bestializer."[18] (Which is not altogether true, however, since Swinburne did enjoy the "vice" of sexual flagellation and definitely expressed homosexual impulses—whether or not he acted on them is unknown.)

The Fryston Hall salon was the ideal testing ground for Swinburne to develop and refine his art. More important than getting to handle forbidden books, he learned a good deal from his fellow houseguests, progressive freethinkers all. The socialite Milnes did have a real talent (and it wasn't a literary one, although he fancied himself a poet and critic): grouping, manipulating, and agitating great characters of his day. He used Fryston as a cultural gathering place, striving to cook up odd combinations of people and delighting in the resulting uncomfortable concoctions. (Some introductions made by Milnes: Nathaniel Hawthorne to Elizabeth Barrett Browning; Louis Napoleon—later to be Napoleon III—to Benjamin Disraeli; the Prince of Wales to Charles Dickens; Swinburne to Oscar Wilde.)

The party of August 1861 was a typically motley group: in addition to Swinburne, Milnes invited the "Chelsea sage" Thomas Carlyle, the Christian socialist and novelist Charles Kingsley, the historian James Anthony Froude, the explorer Richard Burton and his wife, Isabel. Unfortunately, no account exists of what must have been an awkward assortment of breakfasts, country strolls, and conversational evenings. One project that all of these disparate characters shared, and that Swinburne brought to the poetry he was writing at the time, was a questioning of the Christian faith, a move toward either a radical refashioning of belief or a loss of it entirely. Carlyle's rebellion against his Calvinistic upbringing, played out in such works as *Sartor Resartus* and *Past and Present*, led him to forge a deeply influential pragmatic humanism based on a forthright work ethic ("work is prayer") and heroic individualism. Kingsley linked his religion to his desire to ameliorate the plight of the struggling working classes, creating a powerful critique against a Church of England he felt was out of touch with the injustices of industrialism, with its literal starving of the poor on the streets of England's major cities. Froude famously fictionalized his own religious doubts (and those of his era) in *The Nemesis of Faith*, a novel publicly burned at Oxford by the divine William Sewell.

A country well on the road to the secularism of modern capitalism, Victorian Britain found itself in the middle of constant religious upheavals and controversy, a kind of last gasp before a general fall by the end of the century, when to the majority of the population religion became irrelevant. Although Nietzsche wasn't to announce that God was dead until 1882, leading British intellectuals like George Eliot (pseudonym for Marian Evans, the smartest woman in England), Thomas Henry Huxley (who invented the word "agnostic" in the 1860s), and Herbert Spencer (Darwin popularizer) were busy building a humanism based on scientific rationality, empathy, and an ethics of responsibility, through debates, articles in publications like the *Westminster Review*, and a series of influential books, nonfiction and fiction alike. The religious revivals of the 1830s and 1840s (evangelical and High Church) still had their followers, but many saw their faith undermined by the overwhelming discoveries of science. When geologists affirmed that the world was millions of years old rather than thousands, a literal reading of the Bible no longer seemed viable. More trouble for believers came at the end of 1859, when Darwin's *Origin of the Species* depicted nature as a brutal "survival of the fittest" (Herbert Spencer's phrase) rather than the creation of a benevolent god. What place did faith have when humans were not reflections of the divine, but rather just chance hits in evolution? Science (not only naturalism, biology, and geology but also anthropology, sociology, and psychology) became a firmer foundation for faith, just as for Swinburne and his group Art (with an unashamed capital *A*) was more worthy of worship than a stony, distant god. Art cannot be the "handmaid of religion," Swinburne wrote in the late 1860s, but rather it should evoke "the love of beauty for very beauty's sake, the faith and trust in it as a god indeed."[19] He continued with a phrase that he was the first to introduce to the British (imported from the French writer Théophile Gautier) and that would come to have an immense impact on the writing and art of his country and of the United States: "art for art's sake first of all."[20]

BUT OF THE group of eminent men gathered at Fryston that summer of 1861, it was Richard Burton, the secret agent and explorer who introduced the word "safari" to the English language, who was to have the most lasting impact on Swinburne. Swinburne's hot and deep crush on the dashing forty-year-old Burton was never hidden, and Swinburne proclaimed it, with pride, on a large scale whenever given the opportunity. Working up a slavish obsession, Swinburne called Burton "my tempter and favorite audience" and remarked that he had,

> A wider soul than the world was wide,
> Whose praise made love of him one with pride . . .
> Who rode life's lists as a god might ride.[21]

This was their second meeting—Milnes had first introduced them a few months earlier at a London breakfast—and already rumors spread about the eccentric poet and the darkly exotic, rakish adventurer. The two would go off to a nearby room, and "the rest of the company would be tantalized to hear proceeding roars and shrieks of laughter, followed by earnest rapid talk of a quieter description."[22] Their drinking bouts often ended with Swinburne out cold or in a violent state, Burton carrying the small man under his arm (sometimes yelling and kicking) out to the street and depositing him in a hansom cab. Friends (including Milnes) felt Burton was responsible for Swinburne's addiction to brandy, the first step on a descent into ruinous alcoholism. Swinburne's enthrallment to self-destruction, a motif threading through most of his writing, would certainly have carried him down a dangerous path regardless.

It's hard to blame Swinburne for his adoration: Burton had the kind of fascinating, larger-than-life qualities found in certain Victorians that seem to be gone from the world today. His accomplishments include learning nearly thirty languages and dialects and publishing some fifty books in numerous genres—travel narratives, ethnographic studies, poetry, literary criticism, anthologies, short stories, translations. He was the first European to reach Lake Tanganyika and the sacred city of Harar. By 1861, when he met Swinburne, Burton's considerable fame rested on his 1853 trip to the sacred city of Mecca, strictly closed to non-Muslims. Burton made the perilous journey, completed by a handful of Europeans before him, in various disguises (a Persian Shia, a Sunni "Shakykh," a simple Muslim pilgrim). His riveting account, published as *Personal Narrative of a Pilgrimage to El-Medinah and Meccah* in 1855, became an ethnographic classic, going rapidly into four editions and turning Burton into an adventure hero in England. But it also placed him, not for the first time and certainly not the last, in the center of controversy.

Like Swinburne, Burton pushed against the walls of Victorian propriety repeatedly, seeming to enjoy the row kicked up when he offended "Mrs. Grundy" (a common term for prudish restrictiveness). "Mrs. Grundy is beginning to roar . . . and I don't care a damn for her," he wrote to a friend when shepherding his unbowdlerized translation of *Arabian Nights* into print, "if they [social purity forces] want a fight they can have it."[23] Burton's fascination with the sexual practices of other cultures, which he often analyzed in order to criticize his own culture's repressiveness, would keep him in trouble with the moral police throughout his life. His 1856 *First Footsteps in East Africa; or, An Exploration of Harar* was just the beginning: it took up prostitution, lovemaking positions, and male and female circumcision (a "barbarous" practice, he felt). The analysis of circumcision, deemed too racy by his publisher, was cut without his permission just before publication.

Yet it wasn't just Burton's sexual radicalism that was unconventional, or that was to carry the impressionable Swinburne along with him: his religious defiance not only made him an outsider from the Church of England (including High, Broad, and Low Church, and even the Dissenters) but left him challenging the growing number of atheists, some of whom were his friends. It was this spiritual defection that made *Personal Narrative of a Pilgrimage* possible and gave it such cultural importance. In fact, Burton's trip to Mecca was a *genuine* pilgrimage. In many ways the bluff British imperialist—agent for the East India Company and representative for the Royal Geographic Society—Burton had, in all seriousness, converted to Islam, entering the Sufi Brotherhood through years of study, ritual, and practice. For a member of the ruling elite, this was a startling act; Islam was viewed as an inferior, barbaric religion. As the *Edinburgh Review* complained, "There is something indescribably revolting to our feelings in the position of an English officer . . . crawling among a crowd of unbelievers, around the objects of their wretched superstition."[24]

One of Burton's most charming characteristics was his relativism, his ability to insert himself into an unfamiliar culture and see through its eyes (except when it came to Africans, where he was a terrible racist). Throughout the many travels of his lifetime, he would not only throw himself into the language, literature, and everyday life of the new cultures he encountered; he would also enter deeply into their spiritual beliefs. Eventually, his studies and faith led him to develop a thoroughgoing critique of Christianity as practiced in the nineteenth century: "The Moslem may be more tolerant, more enlightened, more charitable, than many societies of self-styled Christians."[25] In particular, he criticized the stifling restrictions on women in Victorian England: "At a time when common sense is demanding the political emancipation of women in England," Burton points to "the superior liberty of the sex amongst the Moslem races." Moslem women had "immense advantages in the management of children, property, and servants" compared with British married women, who had no legal rights to their possessions (indeed were the "chattel" of their husbands) until the Married Woman's Property Act of 1870.[26]

Religion was on Burton's mind when he formed his radical dining club in 1863, an inner circle of members of the Anthropological Society, also founded by Burton. The club was an irreverent, boisterous gathering over rare wine, steaks, chops, mutton, and all manner of meat at Bertolini's Italian restaurant (the haunt of "fast men") near the once fashionable but now seedy Leicester Square. He wanted a freewheeling, uncensored forum to discuss the heady topics of the day: sexuality, gender, and, of course, religion. He dubbed it the Cannibal Club as a kind of outrageous joke: what could be more shocking, and blasphemous, than humans eating their own kind? The club took as its symbol a mace in the shape of an African gnawing on a thighbone. Cannibalism worked as a figure for the moral distance he wanted, as a means to free up space for discussion about everything and anything. When Swinburne joined, he penned a little theme piece for the club, a sort of sacrilegious play on the Christian catechism (the Eucharist is here compared to a cannibal feast), called the "Cannibal Catechism."

> Preserve us from our enemies
> Thou who art Lord of suns and skies
> Whose meat and drink is flesh in pies
> And blood in bowls!
> Of thy sweet mercy, damn their eyes
> And damn their souls!

Two key members of the coterie were prominent atheists. Thomas Bendyshe was the editor of the freethinking periodical *Reader*. Charles Bradlaugh gained notoriety when he refused to take the oath of allegiance upon his election to Parliament because it includes an allegiance to God, which started a widely followed five-year legal fight. (This remains radical even today, when candidates for president of the United States must state openly their strong belief in God.) Swinburne, still willing to pour his identity into different vessels, found the dimensions of his atheism expanded and refined through debates with such brilliant men. Like Milnes's dirty books, the Cannibal Club's religious radicalism (brought to him through the mesmerizing haze of his love for Burton) became a cornerstone for his most important poems. By 1865, he was well on his way to a new heretical questioning in his art: could a worship of the senses replace a belief in God?

ON SATURDAY, AUGUST 4, 1866, Swinburne made his way, with his peculiar, dancing step, down Dover Street to Piccadilly. The grand thoroughfare was as usual a rush of carriages and cabs. He walked with his publisher, James Bertrand Payne of Moxon's, who had issued Swinburne's *Poems and Ballads* a week earlier. Passing the White Horse Cellar, they may have seen that increasingly rare occurrence (with the ever-expanding railroads): a coach pulled by a team of six—heavy with passengers and luggage—setting off for the country. Ancient, silent trees spread over the street on the park side, while on the other bustling houses of trade mixed with stately, old-moneyed mansions: Devonshire House, the Rothschilds pile, Apsley House. The Parisianesque Burlington Arcade arched elegantly over jewel-like wares for sale to the wealthy. The two men were in expansive moods, elated to have finally shepherded the collection into print, after many delays and worries. Yet this would be one of the last times Payne and Swinburne were to meet as friends. The descent into recrimination and scandal was just about to begin.

Pausing at a newsstand, Swinburne decided to buy a copy of *Saturday Review*, an influential literary weekly. Glancing through its contents, he spotted an article on his book by John Morley. Swinburne asked Payne to stop a moment, so he could read the piece. As his eyes moved down the column, his face grew red with fury. With wild, agitated gestures, he began cursing in rage. Payne, alarmed by the obscenity of Swinburne's shouts, directed him into a nearby restaurant. But his angry words were so violently scatological that the waiters kept away in alarm. Payne dryly suggested a switch in language; if he cursed in French, people might take him for an excitable foreigner.

Swinburne's fury was understandable. One of the most savage critiques of a writer ever published, Morley's article was particularly damning because it condemned not only the poems but Swinburne's character as a gentleman. Swinburne "has revealed to the world," Morley seethed, "a mind all aflame with the feverish carnality of a schoolboy over the dirtiest passages in Lemprière [a reference work on classical and ancient mythological history]." He dubbed Swinburne "the libidinous laureate of a pack of satyrs" (a title that would stick). Comparing his poems to pornography, Morley found the volume "crammed with pieces which many a professional vendor of filthy prints might blush to sell."[27] He could take comfort only in the fact that most readers wouldn't understand the "fevered folly" of poems that referenced ancient Greek myths and writers, like "Hermaphroditus" (about intersexuality) and "Anactoria" (on Sappho's jealous love for a woman). Such critical hysteria appeared in reviews on both sides of the Atlantic. Swinburne opened letters threatening to castrate or brand him. *Punch* gleefully suggested he change his name to "Swineborn." Such a virulent rash of attacks proved how perfectly pitched the book was for its times.

The equally fervent admiration for the volume gave further proof of its powers to stir, especially among the young. With this single book, Swinburne became an international figure for religious and sexual rebellion, for the importance of artistic expression above all else. "All literary London is now ringing with the genius, the blasphemies and indecencies of his last book," the historian W. H. E. Lecky remarked.[28] One Oxonian gushed to the writer Edmund Gosse, "It simply swept us off our legs with rapture."[29] Students there and at Cambridge linked arms and chanted the memorized lines of "Dolores" as they stalked college grounds at night. When Swinburne read the poem aloud at parties, the audience "had been moved to such incredible ecstasy by it that several of them had sunk to their knees then and there, and adored him as a god."[30] Young Thomas Hardy, a clerk in a London architect's office with all his great, gloomy novels still before him, was bowled over by the power of Swinburne's verse. He found himself stalking the foggy city streets with book in hand, "to [his] imminent risk of being knocked down."[31]

To his horror, on the very next day, Payne heard rumors that the *Times* would print an article demanding prosecution of the publisher for obscenity. J. M. Ludlow, a leader of the Christian Socialists, called on the attorney general to prosecute. Payne withdrew all copies from circulation. Was he overreacting, as Swinburne felt? Payne couldn't help recalling the conviction of Edward Moxon (the now deceased founder of Moxon's) in 1841 for publishing Percy Bysshe Shelley's atheist, free-love-advocating *Queen Mab*. Payne was more versed in the punishment for challenging the establishment—usually jail time with hard labor—than Swinburne could be. Swinburne railed against that "hound of a publisher," and hastily took the volume off Payne's "villainous hands" and put it into those of John Camden Hotten, who reissued it forthwith to more moral censure, but also to enough support from intellectual powers (the art critic John Ruskin stood behind him, as did Lord Houghton) that no one was prosecuted. (Hotten wasn't the most savory publisher around.[32] His list included *Worship of Priapus*; *The Merry Order of St. Bridget: Personal Recollections of the Use of the Rod*; and *Flagellation and the Flagellents: A History of the Rod*.)

POEMS AND BALLADS proffers an atheist's view of the ecstasy to be found in emptiness. All must be had at once "while time is with us and hands are free" because a "whole life's love goes down in a day."[33] When this brief life is all there is—no afterlife awaiting, no angels recording those minutes half gone as they begin—experiences flame out, in their vibrant immediacy, from the darkness of the hard mortality of forever. Feverish objects of desire burn in ephemerality: "Close lips that quiver and fold up wings that ache," "strange swift eyes where the soul sits free," "buds burning in the sudden spring like fire." In these poems the bitter and blighted can flower into a moment of grace, without ever losing their agonized coloring.

Swinburne's poems of 1866 plumb a world without God, one where only the senses can succour, and then just for a short time and always intermingled with the deep pain of impermanence. Sensual passion (love, lust, longing, the body's needs) expresses most completely the fervent chaos of this world and is one of its only possible points of redemption. In "Dolores," the poem subject to so much venom from some and to such heady reverence from others, a search to fill a spiritual emptiness with "all the joys of the flesh" begins. Hymn to a cruel saint, Our Lady of the Sorrows (usually the title for the Virgin Mary wounded by the seven major tragedies of her life), the poem worships a "poisonous queen" whose "cold eyelids" "hide like a jewel / Hard eyes that grow soft for an hour." She is "Our Lady of Pain," an anti-Madonna who guards not the virtues but sin, "fierce midnights," and "the loves that complete and control."

Unlike chaste Mary, who calms with her covered head and milky skin, Dolores's hair is "loosened and soiled in mid orgies / With kisses and wine," and when men touch her "sweet lips" they "change in a trice / The lilies and langours of virtue / For the raptures and roses of vice." In "Dolores" the "I" of the poem attempts to find an ecstasy so severe in its annihilating extremity that it will allow him to forget the grief of sorrows, loves, and life itself. Our Lady of Pain, while "fruits fail and love dies and time ranges," is immortal; suffering outlasts all. Dolores cracks open life because she is cherished by the light of the most common experiences: "by the hunger of change and emotion, / By the thirst of unbearable things, / By despair, the twin-born of devotion." Swinburne speaks here of the power on the senses of godlessness. The height of passion, the strongest emotions of one's life, might involve a casting out of God, an embrace of his absence. Such heresy most Victorians found overwhelmingly offensive.

"Dolores," the work of a cynical sensualist, an expression of Swinburne's feeling of emptiness and alienation in the modern, industrialized world and a need to give it some chance of fulfillment, makes him the father of Modernist spiritual deadness: T. S. Eliot's wasteland, D. H. Lawrence's frozen, sterile universe. Swinburne's atheism, discovered at Oxford, brought him a desperate sense of loss. When he was a boy, his passion for the Anglo-Catholicism of his family carried him into "unaffected and unashamed ecstasies of adoration when receiving the Sacrament."[34] So much of his writing seeks not to repair the rent created by his unbelief but to feel it more fully, to experience existence by its pain and emptiness (Gosse called him "an evangelist turned inside out").[35] His radical art came as an outward expression of this interior troubling and led him to attempt to unite what the puritanism of his society had sundered: the physical and the spiritual. Christianity needn't be caught up in social purity. Swinburne's verse pointed to ways in which biblical stories and the lives of the saints make central the ecstatic side of worshipping God and Christ: the eroticism of the Song of Solomon, the reverence for Christ's body in religious images, the sensualism of sacrificing one's limbs for higher ideals. Swinburne propounded in his literary criticism "an equal reverence for spirit and flesh as the two sides or halves of a completed creature."[36] Still, Swinburne loved the physical, and often the "spirit" entirely slips away in his life and art.

CHRISTINA ROSSETTI'S VERSE had always been an important influence on Swinburne (placing her firmly in the Aesthetic camp), despite her deep faith and retiring lifestyle and his outrageousness and flaunted unbelief. Stylistically, Rossetti's poetry both influenced and was influenced by Pre-Raphaelitism: her lush sensual verse, with its medieval or fairy-tale qualities, was always in dialogue with her brother Gabriel's work, and that of the circle as a whole. (Her career began when her poems appeared in the short-lived radical journal *Germ*, legendary organ for the Pre-Raphaelite Brotherhood.) Swinburne sang Rossetti's praises in print, discovering in her writing "cadences of refluent sea-music beyond reach of harp and organ, large echoes of the serene and sonorous ties of heaven."[37] Reading her poetry made Swinburne "purr with pleasure and feel as if [his] fur was being rubbed the right way," and he later penned some lines urging her to write more, entitled "A Ballad of Appeal, to Christina Rossetti."[38] Seeing something in her that others didn't, he based the title character of his unfinished novel *Lesbia Brandon* partially on her, a female poet who kills herself "off by inches, with the help of eau de cologne and doses of opium." She appreciated his work, too, although her brother William observed her pasting strips of paper over the blasphemous sections.

Hardly any details exist of the numerous encounters between

Christina Rossetti and Swinburne. They met at least three times in the early 1860s, and either their first or second meeting occurred at the house in Scotland of their handsome mutual friend, the writer William Bell Scott. The only thing Christina had to say about this meeting was rather droll. She found him "as surprizing as usual."[39] Wherever it was, Swinburne must have been on his best behavior in the presence of the prim poetess, since they maintained an occasional and warm correspondence. If Swinburne had pulled any of his usual shenanigans, such as drinking three bottles of port and sliding down the banisters, Christina would certainly have "cut" him thereafter. The two must have had much to talk about, sharing an interest as they did in virgin martyrs, the poetry of Robert Browning, and the habits of house cats.

Their poems of yearning had many meeting points. Christina became devout in her great need to hold on to something she so fervently feared could slip through her fingers. To keep the precious thing, she hid it in the secret recesses of the sensual body, with all its pains and privations intact. Swinburne's spiritual desperation took him in the opposite direction: to "bleak blown space, / Full of the sound of the sorrow of years," the "iron hollow of doubtful heaven."

CHAPTER THREE

The Seductress and the Bluestocking

> Foggy weather is propitious to amatory caprices. Harlots tell me that they usually do good business during that state of atmosphere, especially those who are regular nymphs of the *pavé*.
>
> —ANONYMOUS, *My Secret Life*

PRIL 1862: SPRING brought on a soupy yellow fog that gathered with the darkness, cloaking figures on the nighttime streets. Dante Gabriel Rossetti and his friend and fellow painter George Boyce spent some of these April nights cruising for easygoing, flirtatious women with paintable faces. Sometimes these women were prostitutes: modeling, like acting, not considered altogether respectable for young, unmarried women. The two would generally set off from Rossetti's antique-filled rooms at 59 Lincoln's Inn Fields, strolling a bit before hailing a hansom cab. Rossetti, as he walked, liked to hum a nondescript tune with closed teeth that a friend described as "a *sotto voce* note of defiance to the Universe."[1] The city streets smelled strongly of horse dung and wet straw. The delicate gas flares smoking in the soot-laden air created deep pockets of velvety darkness in corners and along damp alleys. The nearby Thames ran swiftly and silently, still congested at this late hour with watercraft of all shapes and sizes. Large steamships from Europe loomed as dangerous masses for the light boats darting in and out of the current, their bedraggled watermen looking for floating corpses to rifle and any rolling detritus that might be worth something to someone.

Already slightly drunk, the pair would debate where to go. An occasional haunt was the Argyll Rooms on Windmill Street, just off of the Haymarket, one of the most popular dancing and music rooms in 1850s and 1860s London. Visitors to the Haymarket after eleven in the evening found themselves jostled by drunken couples walking arm in arm. Known as Hell Corner, the Haymarket was the notorious center of the West End prostitution trade. In order to arrive at the Argyll, they had to work past "sparring snobs, and flashing satins, and sporting gents, and painted cheeks, and brandy-sparkling eyes, and bad tobacco, and hoarse horse-laughs, and loud indecency," as a disapproving reporter wrote. It swarmed, he went on, with "a very large part of what is blackguard, ruffianly, and deeply dangerous in London."[2] A brass band blared in front of the gin shop. Boisterous women sauntered by, sometimes in small groups, but more often alone. A better class of prostitute could be found at the Argyll Rooms, or at least women who were less likely to pass on syphilis or gonorrhea.

How easy it was to find sex in 1860s London! The man about town could cruise the Strand, Tottenham Court Road, the Queen's Highway, and scores of other pickup spots for women who had that unmistakable air of being available for a price. Perhaps her bright silk dress displayed a wealth beyond her obvious class. A bold stare would suffice, as would lifting her petticoats a little higher than other women did when crossing the muddy thoroughfare. Often it was something intangible that led to the encounter, just as when the city stroller today can guess at the professions of passersby, using a system of almost unconscious signs. "One summer's morning about midday, I was in the Quadrant," describes a Victorian in his memoir *My Secret Life* (while the author of this work remains unknown, many have argued for Henry Spencer Ashbee, a friend of Burton and Milnes),

> In front of me I saw a well-grown woman walking. . . . I followed on, passed her, then turned around, and met her eye . . . . I followed quickly, saying as I came close, "Will you come with me?" . . . Without replying a word, and without looking at me, without hurrying, she walked steadily on till she entered the house No. 13 J***s Street. . . . Inside the house she stopped at the foot of the staircase, and turning round, said in a low tone, "What are you going to give me?" "Ten shillings." "I won't go upstairs then, so tell you at once." "What do you want?" "I won't let any one come with me unless they give me a sovereign at least."[3]

The wealthy and worldly might meet a woman at a better sort of "introducing house" on Bolton Row (near Grosvenor Square)—where the "abbess" or "mistress" would set up an encounter by sending the gentleman a note at his club. Catching his fancy, the woman might become a kept mistress. He would take a house for her in one of the terraces overlooking Regent's Park, give her £4,000 a year (approximately $200,000 today), set her up with a carriage and stud and a box at the opera.

City sophisticates had their favorite brothels. But for the country fellow just come into the city, there were guides like *Hints to Men about Town or Water Fordiana* or *The Man of Pleasure's Pocket Book*, which described the intimate attributes of well-known prostitutes, their addresses, and sometimes their prices. Casinos, dancing rooms, divans, night houses, pleasure gardens, music halls, and cafés worked as more casual sites for picking up a bedfellow, but most commonly the flâneur fulfilled his desire by hitting the streets. As London was beginning to outpace Paris as the shopping capital of the world, so too was it becoming famous for its heady display of flesh for sale. On Waterloo Road women appeared in windows, wearing the flimsiest of underwear. In the streets around Haymarket, if the prostitute didn't already rent a drawing-room floor for an exorbitant price, houses with signs in the windows like "Beds to Let" and "For Private Apartments, Ladies" worked as casual, come-as-you-may bordellos. "A stranger cannot help being astonished at the vast, almost incalculable, number of unfortunate women who haunt the London streets in this quarter as the hour of midnight approaches," wrote the popular journalist Daniel Joseph Kirwan, using one of many euphemisms of the time for prostitutes.[4]

Sex on the street could be literal. Slipping into the shadows of a dank alleyway, especially on a foggy night (which Dickens calls "a London particular"), could bring speedy, anonymous satisfaction. At the bottom of the hierarchy of prostitutes were the "park whores." "Passing a park entrance one misty and warmish night at about ten o'clock," wrote the diarist in *My Secret Life* around this time,

> I thought I should like to feel a cunt . . . . I entered and saw couples sitting on the seats close to each other, and further from

> the walk, couples indistinctly in more compromising attitudes . . . . A square built, shortish female passed me . . . . "Come on to the grass, let me feel your cunt and I'll give you a shilling." In half a minute I had my hand between her thighs . . . . It was getting more misty and I felt secure from observation. . . . Would she let me have her for half a crown? . . . . "Too glad," said she . . . . We went still further off, and found a vacant seat near an out of the way walk . . . . I sat down, and turning her back towards me, she pulled up her petticoats . . . .[5]

WHEN ROSSETTI MET Fanny Cornforth in 1858, he had already been mulling over the social problem of prostitution. Something about it kept him brooding. His sister Christina also found it of great interest. She was, at this time, working to "reclaim" prostitutes while Rossetti visited them, slept with them, paid them, and painted them. Still, his entanglement in the matter was more complicated; he carried that intriguing knot of sex and money into his work. Displaying a startling literal-mindedness, Rossetti used Fanny for his painting of Mary Magdalene and also for *Found*, depicting a London streetwalker discovered by an old beau from the small town of her youth. With Fanny in his life and often around his home and studio, he began reworking what would become the notorious poem "Jenny" (and which was to become, incidentally, one of the "grave poems," buried and then disinterred in Highgate). Started in the 1840s, "Jenny" is a lengthy dramatic monologue spoken by a bookish, bohemian youth who wonders what the "lazy laughing languid" prostitute, who has fallen asleep with her head resting on his knee, might be dreaming and thinking.

What would it be like to be a prostitute—he wonders from his privileged position—to be looked on as a "degraded" means for the "flagrant man-swine" to whet "his tusk"? The narrator doesn't come off well in this speech, despite being clearly progressive minded for his time (he actually pauses to wonder what prostitution is like for the prostitute). His attitude is ultimately condescending, lordly, and oppressive, especially to the modern reader: he seems to think he can know this woman and her life just through his imaginative powers (not by getting to know her), but ultimately he can come up only with a reflection of his own small-mindedness.

Rossetti, with "Jenny," shows an awareness of the pitfalls of turning an individual into a symbol, thereby losing the sense that each person has a unique outlook, life, and experience. Victorian society as a whole found itself often caught in such a muddle, particularly when it came to the intense debates of the time on the "Woman Question," as it was called. Women could be looked up to as the "angel in the house," the title of a hugely popular 1854 poem by Coventry Patmore—a friend and associate of Rossetti and Milnes, who had some work published in the *Germ*—that saw women as the moral guide and chaste guardian of the sanctuary of the home. "Fallen women," according to popular thinking, must be one of two types: they were either victims (of seduction, the "white slave" trade, or wretched poverty) or themselves the aggressive agents of an evil degradation and decadence. ("Once a woman has descended from the pedestal of innocence, she is prepared to perpetuate every crime," claimed the moral reformer J. B. Talbot, author of the well-known *The Miseries of Prostitution*).[6] In actuality, the majority of the prostitutes were neither. Generally self-aware, working-class women who decided to make extra money, most prostitutes took up the trade as a conscious, usually temporary choice, often moving on to other types of work later. Fanny herself was one such woman. A frank, friendly, working woman, she went on to marry a young mechanic, but later left him to return to Rossetti, with whom she was clearly in love.

"The Great Social Evil" (as prostitution was called) stirred up a good deal of hysteria, especially among evangelicals and other religious-minded folk. To many, the active and visible trade represented all the evils of the modern city. Churchmen railed against this new Babylon; statesmen decried it in Parliament; concerned residents sent letters to the *Times*, worried about the degeneracy of the streets. "There must be a great rottenness in Denmark where such a state of things can exist," Kirwan cried.[7] "I can conceive of no city more sunk in licentiousness and rascality than ours," wrote the popular journalist J. Ewing Ritchie in 1858.[8] All that seemed to the English to be wrong with themselves—moral degeneracy, decaying health, flagging patriotism—was projected out onto the "other" of the prostitutes and, to a lesser extent, their clients. The sense that prostitutes contaminated the larger social world, that the moral disease of modernity somehow resided in them—in their bodies, even—was expressed quite concretely with a series of laws. The Contagious Diseases Acts (the first passed in 1864, broadened in 1868 and 1869), billed as an attempt to stem the rampant spread of syphilis and gonorrhea among the military, required that prostitutes submit to genital inspection and, if needed, forced treatment. The acts served to reinforce the idea that it was "natural" for men to frequent prostitutes but immoral for women to *be* prostitutes. Thus, the sexually transmitted diseases passed through these encounters were entirely the fault of prostitutes and their sinful state.

Not coincidentally, the 1860s saw the rise of the first wave of the feminist movement. These early feminists worked to carve out a position for women in the world that didn't involve being defined solely by their familial relationship to men, as wives, daughters, mothers, whores (who fit into this paradigm as providing "sexual release," as the story went, for men not yet married or married and not wanting to let their wives in on their lusty ways). Feminist groups formed around fighting for women's autonomy—whether it was political (the Langham Place circle organized a petition for a woman's suffrage bill in 1865); educational (Girton College was established in 1869); or over their own sexual bodies (Charles Bradlaugh and Annie Besant spread information to women about contraception in the 1860s and 1870s, and the Ladies National Association, led by Josephine Butler, fought the Contagious Diseases Act).

Rossetti hovered ambiguously on the sidelines of radical feminist circles. He counted as a dear friend Barbara Leigh Bodichon, whom he met as the single "Miss Smith" in the 1850s. She was a "jolly fellow," so dedicated to her painting that she thought "nothing of climbing up a mountain in breeches, or wading through a stream in none, in the sacred name of pigment."[9] She joined the Folio Club, the post–Pre-Raphaelite Brotherhood sketching club started by Millais, and later in life Rossetti often stayed at Scalands, her cottage in Sussex. He knew George Eliot, Josephine Butler, and the novelist Elizabeth Gaskell and was a great admirer of Elizabeth Barrett Browning's emancipationist poem *Aurora Leigh* ("an astounding piece of work").[10] But his ideas about such powerful women were essentially mixed; he approved of them overtly, but his art and poetry told a more nuanced story. Seeping up through buried parts of his consciousness came an unsorted welter of erotic fears and attractions. Emancipated women were dangerous to men, many of his paintings proclaim, which was, indeed, a huge part of their erotic appeal.

A HARDY WALKER throughout his life, Swinburne liked to begin some of his days in 1868 strolling from his place on Dorset Street to his favorite brothel at 7 Circus Road, St. John's Wood. He would often stop off at Regent's Park. A friendly park keeper used to spot the poet at his favorite bench, working on a poem (some of the verse collected in *Song before Sunrise* was written this way, Edmund Gosse reports). After a chat with the park keeper, Swinburne would continue on his way to Verbena Lodge, or, as he used to call it in a nice bit of blasphemy, "the Grove of the Evangelist." The poet was lightened of a good deal of "tin" at Verbena, but he wouldn't have taken anything additional away with him as he left, such as the usual parting gifts of syphilis and gonorrhea. Verbena Lodge was one of a number of brothels in mid-Victorian London that catered to flagellation ("a London particular," as Dickens might have said). Swinburne went there to be "birched" by "two golden-haired and rouge-cheeked ladies" dressed as schoolmasters or mistresses, willing to chastise their clients for misbehavior, for large sums.[11]

Swinburne had a way of putting women on pedestals, somewhat like Patmore with his "angel in the house," except Swinburne's idols were neither domesticated nor chaste. He found pleasure in groveling at the feet of sexually aggressive, even violent, women, with rod in hand (or ones he paid to appear this way). The more morally transgressive the woman the better, to Swinburne's mind. He took the fears of his contemporaries, who saw female sexual promiscuity as diseased and perverted, and turned them into hothouse desires, to be carefully explored in his poems, plays, and novels. The theme of the femme fatale preoccupied him throughout his life; his work returns again and again to real-life "fatal" women, like Lucrezia Borgia (reputed to have tipped poison into men's drinks from her ring); Mary Stuart (around whom a good deal of blood was spilled); the Venus of the Tannhäuser legend (a seductress almost impossible to resist who wears out the poor knight with her sinful extravagance). But then he felt much the same about men, although he never, as far as we know, paid them for the pleasure (he got the cruelty of men for free).

Swinburne figured out early on that at its core sexuality was often about power relationships—the men generally having almost all, the women having very little—and made this boldly apparent by inverting it: giving the women in his writings an extravagance of physical, sensual control, knowledge, and, at times, anger. Women in poems like "Dolores," "Laus Veneris" ("Praise of Venus"), and "Anactoria" use the bodies of men and women like canvases in a highly cultivated sensual art. (Venus, for instance, is a weaver of male flesh: "With nerve and bone she weaves and multiplies / Exceeding pleasure out of extreme pain.") Swinburne's female characters mastermind a philosophy of Aestheticism that involves milking each moment of its languid beauty, its sensual delight, and its agony. From the body of the lover they draw out moments of intense meaning, a kind of erotic existentialism.

It was in Sappho that Swinburne found his lasting muse. Sappho was "the very greatest poet that ever lived," he felt. Not only did he write of her; he carried her metric stanza (called sapphic) into his poetry (thus revitalizing it for English poetry) and even worked in some of her actual phrases.[12] In his long poem "Anactoria," based on Sappho's own fragment "Ode to Anactoria," Swinburne has Sappho speak in the first person to her female lover Anactoria, who has betrayed her with a man. In the beginning of the poem, she vents her angry jealousy—"my life is bitter with thy love." While her fury runs hot, she enumerates ways to hurt Anactoria, which become markers of her desire, her yearning to have and keep her. "That I could drink thy veins as wine, and eat / Thy breasts like honey!" But Sappho expands in power as the poem goes on, and Swinburne sets her up as a rival to the Christian God (even though the poet died around six hundred years before the birth of Jesus), just as he does with the pagan goddess Venus, in "Laus Veneris." Sappho talks of reaching into heaven, smiting and desecrating the cruel God, making him feel what it's like to be human: to "mix his immortality with death." Anactoria will die ("thou will be forgotten like spilt wine"), but she, Sappho, will be immortal through her poetry. Becoming the very figure of passion, her image will be seen in "bright fire" and the "immeasurable tremor of all the sea." She will be one with

> all high things for ever . . .
> my songs once heard in a strange place;
> Cleave to men's lives, and waste the days thereof
> With gladness and much sadness and long love.

Into the mouth of the mythic "lesbian" (this word comes from the name of Sappho's home, the Greek island of Lesbos), Swinburne puts the major idea of his life and work—that it's the poet or the artist and not God who speaks for humanity.

Dangerous women with overweening hubris were not only

sexually desirable to Swinburne; they worked almost as a kind of stand-in for him. They spoke his philosophy, his despair, his sexuality. He identified closely with female rebels, especially lesbians (writing with lesbian themes would become his "golden book of spirit and sense";[13] when he died, he wanted to go to the "Lesbian Hades").[14] Gender roles at the time were so heavily codified that they were thought to be biologically based (as is still true today, with minor differences): men were, by nature, productive, carefully suppressive of emotion and weakness, sober-minded, and firmly rational. Women "naturally" complemented them: they were emotional, yielding, highly sensitive, messy-minded, and attractively weak in character. Of course, the reality was quite different, and many people were aware of this. Still, such ideologies kept a strong hold on the imagination. Just think of any of the major heroines in the novels of Dickens and the qualities they valorize (Esther Summerson in *Bleak House*, for instance, or Little Nell in *The Old Curiosity Shop*, Lizzie Hexam in *Our Mutual Friend*), and it's easy to see how persuasive these ideas remained.

Even to Swinburne his hard, self-serving, unyielding women were manifestly subversive. Deforming the "natural order" was part of Swinburne's aesthetic, his sexual identity. Speaking through such "depraved" women, such outsiders, freed him to step out of his role as a Victorian male. From an imaginative androgyny, he gained an ability to look back at his world from the margins. In this sense, Swinburne's treacherous women are all reflections of his own identity, his own dark being growing into power. His femme fatale character, if we follow this line of thinking, isn't about real women at all, but rather about a certain kind of renegade art that he, as a man, created.

While it's indeed difficult to see how his image of the birch-wielding woman in any way empowered actual women of his time (although quite a few made an easy quid out of it), Swinburne must be credited with trying to work his way toward a new mobility of sexual identity and gender roles, a fresh way of thinking about bodies and their sexual capabilities. Lesbianism, for a man who probably never met an avowed lesbian, stood for a kind of promised land of sexual identity, where the old structures might be exploded, or at least rearranged drastically. (Later lesbian writers found inspiration in Swinburne. After reading his novel *Lesbia Brandon*, H.D., the bisexual, early twentieth-century Modernist writer, wrote that she fell into an "electric coma.")[15] Swinburne's hugely popular writings opened the door to difficult questions: What if one could move fluidly, at will, between the masculine and feminine? Even more difficult to contemplate, what if the whole concept of masculine and feminine gender roles dissolved?

IN 1868, WHILE Swinburne was dividing his time between the rhythms of the swishings at Verbena Lodge and those of iambics and dactylics, Dante Gabriel Rossetti was embarking on a new love affair, one that would consume him for the rest of his life. His wife now dead for seven years, the widower was looked on by many women as a catch. Despite rarely publicly exhibiting his work—his ego too fragile to face critical attacks—he was now a famous painter whose canvases fetched high prices from wealthy northern industrialists. His ancient Queen Anne style mansion and studio on the Thames in Chelsea, at 16 Cheyne Walk, had become the social hub of bohemian London. Whom would he choose, of all those eligible single women? But he was never to remarry. His passion for his best friend's wife, Jane Morris, came to subsume all.

Rossetti's reputation as a philanderer began in the late 1850s and continues even today. He was known for haunting the city streets half the night, wearing a soft hat and Inverness cape, in a restless search—at times for a warm body, at other times for something less tangible. A potent air of seductiveness hung around him, making it easy to believe anecdotes of erotic prowess and escapades. Burne-Jones remarked of him, in a comment caught somewhere between awe and bitterness, "I'm sure there wasn't a woman in the world he couldn't have won for himself! Nothing pleased him better, though, than to take a friend's mistress away from him."[16] Such exaggerated pronouncements lent Rossetti legendary status, augmented by the sensualist's style in his art starting in the late 1850s. His supposed libertinism took on such proportions that someone in his circle commented "that procuring abortions was an every day amusement to him."[17] (Swinburne reputedly made this quip, but when Rossetti confronted him, he vehemently denied it.)

To some extent, Rossetti cultivated the image of himself as a seducer and sexual experimenter. Sexual promiscuity became part of the bohemian artist's toolbox, another way to wear the badge of rebellion against middle-class morality. Rossetti and his set helped shape the idea, still new in the Victorian period but so prevalent today that it seems somehow "normal," that the artist (or, today, movie or rock star) must have a complicated, even scandalous, sexual life. Indeed, the whole concept of the artist as troubled, laden with an oversensitive temperament bringing self-destruction—the fierce life nourished by drugs, alcohol, sex—developed in the first three quarters of the 1800s. The poet Lord Byron, an international celebrity during his lifetime, virtually started the whole idea, especially the connection between creative talent and a secret sexual life (Byron was effectually exiled from England when his incestuous relationship with his half sister was exposed).

Romanticism with its idea of the artist as a riotous, free agent belonged to Rossetti and his circle almost as much as to the first generation of Romantics (most of whom died around the time these men were born). In fact, those of the first generation who would ultimately have the greatest impact on later eras—the most subversive and trail-blazing of the lot—were rediscovered by the Rossetti and Burton circles. The posthumous reputations of John Keats, William Blake, and Percy Bysshe Shelley were profoundly shaped by these Victorians, our perception of them today filtered through their consciousness. Milnes produced the first biography of Keats, who was largely forgotten after his death in Rome, at the age of twenty-five, in 1821; Blake's work had disappeared into obscurity when Rossetti bought one of his notebooks of poems and sketches for ten shillings and collaborated with Alexander Gilchrist on the first Blake biography (Swinburne also produced a critical work on Blake); William Rossetti wrote an early biography of Shelley, who had been long out of favor because of his socialist political views.

How true was the picture of Rossetti as profligate? Rossetti slept with prostitutes—how many? Some of his models ended up in his bed—which ones? Does it matter? Historians have carried on long-standing squabbles about the notches on Rossetti's belt. In a strange twist, recently, scholars have speculated that his affair with Jane Morris might have been a platonic passion (using as evidence his recurrent hydrocele, or painfully swollen testicles, probably caused by a case of the mumps). While the minutiae and math are of only mild interest, Rossetti (like Burton) did some sexual research. How could he found the religion of sensual beauty without a life well steeped?

Rossetti needed to plant himself inside the place where the passions of the flesh, heart, and mind had their being. Wanting to find, in his poetry especially, what he called an "inner standing point," he got to know things (like prostitution, say) by being in their innards. The artist stands in "the very world" in which the "heart" of mysteries "beat and bleed. . . . The beauty and the pity . . . can come with full force only from the mouth of one alive to its whole appeal."[18] This aliveness involved enfleshed doing. Even when Rossetti's paintings don't appear at all autobiographical, such as his allegorical or historical ones with titles like *Helen of Troy* or *Venus Verticordia*, they still sprang from relationships with moving, breathing people. All of them were recognizably paintings of women he knew. Of course, the same argument could be made with most realist painters. Yet Rossetti practiced a type of collaboration with his models. Many kinds of closeness became fundamental to him. An assertion of place and presence—of warm skin, flowers just blooming, a woman's particular, favorite dress—make these paintings forcefully about what happened in that room between those two people. Rossetti required the type of women who would imprint their selves and bodies on his paintings, his life, and his ideas about art in general.

JANE BURDEN WOULD later become a famous beauty, but when Rossetti first met her, in 1857, she was a tall, lanky seventeen-year-old, the unschooled and unsophisticated daughter of an Oxford hostler at Symond's Livery Stable. On a night out at a local theater with her sister Bessie, she was spotted by Gabriel, a young Londoner who must have seemed impossibly glamorous to her. Jane certainly stood out in a crowd of Britons. Her dark, foreign-seeming countenance led to rumors (untrue) of gypsy blood. Her thoughtful eyes under a heavy brow peer out of photographs with a kind of sullenness (Henry James later called them "a pair of strange sad, deep, dark Swinburnian eyes"), and her thickly massed black hair tended toward frizziness.[19] She had none of the conventional beauty of the time, none of that safe honey-and-roses plumpness. (Georgiana Burne-Jones compared Janey with Lizzie thus: "Mrs. Morris being the statue and Mrs. Rossetti the picture.")[20] Gabriel, always boldly on the lookout for "stunners," pushed his way through the crowd, dragging Ned (Burne-Jones) with him, and asked her to pose. She said yes, but without understanding what he meant. What kind of work was this, being paid to sit while an artist traced your image in charcoal or oils? Eventually Ned went to see her mother for permission, and soon she was modeling for Rossetti's Queen Guinevere, the woman who betrays King Arthur for the knight Sir Lancelot (all of which leads to the downfall of the kingdom).

This summer and fall of 1857 in Oxford would become the stuff of legend. Rossetti took a group of his new friends—including William Morris (who got the nickname Topsy around this time) and Burne-Jones—to paint Arthurian murals on the ceiling of the Union Debating Hall. Morris and Rossetti had proposed the project to the Gothic architect Benjamin Woodward, who designed the building. The "jovial campaign" it was called, or, later, "those wonderful seething days."[21] It was a grand summer: more important than depicting King Arthur, Sir Lancelot, and Merlin was the artistic camaraderie. Painting on scaffolding and making a royal mess, they could be heard by the students studying next door: bursts of song, shouts of laughter, off-color jokes, the pop of soda-water corks. One of these students, Swinburne, met them all at this time and speedily formed a hero worship for Gabriel and a fast and lifelong friendship with Ned (who called Swinburne, with his flame of red hair, "dear Little Carrots"). Their fellow painter Val Prinsep described nights back at their lodgings on High Street. Gabriel would curl up on the horsehair sofa, humming to himself; Ned would continue scratching out a pen-and-ink drawing. Morris would stomp around the room until Rossetti called out, "I say, Top, read us one of your Grinds," as they called Morris's poetry.[22]

Into the midst of such comfortable all-male domesticity stepped Jane. It's likely she was first smitten with Rossetti, but it was Morris who proposed to her. While he painted her as *La Belle Iseult* (a painting also known as *Queen Guinevere*—both women, interestingly, famed adulteresses), the story goes that he scribbled a frantic note, "I cannot paint you but I love you."[23] She accepted his proposal—many years later admitting she wasn't in love with him. But with her family's poverty and lack of education (her mother was illiterate), it was such a glorious match (Morris, who came from a wealthy family, found every opportunity to rebel against his upbringing) that she couldn't say no. Jane thus entered what must have been a brave new world for her, where leisurely days could be lived for art and beauty alone.

But it wasn't until the spring of 1868 that Jane, now twenty-seven and a mother of two, swept a forty-year-old Gabriel off his feet. Jane and William Morris were living in London, after Morris sold his brick medieval country hall and garden—Red House—designed for him by Philip Webb. The exact details of the start of the affair weren't recorded, but Jane began modeling for Rossetti at Tudor House in March (Morris accompanied her at first, but later they were able to finagle long stretches alone). Fanny, who had moved back in with Rossetti around 1863, soon moved out. Something happened on April 14—did they consummate the relationship? Declare their love? Whatever it was, Gabriel planned to commemorate it with a bracelet (which appears never to have been made). He drew a design for it in one of his small notebooks with "Sept 57 ⊗ April 14 1868" penciled as an inscription. September is when he first met her in Oxford, but the nature of the April 14 event remains obscure. The circled x implies some kind of coded, affirmed coming together or meeting. From this date on, she seemed always before his eyes. It's her face seen in every major painting of his for the rest of his life (and this countenance became so iconic that when Pre-Raphaelitism or early Aestheticism is talked about, even today, it's her face that's conjured up instantly). Most of the sonnets in *House of Life* praise Rossetti's obsessive love for Jane, her "sovereign face," which he makes into a "shrine" by his paintings and "song." In one of the flurry of love letters that passed between them, he wrote, "More than all for me, Janey, is the fact that you exist, that I can yet look forward to seeing you and speaking to you again, and know for certain that at that moment I shall forget all my own troubles."[24]

Worshipping at her shrine is a Christian way of stating the pagan: she was his muse. But Janey met him at least halfway. Never merely a passive inspiration, a vision of beauty to be taken up and recorded in oils, verse, or tapestry, Janey was an artist and force in her own right. And this despite being another of those Victorian women with mysterious ailments that kept them mostly confined to the sofa, like Elizabeth Barrett Browning and Lizzie Siddal. A highly skilled embroiderer, Janey picked out in darkly glowing colors strange medieval landscapes for Morris's design company (the first Arts and Crafts group). More lasting, though, was her mastery of a defiant and wholly original personal style. She fashioned herself into a bold character, making living a creative act, something like the artist personae of Swinburne, Rossetti, and Burton (later exemplified by Oscar Wilde and Virginia Woolf). Jane, too, could play at Byronism.

Taking the part of the mysterious, gravely silent cipher, she seemed, to others, to hide a brooding interior and a tormented, unknowable past. She topped it off with a secret sexual life (there were others besides Morris and Rossetti), unusual for a woman of her time. Designing, dyeing, and sewing her own dresses, Janey shunned the current ultra-feminine fashions with their crinolines, corsets, and bustles. Her medieval art robes, usually of a rich, unadorned fabric, draped her shapelessly and boyishly. To this simplicity, she added jewelry designed by herself or others in the set. At a time when women carefully constructed and constrained their hair, Janey wore hers loose, large, wild. Progressive female artists in the 1870s and 1880s who followed the aesthetic creed adopted this look, which they picked up either from knowing Jane or from seeing her in Rossetti's paintings. When she sat for Rossetti, she presented this cultured artistic self (wearing her handmade dresses and jewelry), a self wholly remade from the working-class teenager of Oxford. Rossetti drew out of the deep well of Janey to make his paintings. They are testaments to his attempt to finally know her, to pin down what she was and figure out how he could have it. But her magic was, for Rossetti, inexhaustible and ultimately impossible to plumb, even though he spent some fifty sketches and full-scale oils—and a raft of love sonnets—trying.

On a visit to the Morrises in 1868, Henry James recognized

the collaborative nature of Janey's involvement. Steeped in Pre-Raphaelite and Aesthetic pictures, James commented on Janey's complicated relationship to both producing and inspiring the style associated with Rossetti, Morris, Burne-Jones, and their cohorts.

> Such a wife! . . . she haunts me still. A figure cut out of a missal—one of Rossetti's or Hunt's pictures—to say this gives but a faint idea of her, because when such an image puts on flesh and blood, it is an apparition of fearful and wonderful intensity. It's hard to say whether she's a grand synthesis of all the Pre-Raphaelite pictures ever made—or they a "keen analysis" of her—whether she's an original or a copy. In either case she is a wonder.[25]

If Rossetti hadn't discovered Janey, would he have been able to call up those otherworldly visions, marvelously alive with the character of the sitter?

Gabriel's most important oils of Janey depict women who amass destruction around them. When he developed his mad love for her, Rossetti had already embarked on his series of sirens, seductresses, and femmes fatales. There was *Helen of Troy* in 1863, his painting of the woman whose face launched a thousand ships, with Fanny as his model. Then came *Venus Verticordia* (1863–68), which Rossetti translated as the Venus who turns men's hearts away from fidelity (à la Swinburne), modeled by Alexa Wilding. Wilding then sat for *Lady Lilith* (1866), Adam's witchlike wife before Eve. Out of his collaboration with Jane came the crowning masterpieces of his career: *Pandora*, who unleashed a world of trouble when she opened that box (one completed in 1871, another in 1878); *Astarte Syriaca*, the

Syrian Venus (1877); and *Proserpine* (1882), a variant spelling of Persephone, whose beauty ultimately led to her kidnapping and that curse we must experience every year: winter.

Rossetti dwelt on the theme of women who bring winter and chaos. A cluster of contradictory impulses came into play, all feelings Rossetti had at various times in his life: fear of women, resentment of their power over him, a need to play the master, a deep interest in women who might destroy him. Rossetti's attraction to destructive women works as the flip side of his love of dead and dying women, both being a fascination with the place where death and sex meet (woman as killed or killer). Rossetti wanted to lose himself in and with women. He wanted to "die" in them. Thus, the full meaning of Janey's being a "stunner": he desired a lover to come and knock him out, bewilder him, put him in a trance.

Jane starts forth as a strong, dark presence in Rossetti's late pictures. As their mutual aesthetic developed, Jane's figure became androgynous, with the thick neck, heavy arms, and shoulders of a man (photographs of Janey belie this constructed image). Limbs in *Astarte Syriaca*, for instance, appear surprisingly muscled. Hands and sometimes faces and necks become curiously distorted, fingers frozen in a spiderlike curl, plucking rare instruments or grasping at objects (Pandora at her box, Astarte at the girding on her robe, Proserpine at the fateful pomegranate bursting with seeds). Gender is disrupted. Rossetti troubles the Victorian certainty that gender is simply a binary matter: male and female. But anxiety surrounds this possibility. Strong women, were they monstrous—Circes, sirens, Medusa? Conventional Victorian society tried to push such women to the margins, making them seem like outsiders and strange anomalies. But this constant pressure to keep them out, to make them grotesque even, proved their deep centrality to Victorian identity. Women had to be asserted as angels, because the reality—women working to gain real power—had the dangerous potential to explode. Rossetti mined these cracks and fissures.

Rossetti's androgynous pictures also envisioned his own identity confusions. Masculinity seemed something he both wanted to hold on to and ached to give away. On the one hand, he could sensually succumb to an Astarte. Yet when he was attacked in the press, after he published his volume of poetry that contained *House of Life*, for being unmanly, emasculated, and dealing in matters "that healthy men put out of their thoughts," his sanity began to unravel.[26] Such an accusation seemed the stuff of nightmares, and he sank into a delusional and paranoid state, which led to a suicide attempt by an overdose of laudanum. He did recover after four months, but he never emerged fully from his addiction to chloral and whisky, taken in horse doses. His sense of himself as a man in the Victorian world, and what this meant in relation to his passion for women, stayed knotted up inside him, picked at always in his art but never disentangled.

IN MAY OF 1863, Burton languished at the backwater post of Her Britannic Majesty's Consul of Fernando Po, in West Africa. "I felt uncommonly suicidal through that first night on Fernando Po," he wrote in despair.[27] Stuck on the island of yellow mud, rotten shacks, and fever (a "white man's grave" because dysentery, typhus, and yellow fever regularly "clears off almost all the white population") as a result of his knack for offending authorities by sending them starkly worded, unwelcome truths, he was bored with his official duties, which were far beneath his abilities.[28] He did what he would always do in these situations: he went exploring. What currently sparked his interest were rumors of a band of Amazonian women warriors, the personal bodyguard of King Gelele of Dahome. A French traveler had assessed their number at twelve thousand; others had described their muscular beauty and prowess on horseback. Burton, a critic of the confining dress of English females and the "pure purgatory" of English country-house life for women, was fascinated by the possibility of military women. In the event, he was somewhat disappointed—their skill and majesty didn't live up to myth.

Characteristically, his interest sharpened when it came to gender and sexuality. The Amazonians explained that in taking up their warlike lives, they had become males (usually dressing like them), thus giving up entirely all pretensions to being female. What did this mean? Burton mused. Deeply compelling to him, as to Swinburne, was any type of gender or sexual "play," such as androgyny or intersexuality (or hermaphroditism, as it was then called). In analyzing their "masculinity" (characterized by ferocity and a propensity to violence) in his book *A Mission to Gelele, King of Dahome*, Burton felt that it emerged from suppression of sexual energy. Anticipating Freud (as Burton commonly did), he found the source of their "unfeminine" ways in the celibacy required in their line of work. Sexuality became rerouted into violence: "All the passions are sisters," Burton stated. "I believe that bloodshed causes these women to remember, not to forget LOVE."[29] A rather un-Victorian view, this: to block such weighty and potent sexual desire is to provoke a lust for blood in women.

In the fabric of a newly encountered culture, Burton's deft eye picked out those who were anomalous, marginal, outcast.

This kept him focused on women and the position they occupied, most often outside the structures of power. He studied the weave of sexual dominance and submission that he felt, in one of his pet theories, was integral to the functioning of a culture (a theory he also applied critically to his own society). Such interests emerged directly out of his own sense of self. Burton relished his mastery over others, like any stalwart Victorian imperialist. Most thoroughly of the men under discussion here, he stepped into the shoes of the Romantic adventurer, the Byronic antihero. An acquaintance described him as "dark, swarthy, loud-voiced, self-asserting. . . . The sense of power . . . was borne out in every glance . . . ." In fact, he was "the very type of a romantic young lady's ideal pirate, or captain of a robber band."[30]

Sexual experience worked as a crucial component to Burton's carefully orchestrated masculinity. Anecdotes about his far-flung sexual avidity were seeded throughout his published writings and his talk. He wrote openly about the series of mistresses who passed through his tent when he lived in India, even though such a reputation worked at times as a detriment to his career. His ethnographic studies of brothels, prostitution, and casual sex contained such insider's detail that it was clear that Burton—a voracious, sensual man—was throwing himself into his work rather than maintaining proper scientific objectivity. (The syphilis Burton contracted around 1853, most likely from sleeping around in Sindh, would plague him on and off for the rest of his life, reaching the tertiary stage in the end.)

Burton swaggered in company, painting a blackened picture of himself in order to shock and entice his dinner mates. Rumors circulated, such as the one that Burton had shot a boy who discovered that Burton was a Briton disguised as an Arab (such gossip of "dark horrors" popped up throughout his lifetime, none of it true), and when asked about them at parties, he would usually make some cynical joke that left his listeners unsure what to believe. Dr. George Bird: "Now, Burton, tell me, how do you feel when you have killed a man?" Burton: "Oh, quite jolly, doctor! How do you?"[31] Meeting up with Burton in Brazil (a dark episode in Burton's life, when disappointments led him to heavy drinking), Wilfrid Scawen Blunt (incidentally, Jane Morris's lover after Rossetti) found himself disturbed, galvanized. "In his talk he affected an extreme brutality, and if one could believe the whole of what he said, he had indulged in every vice and committed every crime." Blunt feared Burton's spell. "If I had submitted to his gaze for any length of time . . . I have no doubt he would have succeeded in dominating me."[32] But Blunt later came to understand that Burton slipped fluidly in and out of disguises. Burton performed his masculinity, with a theatrical flair and a heavy dose of self-awareness. Or, as Blunt put it, he was "a sheep in wolf's clothing."[33]

Burton's love of role-playing took on its richest coloring in his relationship with his wife, Isabel. Both husband and wife wrote extensively of their lives and travels, much of the prose packed with personal detail. Their overblown personalities developed in the public eye. Although Isabel burned many of their papers after Burton's death (and had executors burn more after her own), a fairly intricate record of the drama of their marriage remains—its mesmeric and telepathic eroticism, showy exoticism, and mystical feverishness.

It was Burton's commanding presence as a young officer that enthralled Isabel Arundell when she first caught sight of him, on fashionable promenade on the stone ramparts of Boulogne in 1852.[34] He stepped, with exact symmetry, into the model of the perfect man she had already laid out in her teenage diary—the only kind of man, she vehemently proclaimed, she would marry or else become a nun. This ideal persona formed her destiny, Isabel superstitiously believed, convinced a gypsy had foretold it all when she was still a girl. Her first encounter with Burton was recorded in her diary in her usual dashingly romantic, gothic style. "The most remarkable part of his appearance was two large, black, flashing eyes with long lashes, that pierced one through and through. . . . I was completely magnetized; and when we had got a little distance away, I turned to my sister, and whispered to her, 'That man will marry me.'"[35] For four years Isabel remained "spellbound" by Burton, who escaped the empty rhythms of English high society—its visiting cards, dressing for dinner, narrow-world gossip—and who speedily forgot about Isabel, who, as a woman, couldn't get out of the tiresome social rounds. No wonder Isabel would later exclaim, "I wish I were a man: if I were, I would be Richard Burton. But as I am a woman, I would be Richard Burton's wife."[36] Burton himself, the lucky man, was off pilgrimaging to Mecca, exploring the sacred city of Harar, and getting speared through the face in East Africa.

Richard finally came back to London in 1856, with the season in full swing. The two ran into each other at Hyde Park's botanical gardens. Fashionably dressed, with his long mustachios and in a frock coat with velvet collar, Burton's civilized veneer barely covered his unusual physique: he was extraordinarily broad-shouldered and barrel-chested. A friend noted he had the "frame of a Titan," adding, "He was the only man I ever knew who could fire the old-fashioned elephant gun from the shoulder without a rest."[37] Isabel, herself a famously aggressive character (rumors abounded about her dexterity and cruelty with a whip, when the Burtons took over the consulship in

Damascus in 1869), wanted to be pulled under by such a tide of inexorable dominion. "Richard has the upper hand now, and I feel that I have at last met the master who can subdue me," she wrote in her diary. She continued (referring to women in general along with herself), "They say it is better to marry one who loves and is subject to you than one whose slave you are through love. But I cannot agree to this. Where in such a case is the pleasure, the excitement, the interest?"[38] Burton provided such stimulation in spades; being with him brought on something akin to "a fever or a momentary madness . . . I am frightened at . . . his dangerous but irresistible society."[39]

Burton, who could be profoundly romantic despite his cynicism and casual promiscuity, took only two weeks to propose. "He stole his arm round my waist, and laid his cheek against mine and asked me, 'Could you do anything so sickly as to give up civilization? . . . [I]t will mean . . . giving up your people and all that you are used to, and living the sort of life that Lady Hester Stanhope led.' " Isabel replied, "I would rather have a crust and a tent with you than be queen of all the world."[40] Because Isabel's family held such high status in England (she descended from ancient dukes and earls), and Burton's reputation in polite society at the time was mostly gutterish (summed up by an early Burton biographer: "Pious mothers loathed Burton's name, and even men of the world mentioned it apologetically"), they eloped in secret in 1861.[41]

Their marriage was a great success. They established a fruitful and productive partnership that flourished for the rest of their lives. Inextricably bound up in their relationship was the need to re-create the dreamy trance, the tumult, of their role-playing in the beginning. The roles they would take—with Burton usually as the "top" and Isabel as "bottom" (although

Isabel was a "bottom" who liked to "top")—were often salted with a little gothic magic and performed for an audience. A rather cryptic observation of the two came from Madame Mary Mohl (a disciple of Florence Nightingale), who was with them at a house party at Fryston. "He acts a ferocious musselman to her lovely oppressed and impassioned slave and I suspect they chuckle over our simplicity instead of fighting in their secret compartment and if she told you he had beat her I would believe it unhesitatingly."[42] Mohl moves back and forth between belief and nonbelief. From her comment and others, Richard and Isabel's delight in such playacting shines through, as does their recognition of its replication of conventional gender roles. Still, it was also clearly a constitutive force in their relationship, required for its basic functioning.

Richard liked to prove his hypnotic power over Isabel by mesmerizing her, usually in front of others. Mesmerists (named after Anton Mesmer) thought the universe was infused with an invisible fluid, akin to electricity, that could be manipulated to control others. A popular pseudo-science and parlor trick of the day, mesmerism could also be used medically—as a way to pull out the tooth of a hypnotized person without pain, or to persuade them to give up physical or psychological ailments. Blunt wrote some lines in his diary on Burton's mesmeric influence on Isabel. "Her devotion to him was very real, and she was . . . entirely under his domination, an hypnotic domination Burton used to boast of. I have heard him say that at a distance of many hundred miles he could will her to do anything he chose as completely as if he were with her in the same room."[43] For Burton (and for Charles Dickens, who loved hypnotizing women), mesmerism certainly had a sexual element to it. Isabel reports that in choosing the people he would mesmerize, Richard "always preferred women and especially of the blue eyed, yellow-haired types."[44] He started in on Isabel as soon as they were married, forcing her when under his influence to tell him everything on her mind ("I have often told him things I would much rather keep to myself").[45] He never allowed anyone else to put her under, stating on one occasion, in the heat of an argument, that he would kill her and the man. Isabel also held such jealousies, becoming enraged when he mesmerized other women.

Both Richard and Isabel, as highly intelligent observers of culture, saw their identities as Victorian men and women to a large extent *as roles*—the man a controlling hero, the woman a self-effacing helper. Burton's open exploration of gender relations and sexual role-playing in his published writing put him in the vanguard of thinking about gender and sexuality. Still, he didn't throw his weight behind the women's movement for equality (although he did feel women should be freer than they were, especially in the areas of sexual education and legal rights over their property and children). His feelings toward nascent feminism were mixed, at best, and some of the beliefs put forth in his writings make modern feminists cringe (like his admiration for polygamy or his joking promise to Frederick Hankey to obtain for him a "peau de femme" when in West Africa, so Hankey could bind his book with human flesh). Yet the Cannibal Club itself became a forum for men who were women's rights activists or were openly supportive of the cause. Charles Bradlaugh, with Annie Besant, published pamphlets for distribution to working-class women about birth control that got them arrested and prosecuted, in 1877, for depraving public morals. Lord Penzance worked for the reform of divorce laws so that women had an easier time escaping abusive husbands.

Asked by John Stuart Mill, Milnes joined the Women's Suffrage Society in 1867. Milnes was financially and emotionally supportive of the work of Florence Nightingale (who wrote, "Why have women passion, intellect, moral activity—these three—and a place in society where no one of the three can be exercised?").[46] Indeed, he fell in love with her, proposing marriage more than once. Her repeated refusals left him in the role of staunch supporter and friend throughout their lifetimes.

Isabel willingly took the role of Burton's devoted assistant, spending time and energy furthering his career. Yet she was never a stereotypical "wife." She grew into the position of his highly skilled literary agent and editor, guiding most of his manuscripts into print. Along the way, she became a popular author herself, writing books that sold more copies than her husband's, at least during her lifetime. In a preface to his *Highlands of the Brazil*, she wrote that she was "compelled to differ with him on many . . . subjects; but . . . not in the common spirit of domestic jar, but with a mutual agreement to differ and enjoy our differences, whence points of interest never flag."[47] She actively supported Florence Nightingale's feminist work and could write scathingly of the circumscribed life forced on English women (and in other cultures; she often toured harems and wrote about what she observed there). Those poor English women were "breeding fools," and they "chronicled small beer."[48] She felt she had escaped such a life, living with Richard abroad and shaking off the constraining "harness of European society." Her life in the East represented a measure of liberty: "I shall have tents, horses, weapons, and be *free*."[49] Toward the end of her life, Isabel began signing many of her letters "Hermaphrodite."

MEN TOGETHER

CHAPTER FOUR

The Grove of the Evangelist

> . . . but he was a stunning tutor; his one other pet subject was metre, and I firmly believe that my ear for verse made me rather a favourite. I can boast that of all the swishings I ever had up to seventeen and over, I never had one for a false quantity in my life. . . . One comfort is, I made it up in arithmetic, so my tutor never wanted reasons for making rhymes between his birch and my body.
>
> —SWINBURNE in a letter to Milnes, February 1863

UGUST 16, 1862: It was a typical Saturday morning, high summer, with most everyone out of town and the Thames stinking and smoking under the baking sun. Shouts of laughter rang out from Swinburne's rooms, near the British Museum (which also contained, at the time, the British Library). He was reading to Rossetti and George Boyce, from a volume he had been trying to get his hands on for years. He relished the declamatory pose. A gifted reader and speaker, Swinburne compulsively recited at parties—Shakespeare, Sophocles, Dante (all from memory), his own poetry—leaving listeners in a wondering trance. Now he was at it again, but this was not the usual well-thumbed classic. Rather, this banned book was borrowed from Milnes's porn library, smuggled into London from Paris (probably nestled in the warm curve of Augustus Harris's back, under the auspices of Hankey). The book was the Marquis de Sade's *La Nouvelle Justine* (the extended, graphic version, published in France in 1797, that landed Sade in prison for many years), which follows a girl as her excessive "virtue" is repaid repeatedly by "vice," equally extreme. It is a book of dark humor—comedy as black as can be—where rape isn't depraved enough, but rather must be ratcheted up to sodomy by monks who not only feverishly flagellate their victims, but also consume their feces (Swinburne calls this latter practice "those rank and rancid preparations which served as *entremets* at the great dinners and suppers of Gomorrah").[1]

Sade set out to offend, and he accomplished this in spades. Yet despite being such strong stuff, in its absurdity it's hilarious. It came as especially hysterical to those living in Victorian England (and Enlightenment France, for that matter), when treacly proclamations about virtue served as cover for a culture of violence and suppression—against those they colonized (the "Indian Mutiny" of 1857, for instance) and the poor of their own cities (the Poor Laws and the workhouse, which punished brutally the "crime" of poverty). Swinburne and his clan, with their gallows humor, took Sade in high glee: savoring the "mystic pages of the martyred marquis" (Swinburne). "I never laughed so much in my life: I couldn't have stopped to save the said life . . . . I wonder to this minute that we did not raise the whole house by our screams of laughter."[2] (Burton, however, did not love Sade. Asked to translate *Justine* from the French, for Leonard Smithers's imprint Erotika Biblion, he begged off. "I shall have nothing to do with . . . *Justine*. The French of Dr Sade is monstrous enough and a few pages choke me off. But what bile it would be in brutal Anglo-Saxon.")[3]

It seems inevitable now, given his penchant for the rod since youth, that Swinburne would discover Sade. Still, it took longer than one might imagine. Swinburne had taken Sade as his master and upheld him as the "acme and apostle of perfection."[4] That was, until he read him for the first time, on this Saturday morning. Immensely disappointed, he wrote to Milnes to explain why: "I looked for some sharp and subtle analysis of lust—some keen dissection of pain and pleasure." Instead, he finds sexual atrocities piled up, a kind of catalog of outrages against the human body: "he takes *bulk* and *number* for greatness." Funny, yes, but it lacked a cutting philosophical point. "Shew us how and why," Swinburne pleads, "these things are as they are."[5] Swinburne would come up with future masters (Baudelaire, Burton, Giuseppe Mazzini, leader of Italian liberation), but his task now was clear: he would need to take the measure of "the feverish famine in [his] veins" that flowed out from being in love with longing.[6]

BORN TO BE BULLIED, Swinburne, with his delicate frame, soft voice pitched high, and dancing gestures, had found Eton a bruising place. The toughs of the school had descended on him. Corporal punishment wasn't only a part of boy culture; it was built into the foundations of public school education.

Swinburne's tutors had birched him for minor infractions such as reading Edgar Allan Poe's "Descent in the Maelstrom" or Nathaniel Hawthorne's *The Scarlet Letter* instead of working on his Thucydides. According to accounts by boys who attended midcentury, "some half-dozen boys were flogged everyday. It was entirely public; any one who chose might drop in."[7] Boys as old as eighteen or nineteen might be put on the "hard old wooden Flogging-Block" with their pants dragged down and two boys pulling up their shirt tails and imprisoning them there. Many watched the "swishing," particularly the boy's close friends and enemies, to see how he "stood it." The Eton rods used for the "execution" (as the beatings were called) were huge—two feet of thickly bundled birch twigs with a three-foot handle. Beaten boys garnered nicknames: "Pepperbottom" (from the markings that were left by a rod made of fir twigs with buds still attached) or "Wagtail" (a reference to the writhing movements of the boy while being birched).

Swinburne would later recall his Eton floggings with a troubled nostalgia, in words of fear and fondness. He lingers over details lovingly, painfully, with literary embellishments. In fact, all of the accounts we have of his Eton birchings are colored by his later sexualizing of punishment. It's impossible now to pick the facts out of the haze of fantasy. At the time there must have been trauma and humiliation (some of this comes out in Swinburne's novel *Lesbia Brandon*, where Herbert Seyton's sobbing and flinching at his flagellation by his tutor was probably based on Swinburne's experience). But he tells of his chastisement with a complicitous bravado, a conscious aestheticization. Rather quickly, Swinburne took his shame and expanded it—complicated it—into a wellspring for invention. When he recalls a beating by his tutor James Leigh Joynes, in an 1863 letter to Milnes, he claims it's all based on fact. Joynes would,

> perfume the flogging-room with burnt scents; or choose a *sweet* place out of doors with smell of firewood. *This* I call a real delicate torment. . . . Once, before giving me a swishing that I had the marks of for more than a month . . . he let me saturate my face with eau-de-Cologne.[8]

The clever refinements—the mingling of the opening of the senses and the markings on the flesh—are vintage Swinburne, whether they are copies of Joynes's "lesson" or Swinburne originals. Milnes jotted down a conversation with Swinburne about another Eton incident, where a tutor "swished" Swinburne over a fallen tree trunk. The beating went on until

> the grass was stained with his blood and another time when wet out of the water after bathing: the last much more painful! . . . Tutor telling him he had no pleasure in flogging boys who were not gentlemen: the better the family the more he enjoyed it. The tutor once flogging him in three different positions till he was quite flayed. A. S. very fair, the tutor often flogging a very dark boy by way of contrast, making them hold each other.[9]

The detail of the dark skin next to the pale, both striped red, has the visual intensity of a Swinburne poem; it emerges from the same creative register as "Dolores," "Laus Veneris," and "Anactoria."

Eton was lodged in Swinburne's head. His friend George Powell got a piece of an Eton rod, which Swinburne encased in a locket like a holy relic. Swinburne had a photo taken of the flogging block. In 1891, on Eton's 450th anniversary, Swinburne, now famous throughout the world, was asked to write a poem to celebrate the occasion. He speedily penned "Eton: An Ode," decorous if a bit dull. At the same time, he wrote a second, secret one: "Eton: Another Ode," which isn't dull at all and more honestly praises what he learned there: "Lad by lad, whether good or bad: alas for those who at nine o'clock / Seek the room of disgraceful doom, to smart like fun on the flogging-block!"

Swinburne's flagellation writings fill volumes. He wrote rafts of letters that contain stories about schoolboys being whipped—to Milnes, Charles Augustus Howell (who later sold some of these letters, and was the one, incidentally, who exhumed Lizzie and the manuscript for Rossetti), his publisher John Camden Hotten, Simeon Solomon, his cousin and first love Mary Gordon (in code—a kind of childish gibberish), and others. Flogging figures in much of his prose and seeps into his poems. In addition to his "proper" literature, he also wrote a good deal of flagellation pornography ("Eton: Another Ode" falls into this category). The titles themselves scintillate with a slightly sinister bawdiness: "Redgie's Return: A tragicomedy in 3 acts, 4 double acrostics, 16 scenes and 4 floggings"; "The Schoolboy's Tragedy"; "The Flogging Block. An Heroic Poem by Rufus Rodworthy (Algernon Clavering) with annotations by Barebum Birchingham." Some of his porn was printed in the serial *The Pearl* and the anthology *The Whippingham Papers*, but most of it remained carefully suppressed.

Swinburne was keen on skin. In his pornographic writing, the flesh of the buttocks isn't to be caressed, but rather imprinted. White cheeks form a kind of page; the marks a kind of writing. In "Arthur's Flogging," the metaphor runs throughout the poem:

> The fair full page of white and warm young flesh
> Was ruled across with long thick lines of red,
> And lettered on the engraved backside with fresh
> Large characters, by all boys to be read.

A different way of considering this relationship came from Swinburne's friend (and Cannibal associate) Frederick Hankey. In an attempt to dovetail his two passions—sexual pain and bibliophilia—Hankey talked often about binding books with the soft pelt of a woman. In a boast to the Goncourt brothers, who found him appalling ("a madman, a monster"), he lamented that human skin took six months to tan, so he was forced to wait to bind his *Justine*. Anthropodermic bibliopegy was not uncommon in the nineteenth century: for example, two American thieves arranged to have their autobiographies bound in their own flesh, after their death. The London master binder Joseph Zaehnsdorf was kept busy by doctors, lawyers, and others using unclaimed corpses of the poor for the purpose (most Victorians would not find this practice depraved, but rather thrifty). Hankey, whom Swinburne described as "the Sadique collector of European fame," would today be called a "sadist," although this word wasn't coined until 1886 by the sexologist Richard von Krafft-Ebing.[10] Krafft-Ebing also came up with "masochism," named after the Austrian writer Leopold von Sacher-Masoch, whose masterpiece, *Venus im Pelz* (*Venus in Furs*), tells the story of a man who has "the passion to play the slave" (which involves flagellation, of course). This would have been the book for Swinburne, but it wasn't published until 1870 (in German), and there's no evidence he knew of it. Both Freud and Havelock Ellis, around twenty years after Krafft-Ebing, took these two words, stuck them together, and gave them a foundational role in their theories of sexual development.

Swinburne's porn revolves with obsessive intensity around the same few iconic moments as other "fladge" porn of the period. Such writing was immensely popular midcentury: around 50 percent of all pornography produced from 1840 to 1880 centered on flogging. It also is the richest in terms of variety of genre. There are novels; poems; plays; lectures (such as the "Experimental Lecture by Colonel Spanker on the exciting and voluptuous pleasures to be derived from crushing and humiliating the spirit of a beautiful and modest young lady; as delivered by him in the assembly room of the Society of Aristocratic Flagellants"); "histories" of the practice (for example, *Mysteries of Flagellation*); confessional memoirs (such as *The Spirit of Flagellation; or, The Memoirs of Mrs. Hinton, Who Kept a School Many Years at Kensington . . .*); epistolary collections (for instance, *Sublime of Flagellation in Letters from Lady Termagant Flaybum, of Birch-Grove, to Lady Harriet Tickletail, of Bumfiddle-Hall*); and even medical tracts. Flagellation porn was of high interest to Cannibals: Simeon Solomon and Edward Sellon dabbled in birching narratives; the novelist George Augustus Sala was reputedly the author of *The Mysteries of Verbena House; or, Miss Bellasis Birched for Thieving*; Milnes brought out (through Hotten) *The Rodiad* and others. His library contained many shelves of specimens.

Like pornography in general, these works follow a strict formula. Intercourse is of little to no interest. The whipping doesn't lead up to anything: the whipping *is* the thing. Fladge porn has its own scenes and rhythms of intensity. The points of high meaning—details unfolded slowly and were dwelt on with care—work as replacements for those core events (penetration, orgasm) in regular pornography. The protagonist (it could be man, woman, or child, or a confusing mixture of all three, as cross-dressing, performance, and androgyny are common) commits some wrongdoing, such as sloppiness, insubordination, impertinence, or petty thievery. The reader is usually meant to identify with the supplicant. The moment when the rod is called for is highly charged: "Martha lays a fine bunch of fresh birch twigs (especially tied up with ribbons) at my feet, I have to pick it up and kiss it in a most respectful manner, and ask my schoolmistress to chastise me properly with it." The implements are various: shafts with a dozen whip thongs on each of them, cat-o'-nine-tails with needle points worked into them, thin bending canes, leather straps, battledores, currycomb tough hides, prickly evergreen, holly brushes, furze brushes, green nettles.

The protagonist takes, willingly or almost willingly, a shaming and powerless position—sometimes bent over the lap of the flagellator (with his or her face pressed up against the thighs of the punisher), other times placed over the back of a helper ("horsed") or tied to a piece of furniture or bed. Often accomplices will hold the sufferer down: "I knelt in front of the square ottoman; the ladies held my hands across it."

While force is sometimes a factor, the movement of the narrative is toward the protagonist's accepting not only that the punishment is deserved but that the beating meted out is ultimately a great pleasure. As one "lover of the birch" describes just before she discovers her love, she "was filled with a delightful sense of shame when she recollected the part of her body which would receive the castigation and the exposure it would entail."

The central fascination in flogging literature is with the buttocks and their exposure, vulnerability and even innocence. A lingering description of the uncovering of the "white angelic orbs" is a requirement for the formula: "unfastening her drawers, Jane drew them well down, whilst Mrs. Mansell pinned up her chemise, fully exposing the broad expanse of her glorious buttocks, the brilliant whiteness of her skin showing to perfection by the dazzling glare of the well-lighted room."[11] The flesh of these girls and boys (or women and men) shines with a luminous purity; they are the virgin cheeks of a child. Desire stops just here—with the besmirching of the downy cheeks of the buttocks. The smooth surface awaits the lash with trembling innocence. As the birching commences, the writhing and flailing about of the buttocks matches the rhythm of the beating, creating a kind of erotic dance. Lovingly described as they turn pink, crimson, or even marked and bloody, the buttocks in most narratives of flogging are the sexually desired body part, and in their stimulation and the regular rhythm of the beating lies the erotic core of flagellation narratives. Orifices (or genitals of any sort) have no place here; they are replaced by the redness of welts, "stripes," raised markings, or simply blushing and the smooth round curves of the buttock cheeks.

SOMETIME IN THE 1870S, the author of *My Secret Life* made a visit to a flagellation brothel in London, one of many that catered to the taste. Not himself a lover of the birch, "Walter" (as the author calls himself) goes as a kind of sexual tourist. Arranged in advance with the "abbess" of the establishment, the setup has Walter entering, masked and with his current lover, called H. A half-masked man is already kneeling on a large chair and is bent over the foot of a bed. "He had a woman's dress on," Walter explains, "tucked up to his waist, showing his naked rump and thighs, with his feet in male socks and boots. On his head was a woman's cap tied carefully round his face to hide his whiskers." Two women stand behind him, one dressed as a ballet dancer, with short petticoats and bare thighs and breasts, and another with bright yellow hair, naked except for boots and stockings ("a bold, insolent looking bitch"). The "patient" "whispered to the abbess that he wanted to see my prick." Walter, "determined to go thro the whole performance," lifts his shirt to show it, but doesn't comply with the "patient's" request to feel it. The abbess: "Be a good boy or Miss Yellow will whip you hard." The man whispers: "Oh—no—no—pray don't." The abbess: "Now she shall whip you, you naughty boy." The rod descends heavily upon his rump, punctuated by his whispers and then his loud cries. As he is whipped, Walter agrees to "frig" the recipient. Eventually the "patient" "spurts a shower of semen." H. and Walter retire to a nearby room to finish each other off. Walter's pat analysis of the experience: "The abbess treated him like a child."[12]

Flogging brothels dotted the landscape of mid-Victorian London. Milnes visited them, as did, according to rumor, senior army officers of the Horse Guards, the Prince of Wales, and the King of the Belgians, when he was in town. Prostitutes generally dressed up as governesses, schoolmistresses, and abbesses. Male visitors could pay to birch a prostitute. A well-known keeper of a flagellation brothel on Charlotte Street, Mrs. Theresa Berkley, became something of a legend for her creative role as a flagellant "governess." She perfected a flogging device—a standing, adjustable, padded easel with holes in convenient places and rings for tying the client down—dubbed the "Berkley Horse" (also sometimes referred to as a *chevalet*).

Dominance and submission had a foundational status in Victorian Britain. Flogging was not only common practice in schools and nurseries; minor crimes, such as vagrancy, were punished by whipping. In prisons, the army, and the navy, thirty to three hundred lashes with a cat-o'-nine-tails were not uncommon, and occasionally men died from such castigation. A powerful leader in the Victorian Anglican Church, Edward Bouverie Pusey, taught the benefits of mortification (self-whipping) "for about a quarter of an hour a day" (his many followers, such as Christina Rossetti and Charles Kingsley, were called Puseyites).[13] Such abasement was to remind one that "our bodies become sacred; they are not ours; they are Christ's."[14] To those on the Continent, the British appeared to be flagomaniacs, and birching became known as *le vice anglais*. Whether corporal punishment should form a part of a modern, civilized culture became a major topic of discussion, and a number of magazines and newspapers ran series of letters to the editor arguing both sides. The possibility that flagellation had erotic uses didn't form a part of these public discussions, however, giving it a strange dual status. On the one hand, most thought it was a healthy disciplinary measure for children and adult miscreants. Yet, on the other, with a slight twist of audience and context (found in the parallel, underground world of pornography and prostitution), it could be a "depraved," "perverse" practice on a par with those other demons—masturbation and sodomy (pederasty was not deemed a demon quite yet).

Such a fine balance of meaning opened the possibility that the exact same text could serve as serious and edifying and, at the same time, titillating reading. Prime examples were two series of letters that ran in the *Englishwoman's Domestic Magazine* and the *Saturday Review* about the wisdom of birching children.

The carefully rendered details in some of these letters made them no different from fladge porn. A passage from one letter, arguing for the abolishment of birching as a brutal practice, could have been excerpted from a porn text:

> I was made to kneel on a low deal table on my knees and elbows, with my face against the table, and my back quite arched in—to give a proper prominence to the part to be chastised. My skirts were then drawn over my head and my flesh bared.[15]

The debate was so heated that it's certain that the (mostly female) readership enjoyed the accounts in more than just a purely intellectual way. Later it came out that most of these letters were frauds—fictions made up for the fun of it. Given this climate, it's easy to see how Swinburne's poems of erotic discipline created such a furor, exposing as they did the sensual possibilities of an everyday practice, one that needed to be seen as pure, manly, and a forthright part of a solid gentleman's education.

Some of the frisson of birching issued from the bringing together of the "manly" and the infantile. The gentleman of the era, required to maintain a steady stream of productive energy, with a strong handle on his women, the lower classes, his servants, found release in giving up his masculine role of responsibility. Degradation, groveling, handing over the power of decision and righteousness, and preparing to be punished for failure all served as pleasurable means of role swapping. Control could be turned over to the flagellatrix, a surrogate or placeholder for anyone who might step into the role of powerful chastiser, whether it be the tutor, a real-life dominating woman, or possibly even—to be Freudian about it—the mother (another Freudian possibility to be explored later: she is the father).

ON A FRIDAY morning in September 1868, the sea off the coast of Normandy turned wild with a hard wind, due east. Swinburne stripped off his clothes and abandoned himself to the waves. Tossed about in foam and sea rack, he struggled to keep his head above water. What a splendid death this would be (he later imagined in a poem about the experience), with the sea a kind of embrace of immensity. "When thy salt lips well-nigh / Sucked in my mouth's last sigh, / Grudged I so much to die / This death as others?" He almost did die on that day. Carried out to sea by a treacherous undercurrent, Swinburne faced drowning. But his shouts and yells attracted the notice of an official on the cliff edge who hailed a fishing smack. The French fishermen dragged him onto the boat and wrapped him in a spare sail. He declaimed poems by Victor Hugo to them, as entertainment on the way back to shore. An eighteen-year-old Guy de Maupassant happened to be on the scene and waded in to help, starting the legend that he had saved a drunken Swinburne from drowning.

For Swinburne, the sea had always provided a means of transcendence. He spent his childhood on the Isle of Wight, in a house so close to the shore that through its briny windows would come the booming sound of the waves. Swinburne couldn't remember an earlier enjoyment than

> being held up naked in my father's arms and brandished between his hands, then shot like a stone from a sling through

> the air, shouting and laughing with delight, head foremost into the coming wave. . . . I remember being afraid of other things but never of the sea.[16]

The sea, swimming, and writing formed a sensual nexus. So many of his poems are songs to the sea and end with lines like "Till supreme sleep shall bring me bloodless ease . . . And shed around and over and under me / Thick darkness and the insuperable sea" (Sappho in "Anactoria"). Or, "When, refreshed as a bride and set free, / With stars and sea-winds in her raiment, / Night sinks on the sea" ("Dedication"). Long passages of luxurious writing are devoted to Herbert Seyton's experience of the sea in *Lesbia Brandon*. He would swim until "the soul of the sea entered him and filled him with fleshly pleasure and the pride of life."[17] The ocean appears as a tumultuous lover. He "sprang at the throat of waves that threw him flat, pressed up against their soft fierce bosoms and fought for their sharp embraces."[18] Swimming provides a sense of the body liberated, as open fully to the life of things. It fulfills a wanting to dissolve, to disappear into the universe, to be dispersed to the winds.

Swinburne's love of the sea was another strand in the web of his desire to be mastered by a force stronger than himself. More than once did he let the sea almost drown him, just as sex for him was a craving for a loss of control, for a kind of immolation where pain and pleasure inextricably burned together. He needed to be taken out of himself, and sometimes violent means had to be used. The adult Swinburne's self-destructive nature played itself out on many fronts—he left single-copy manuscripts in cabs, tried to murder himself with drink (and came close to succeeding). He flirted with imprisonment for publishing writings he knew would be deemed morally depraved.

Life put Swinburne under the lash. A good deal of his impetus to self-ruination came from being handed a damaged deal. And much of his writing sprang from this personal despair. For example, the mood of his poems of 1866 came out of such calamities as the death of his beloved grandfather in 1860, the suicide of Lizzie Siddal Rossetti in 1862 (whom he counted as a dear friend; he spent part of her last evening with her), and the death of consumption of his favorite sister, Edith, in 1863. His love life was at all times bereft in some way. In 1862 he proposed to a woman and was turned down (biographers disagree on who this was, possibly Jane Faulkner), which spurred him to write the anguished "The Triumph of Time." In 1865 Mary Gordon, his cousin and the love of his life, married someone else. Then came the fladge brothels. To turn him away from them, Rossetti, Burne-Jones, and other friends set him up with the boyish-looking American actress Adah Menken (who called herself "Dolores" in letters to him, after his poem that made him famous). Both of them being major celebrities, the affair caused a big scandal (and lots of unkind tittering because Swinburne's friends knew of his sexual proclivities), especially when photographs of the two together became public. Menken ended it after six months because, rumor has it, he wasn't much good in bed (she told Rossetti she couldn't quite keep him "up to scratch," adding, "I can't make him understand that biting's no use!").[19]

Thus, the prime lament in his writings: communion with others comes wedded at all turns with yearning pain. The closer one wants to get to the beloved, the more the agony of inexorable apartness is felt. Sexuality, for Swinburne, especially foregrounded this tragedy—two become one but only for a moment. His poetry celebrates the failure of love's fulfillment, the madness that comes from pining for a lost kiss. He came to relish the point when love takes on a sickly hue, becomes a decadent lust. Such sexuality—the beatings, the blood, the raised welts—describes (in Swinburne's writing) the condition of the soul in its rage, alienation, and spiritual frustration.

AT THE END of October 1859, Burton was in Paris. He took a few days to knock about in the luminous city, on his way to a Vichy spa for treatment for his gout (despite having the frame of a titan, he suffered from many ailments throughout his life, most the result of permanent damage from dangerous fevers caught during hard living in the tropics). Burton also had reason to escape London for a bit. After his return from a much publicized attempt to find the source of the Nile with John Hanning Speke, Burton had to defend himself against a steady stream of lies and calumny from Speke. A former friend, Speke (who was, at the time, psychologically unbalanced, possibly from marsh fever, which would lead to his fatally shooting himself in the chest, in 1864, with his Lancaster breechloader) set out to ruin Burton's reputation and to snatch all the laurels of the daring and unprecedented expedition for himself (history has proven that the credit goes to Burton). France provided a brief respite.

While there, Burton paid what might be deemed an anthropological visit to the "clitoris of Paris." This was Hankey's apartment at 2 rue Laffitte, probably so called because of his excellent collection of erotic books and paraphernalia (dildos of different sorts, chastity belts, statuary such as "a Sapphic group by Pradier of two girls in the very act—one has her tongue up où vous savez," and the like).[20] Burton appreciated Hankey (the "sadist" to Swinburne's "masochist") as another braggart in the matter of vice. He listened to the lurid yarns Hankey spun about his exploits in his unshockable, worldly way. Hankey liked to talk about his fondness for cannibalism and his plans to see a murderess hanged in London while having two prostitutes stimulate him (watching public hangings was common practice—Dickens did it, for instance, as did William Makepeace Thackeray). Burton may have witnessed one of Hankey's notorious "tableaux vivants" in his flat, which served as a meeting place for literary luminaries—Swinburne when in town, also Théophile Gautier and Gustave Flaubert. Hankey paid prostitutes to stage sadistic theater, much of it women practicing on other women (he had a taste for the "sapphic"). Then he would describe these escapades in his pornography, such as the play *L'École des biches*.

Burton looked on Hankey's shenanigans with part cynical ribaldry, part anthropological interest. Burton himself savored his own power and dominance, but his desires were given more subtle play. They became a current running through his carefully established relationships (such as that with Isabel). His own dabbling in control and command, though, attuned him to how commonly it was woven into the intricate pattern of relationships, communities, and entire social structures. He theorized that Hankey's fantasies of sexual cruelty were a kind of "superstition" (his word) of the type found in many cultures. Having witnessed probably every form of human cruelty in his wanderings through numerous wars, including torture and human sacrifice, Burton found Hankey a curious example to add to his studies. Hankey's "religious" impulses involved, Burton noted, wanting a Bible bound in human flesh, but also maintaining a "strong sense of the wickedness of killing animals for food."[21] Burton discovered such illogical belief systems, or moral blind spots, at the core of most cultures (the British especially). His writing so startled his contemporaries (and continues to do so today) because of his dauntless rendering of the minutiae of sexual power struggles, even the most brutal of nonconsensual acts. He could be sharply censorious. He found institutionalized misogyny such as clitorectomies and infibulation in East Africa barbarous. And horrible was the way Egyptian wives would murder unfaithful husbands, by "tying them down and tearing out the testicles."[22] But at other times he described extreme acts of force in an objective, scientific way, such as husbands using horsewhips on their wives in Somalia as a natural end to the honeymoon or the castration of boys in the Middle East to provide eunuchs as harem guards.

Like Swinburne, Burton felt temperamentally compelled to return to those topics over which his fellow Englishmen wanted to throw a permanent veil. Indeed, he believed "abundant harm" was done by pushing sexual practices into the shadows because of "shame or disgust." Certainly the sexual uses of dominance and submission were just such issues. Burton's motivations were dual, however. Yes, he felt a kind of moral imperative to enumerate all that which (sexually speaking) his countrymen wanted to pretend didn't exist. But removing the veil, cataloging tabooed subjects in careful detail, certainly stirred him in many ways. Threaded through his love of sharing these scandalous stories with his fellows (Milnes and Solomon in letters when he was away, papers at the Anthropological Society, Cannibal Club meetings when in London) are strands of absorption and attraction. The veil itself held its sensuality; hardly anything could be more stimulating than being the one *to expose.*

Burton carried the scandalous nature of his work further by writing his most extended study on the topic *not* about the sexual brutality that occurred between men and women but about that which happened between *two* men. He realized "his neighbors" considered it to be *le vice contre nature*. To this he responded that nothing "can be contrary to nature which includes all things."[23] *Le vice*, in this case, was male-male sodomy and pederasty, both practices that could have been tailor-made for Burton's gifts as a scholar of that which "didn't exist," yet was hidden in plain sight.

His deep preoccupation began in 1845, as he tells it himself in the famous "Terminal Essay" of his translation of the *Arabian Nights*, when he was a young officer in the infantry of the East India Company. Stationed in Karachi, the capital of Sindh (invaded and conquered by the British in 1843), Burton called the barren land a "get-between a dust-bin and an oven." He spent his days soaking up languages: one of his teachers described him as "a man who could learn a language running."[24] For a time he lived in a single-poled tent, and he suffered through 125-degree afternoons by draping his table with a wet cloth, sitting underneath, and studying Persian despite the sweat and dust that coated his writing paper. Evenings found him exploring the city, a carrion-smelling clutch of mud houses and walls. He sampled the opium dens, tried hashish and the different classes of prostitutes, embarked on a study of Tantric sexual rites. This was the period of his life when he first began to experiment with disguises. Only possible because of his extraordinary facility for absorbing languages, gestures, and bodily customs, Burton's masks were strategies for moving among people as something he wasn't, in order to glean information otherwise inaccessible to a Briton. Around this time, he often went out as a half Arab, half Iranian merchant. Thus, he could account for his strange accent among the Sindhis and, as a seller of wares, enter private spaces (including the harem) and be told all manner of gossip. While Burton utilized his skills as a dissembler in order to study cultures from the inside, impersonation came to be an occasional requirement for his being in the world. Here, in his early twenties, began a practice he continued throughout his life. Feeling trapped, bored, troubled, he would wander off in a completely new identity, merging with another culture, caste, or race, sometimes for months on end and at great personal risk. His need for a fluid self explains his attraction to the character of Caliph Harun al-Rashid in the *Arabian Nights*, who, as ruler of Baghdad, would set off in disguise in order to learn what the common folk of the city did with their days, to hear their clever tales of derring-do and magical transformation.

Burton's practice of "going native" earned him the title among his messmates of the "white nigger." Not always used in an affectionate way, this label represented a growing suspicion of Burton within the British elite, something that would plague him throughout his career. Where lay the allegiance of a man who would suddenly take the disguise of a dervish and go out into the desert? Could a man who went so far as to undergo circumcision in order to pass as Muslim be trusted by the colonizers of these very people he liked to mix among? Some of his superiors, however, knew how to utilize Burton's valuable skills. General Charles Napier employed Burton as a spy, sending him out on far-flung missions (the details still remain secret today) to further the British side of the ruthless colonial competition with the Russian empire for large swaths of Asia, called "the Great Game."

Napier had been hearing rumors about brothels in Karachi

that catered to men who wanted to have sex with boys. Worried that his troops might be involved in such "moral turpitude," he sent Burton off in disguise to infiltrate the houses and report back. In his merchant getup he passed many evenings visiting them in order to obtain "the fullest details."[25] The final report he made to Napier has been lost, but some details are in other writings by Burton. Visitors could hire boys and eunuchs to fulfill all types of desires. The young prostitutes would be prepared carefully for their duties, through diet, baths, depilation, unguents, and cosmetics. Boys demanded double the price of eunuchs because, as Burton discovered, "the scrotum of the unmutilated boy could be used as a kind of bridle for directing the movements of the animal."[26] Pederasts, Burton believed, can usually be detected by looking in their face. The colors there have faded, the features have become puffy, and the complexion altogether unwholesome.

So began a lifelong interest in sodomy. One type of anal congress that became a focus of Burton's study (among others that will be explored in later chapters) was the act as a means to assert one's power and position in the world. His investigation of cases in and around Karachi narrowed to sex between men of different races or castes. Burton tells a tragic story of two lovers caught up in the Hindu caste system. Both were sepoys (Indian soldiers allied to the British occupiers), but one was a Brahman and the other of a low caste. In their sexual encounters, the pariah soldier always took the part of the "patient," as Burton calls it, and the Brahman the "agent." The "doer" (Al-Fá'il), Burton explains, was not an object of contempt like the "done" (Al-Mafúl). This relationship ran smoothly until the lower-caste man, "in an unhappy hour," took over the agency, becoming the one actively sodomizing. [27] The high-caste soldier, unable to handle the shame of this inversion of societal class positions

> loaded his musket and deliberately shot his paramour. He was hanged by court martial at Hyderabad and, when his last wishes were asked he begged in vain to be suspended by the feet; the idea being that his soul, polluted by exiting "below the waist," would be doomed to endless transmigrations through the lowest forms of life.[28]

Exploring sodomy was a way to discover how men related to one other, enmeshed as they were in their cultural milieu and their religious "superstitions." What might have been simply an act of love in this case couldn't break free from a society where masters had to be masters. Indeed, even the ghostly soul could be doomed to wander because of the sphincter's guests.

Burton collected cases of the British invaders raped by their colonial subjects. This gave him quite a different angle to view imperialism, one that the elites of the British Empire were certainly loath to take a look at: the rage and resentment of those oppressed, which could explode into acts of sexual violence. Burton recounts the experience of a missionary who, having infuriated a Persian prince-governor with his "conversion-mania," was raped by him.[29] Having a strong distaste for missionaries, Burton seemingly couldn't help himself; he had to add a dash of ribaldry. He reports a conversation with a Persian about male-male anal rape. Asking the man how penetration is possible when met by the resistance of the strong sphincter muscle, Burton received the reply "Ah, we Persians know a trick to get over that; we apply a sharpened tent-peg to the crupper-bone (os coccygis) and knock till he opens."[30] As one who had witnessed the atrocities of the British Empire, in their takeover of lands and people, Burton found this gentle-seeming "knocking" worth a chuckle. Another story told in a similar tone involved Shaykh Nasr, governor of Bushire, a fellow "famed for facetious blackguardism." He enjoyed inviting young European men serving in the Bombay marine to drink with him. Imbibing until they became insensible, the next morning the "middies mostly complained that the champagne had caused a curious irritation and soreness in la parte-poste."[31]

WHEN THE TEENAGE Maupassant "saved" Swinburne from drowning in the French sea in 1868, he won an invitation back to the farmhouse in Étretat that George Powell had taken with Swinburne. Some years later, Maupassant described his visits there to a gathering at Flaubert's house, which included the Goncourt brothers, who assiduously recorded the account in their journal. Maupassant had something of a crush on the "immensely learned" Swinburne, and thus his portrayal of the two men is erotically charged, with macabre garnishes. Indeed, Maupassant implies that a seduction commenced, and he deemed himself lucky to escape with his virginity intact. It all began over lunch. Powell kept "titillating" his pet monkey, who would then gambol over to rub up against the back of Maupassant's neck, when he bent forward to drink. After the table was cleared, Swinburne and Powell brought out their collection of obscene photographs from Germany. They were all of men. In one memorable image an English soldier masturbated on a pane of glass. Meanwhile, Powell, who was at this point "dead drunk," "kept sucking the fingers of a mummified hand."[32] Swinburne said lots of interesting things about snakes. On his second visit, the monkey was dead, and Maupassant was given a liqueur that nearly knocked him out. "Taking fright, I escaped to my hotel, where I slept like a log for the rest of the day." But he went back one more time in order, he claims, to find out whether they were really perverts and sodomites. He noticed an inscription over the door that read Dolmancé Cottage. He asked them whether they realized Dolmancé was the name of the hero of Sade's *Philosophy in the Bedroom*. They replied yes, "with terrifying expressions on their faces." Maupassant left quickly. "I had found out what I wanted to know, and I never saw them again."[33]

While we don't know whether Swinburne enjoyed sodomy with his male friends (or with his female ones, for that matter), it's clear an erotic frisson charged the intimacy between him and many men in his circle. In the scene of reading described at the beginning of this chapter, much of Swinburne's hilarity came from savoring such a dirty book with his friends. (They made a day of it. After reading Sade, they visited the International Exhibition, where they had some ices at a stall "near the Egyptian things" and encountered a "very lovely girl." It was Gabriel, of course, who went right up to her and "obtained a promise to sit for him.")[34] Swinburne continued to draw out the delight of sharing Sade by writing rambling, imaginative missives that replay or rewrite scenes from *Justine*. He used Sadean nicknames—Milnes was "Rodin," for instance—and began letters with a blasphemous invocation: "Salvation in Christ Priapus and His Church by the intercession of the Most Blessed Donatien de Sade." His flagellation writings were *for men*. His whipping stories either appeared in personal letters sent to men for mutual titillation or they were pornography written for other men to enjoy. Biographers have speculated that Swinburne practiced flogging with some of his buddies (not Rossetti, though, who could be rather vanilla in bed and found Swinburne's penchant for the rod distasteful). There's no hard evidence, but it's possible he had the luck of a little play with Burton and the birch. Given Burton's willingness to try everything, the scene does spring to life in the imagination. Swinburne sometimes brought Powell along with him to Verbena Lodge, so cross-dressing and male-male fun perhaps mixed with the beatings.

Even when women wielded the rod, Swinburne's fladge experiences never strayed far from Eton: man beating boy. Scholars have made convincing arguments about Victorian flagellation (real and fictional) as, in the words of Steven Marcus, "a kind of last-ditch compromise with and defense against homosexuality."[35] The evidence to bolster these heavily Freudian arguments is strong. The female floggers in birch porn work well as stand-ins for men (and if it's a girl being beaten, she is, according to this logic, a boy) as they are variously described as "strong-backed," or "scornful," or with a "square cut chin." The flagellatrix, in these theories, represents a father figure. While these works never include sodomy, the attention paid exclusively to the buttocks and the instrument in use usually called a "rod" (which often must be kissed) makes the act latent.

Yet this Freudian conclusion needs some tempering. The word "homosexual" wasn't coined until the 1880s. And the idea that this term (or any term) was a way to pin down someone's identity had to wait until the 1890s, at the very earliest. In Swinburne's case, it was plurality that kept him stimulated. Limiting him to duality—homosexual or heterosexual (or even to a triad, if bisexual is thrown in)—feels like a restriction.

Gender and identity blur when the buttocks are the erotic focus: these stippled cheeks constitute an androgynous field of play. Why can't the one with the rod be many things: a masterful woman, a mother, a father, a male lover? The implement of the birch itself stands as a symbol for such openness. Its bristling multiplicity distinguished it, rather than an erect, unified hardness. The "rod" was usually a gathered and tied bundle of twigs. The thin, bendable pieces would break off as the beating went on. Unlike an actual rod, a thick bundle could never be accurate in terms of its placement, so twigs might tickle the entire area, including the genitals.

Swinburne's love of flogging assuredly had its roots in a desire to find again the free play of childhood, a time before masculine responsibilities, before compulsory heterosexuality, before everything had to be fixed finally in its place. While it's impossible to know exactly what Swinburne did at Verbena Lodge (cross-dress? Enjoy other men?), certainly men went there to be treated like children: according to an advertisement, it had a "schoolroom" setting complete with "governess." His flagellation writings, too, are all about childhood. Unlike many other works in the genre Swinburne's always feature a young boy writhing under the rod, wielded every time by an adult male. His pornography has a fundamental lightness—its tone jocular, silly, and playful: "I sing of Arthur's Flogging; I, who heard / The boy himself sing out beneath the birch."[36] The swish had the beat of poetic meter, the cadence of long summer days with nothing ahead but romping.

CHAPTER FIVE

Cannibals and Other Lovers of Men

What think you I take my pen in hand to record?
. . . merely of two simple men I saw to-day on the pier
  in the midst of the crowd, parting the parting of
  dear friends,
The one to remain hung on the other's neck and
  passionately kiss'ed him,
While the one to depart tightly prest the one to
  remain in his arms.

—WALT WHITMAN,
Leaves of Grass

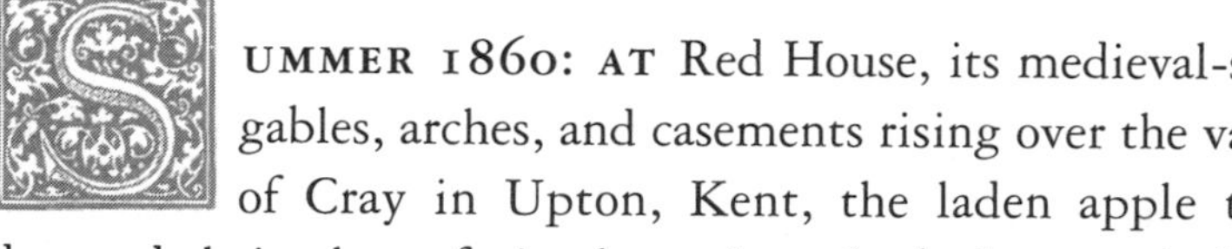

SUMMER 1860: AT Red House, its medieval-style gables, arches, and casements rising over the valley of Cray in Upton, Kent, the laden apple trees dropped their glossy fruit plump into the bedroom windows. Honeysuckle and jasmine climbed the walls, waxy against the warm red brick, and when the roses filled out the trellises, they enclosed an inner garden. William Morris, full of romantic dreams of a preindustrial life—somehow more simple and egalitarian, homier and even socialist—had his friend Philip Webb design Red House on a thirteenth-century plan, with cleanly Gothic peaked roofs of red tile and open barnlike rooms, the porch and gardens comfortably welcoming. The stout walls of Red House enclosed an ideal as well as a dwelling place: Rossetti saw it as "more a poem than a house."[1]

Soon after moving in with Janey in June, Morris set out to make Red House "the beautifullest place on earth," as Ned enthused.[2] Friends arrived to help. The wagonette with leather curtains (designed by Webb) pulled up to Abbey Wood train station, and visitors climbed in. "Then the scrambling, swinging drive of three miles or so to the house; and the beautiful roomy place where we seemed to be coming home," one guest recollected.[3] Ned and Georgie stayed the summer to paint "the inner walls of the house that Top built."[4] Ned started in on a mural for the drawing-room walls, telling the ancient story of Sire Degrevaunt, with a wedding feast featuring Morris as the round-shouldered, busy king in blue robes, Janey as the demure, wimpled queen. Morris painted a "false" tapestry below, covering it with quiet trees and watchful parrots. Small pennons were painted among the leaves, carrying his motto "If I can." Charley Faulkner, a mate from the Oxford days, painted the ceilings with red, blue, and green diaper patterns; Janey helped weave dusky hangings, with lords and ladies moving about in shadows, for the bedroom walls. Rossetti swept in with his characteristic "Hullo! Old fellows!" When he read Morris's motto, he daubed into the empty spaces his version: "If I can't." A scene ensued, and Ned observed wryly of the two quarreling, "It might have puzzled the discriminator of words to say which of these two was most eloquent in violent English."[5]

Bear fights broke out on the carpet, and bowls were played on the lawn. Apple skirmishes left Morris with a black eye. Games of hide-and-seek were taken up in the evening. Janey laughed so hard she, "like Guinevere, fell under the table."[6] Morris would come up from the cellar before dinner, recounted an old friend, "beaming with joy, with his hands full of bottles of wine."[7] Topsy had a boisterous streak, but he was more often bluff and shy, at the same time. He thrived amid a band of friends. Full of gruff eccentricities, Morris, not polished and seductive like Gabriel, practiced plain-speaking. When his socialism led him to wear a working smock, Morris disappeared into a crowd of laboring men. Feet planted, Morris had a stolidity about him and the kind of vigorous Victorian work ethic mostly lost to our modern world today. When he was dying, a doctor named the cause as "simply being William Morris, and having done more work than most ten men."[8]

WITH RED HOUSE, Morris began a lifelong experiment in communal living and working. Work was not to be, in Morris's schema, unpleasant toiling one did for others, in order to buy the necessities of life, but rather a deep pleasure of fellowship, interwoven into the games and good will of being with kindred spirits. The couple or family should not retreat into private domestic spheres, but rather the teeming outside—work and relations with nonfamily—should round out the home life. In Morris's socialist utopian novel *News from Nowhere*, any kind of labor has become "a pleasurable *habit* . . . because there is conscious sensuous pleasure in the work itself."[9]

By the time he moved into Red House, Morris had given up canvas painting. He was first known for his bumpy, gloomy Arthurian poetry, which would later be admired by the Modernists: Joyce has his character Stephen Hero use Morris's verse as a thesaurus. But soon Morris would become the Victorian period's most renowned designer of textiles, wallpapers, and furniture. Already with the furnishings of Red House, Morris began to research outdated means of production—hand looms, plant dyes, woodcuts—with a craving to revive "primitive" crafts as a revolt against the cold impersonality of the mass production of the time. Of all the men in his set, Morris was the one who most cherished little objects against the skin, felt textures—weaves and naps, coarse-grained woods, colored glass. Craft meant creating things made so well they would last a lifetime and not need to be disposed of or replaced. (Morris was an early environmentalist and formed one of the first groups to save historic structures.) Morris's tactility always involved sharing, most often with other men; he created objects in close collaboration. To be fashioning a perfect object with another craftsman was, for Morris, an emotive, highly erotic experience. His friends with homosexual leanings, like Webb, especially felt possessed by Morris's collaborative acts. Out of their intimate tandem sprang Red House. In describing his devotion to Morris, Webb spoke fervently of being "branded," like an animal, by the letter *M*. The things Morris and Burne-Jones made together—books, windows, textiles, furniture, homes—speak of a love expressed by shared rich textures, by heavy sensuous colors laid down first by one man then passed to the other for further layering and close-worked additions.

AS THE DAY evolved into chill night the coal-gas lamps flared up, adding their black smoke to London's choking fog, full of bad smells. On March 14, 1865, Richard Burton strolled along the shabby streets around Leicester Square just as they began to fill with their fitful and slightly sinister nightlife ("at night a change comes over the spirit of its dreams," wrote a journalist about the square).[10] This area had once been glamorous, when Frederick, the Prince of Wales, held court in Leicester House many years ago, but now it was barely respectable. Expatriate Europeans emerged from cheap lodging houses or cold garrets. Billiard room sharks slouched to betting houses. Rouged French and German girls sat at the bar of the Café Chansante to be picked up by grubby medical students, who could rarely pay the girls' full prices. Hard by was the Alhambra, run by a Mr. Smith, who put on rowdy entertainment for the tipsy and uncultured, like "Music for the Millions" and the kind of striptease called *poses plastiques* that Rossetti liked. Gentlemen cruised for guardsmen or effeminate, male prostitutes called mary-annes.

Slumming was a Burton specialty. Disappearing into the cityscape, the Victorian gentleman could slip into a seamy neighborhood, out of the glare of Victorian propriety. Dirt took on a certain dusky glamour. Girls and boys of the lower classes might escape the era's oppressive "virtue" and be up for all kinds of activities. Upper-class men tried on or succored addictions: opium, hashish, gin, flagellation (Burton, Rossetti, Swinburne, and Solomon were all abusers of one sort or another). Slumming could be dangerous, and this too lent it its sheen. Garotting, rife throughout the 1860s, became easier in squalid neighborhoods: a few toughs could waylay a man with a nice coat and hat in a shadowy corner. He would be lucky to survive strangling with hands or wire for his fob watch. Cholera teemed among the poor: from July to November 1866 nearly four thousand people died in the East End alone. Syphilis and gonorrhea took on epidemic proportions. Burton thrived on such risk.

Tonight, though, Burton, in his gentleman's veneer, was on his way to a Cannibal Club meeting. When anticipating the charge of kinship in the presence of like-minded men, Burton felt expansive, open to influence. Despite his general dislike of England and its people—one reason for the self-exile of most of his life—he did enjoy male clubbing, and London was the place to do it. (The fitting name of a later club Burton joined: the Bohemians.) Essentially a raconteur, Burton fed on sharing stories and ideas. But then he also required large tracts of unmappable time, moving about in the guise of someone else. Oscillating between the two kept his needs satisfied and rounded out his creative life.

Cannibals met and dined at a slummer's paradise. Bertolini's, an Italian and French restaurant, occupied a floor of the Newton Hotel on St. Martin's Lane, just off Leicester Square, where Sir Isaac Newton resided in the seventeenth century. An underground alley ran beneath the restaurant, its use now obscure. The old floors were lightly sanded stone; the air hung with smoke. The food at Bertolini's was subject to lewd jokes among members, as was the fact that more gravy could be found on the tablecloths, knives, and waiters' clothes than on the steaks (Tennyson called the establishment "Dirtolini's"). Rossetti took "loose" models there. Other literary figures of the sometimes bohemian set frequented it—Thackeray, Dickens, a young Hardy—along with foreigners and prostitutes of the better sort.

Annie Miller, the model Holman Hunt and Rossetti fought over, handed her slipper to Lord Ranelagh late one night at Bertolini's. He drank champagne from it.

Cannibals came together through conviviality and talk, rather than the handcraft of the Morris circle. Easy badinage created an atmosphere of mutual support for transgression of all sorts: an accepting circle that shut out the cold disapproval of the world outside. At meetings, Burton would bring up some unorthodox topic, and the unstructured bantering would begin. Some Cannibals were famous wits—Edward Sellon and Milnes, who was full of bons mots and mottoes, such as "look at life through the purple veil of the grape!"[11] Others were brilliant conversationalists—Burton and Swinburne, of whose talk Henry Adams remarked, "The idea that one has actually met a real genius dawns slowly on a Boston mind, but it has made its entry at last."[12] Bradlaugh and Bendyshe were intense debaters of ideas, with cravings to reform the political world around them. James Campbell Reddie, George Augustus Sala, and Charles Duncan Cameron, all central figures in the London pornography trade, were full of talk about censorship and ways to combat it. Young Simeon Solomon usually just sat and absorbed. Issues scandalous to the society at large could be explored here without shock or fear of censure (rather, with seriousness, cutting humor, or contrariness but always openly). This is not to say that members all agreed with one another—Cannibals were a set of strong believers in their varied, idiosyncratic ways—but rather that they wanted to hear and talk about it all.

This winter of 1865 two subjects came up repeatedly and got serious airing at meetings: the American poet Walt Whitman and phallic worship. The first kept Swinburne obsessed, and he drew Burton, Milnes, Solomon, Rossetti, and Morris into his circle of interest. In 1860 Whitman produced a third edition of his collection of poems, *Leaves of Grass*, adding 246 new poems to the second edition of 1856, including the cluster of poems—*Calamus*—that celebrate sensual love between men. Lines like "We two boys together clinging, / One the other never leaving . . . / Power enjoying, elbow stretching, fingers clutching"[13] worked on Swinburne like electric fire. Whom else to bring these lines to than Cannibals, the men he loved? He would get drunk (these days, a lot) and rant about Whitman with a feverish excitement. Arthur Munby, a photographer and solicitor who himself was obsessed with slumming (he fetishized and photographed working women's strong arms, and he married a maid of all work), recounted in his diary seeing a tipsy Swinburne at the Art's Club, who "kept up a long and earnest talk, or rather declamation, about the merits of Walt Whitman" and then went to leap "about the room, flinging up his arms, blowing kisses to me, and swearing great oaths between whiles."[14] He wanted to pass around Whitman just as he did Sade: have them on his lips. At work on his *Poems and Ballads*, to be published in about a year, Swinburne needed to air ideas about the body and its uses, to filter and strain them through others who had the ability to lay aside Victorian respectability and give his thoughts back to him further developed and with a stronger foundation. Cannibals knew that Whitman was probably a "sodomite" (or "Platonist"), and speaking about him worked as code for conversing about this illicit desire. Indeed, he was the "passionate preacher of sexual or political freedom" to Swinburne.[15]

Phallic worship made the rounds of the Cannibal table (as a conversational topic) during these months. One of those "superstitions" of the East (India especially) that fascinated Burton, adoring the Linga (usually a smooth, black stone fashioned like a penis) meant seeing it as a symbol of fertility. Men bowing down to the phallus, as a generative, creative force, worked as rebellion against the dominant understanding of male-male sexuality as "against nature" because not procreative. Two penises produced nothing, this conventional thinking went, and thus decadence and depravity could be the only result. Through studying the spiritual practices of other cultures, Cannibals could imagine intimacy between men as fecund. The fellow Cannibal Edward Sellon (also a major producer of pornography) gave a paper at a meeting of the Anthropological Society on January 17, 1865, entitled "On the Linga Puja, or Phallic Worship of India." It caused a great stir. Among other theories, Sellon speculated that the Ark of the Covenant "contained nothing more nor less than a Phallus."[16]

Burton had formed the Anthropological Society with Dr. James Hunt in 1863 in order to find "a liberty of thought and a freedom of speech unknown . . . to any other Society in Great Britain . . . . Our object of study being MAN in all his relations, physical, moral, psychical, and social, it is impossible to treat the subject adequately without offending in general the *mauvaise honte*, the false delicacy and ingrained prejudices of the age."[17] Papers read at the society often had an intimate relationship with what went on at the Cannibal Club. The club usually gathered in between daytime council and evening paper-reading meetings of the Anthropological Society. The Cannibal Club, being of closed membership and entirely under the freethinking aegis of Burton, went even further with these liberties. It developed into a space for experimentation, a more intimate forum of support for the marginal. Such incendiary dining clubs in Britain could subvert received wisdom. For instance, another of the 1860s dining clubs changed the face of evolutionary science:

the X Club with Thomas Huxley, John Tyndall, and Herbert Spencer.

Even among Cannibals, love and sex between men existed on a secret plane, with its own language and code words. The sea, for instance, came to evoke two male bodies conjoined in a common element. Swinburne wrote of Whitman, "I knew that the man who had spoken as he has of the sea must be a fellow seabird with me; and I would give something to have a dip in the rough water with him."[18] Another term that became linked, somewhat obscurely, to male-male desire was "cannibalism." Burton made this connection, and even he himself didn't fully understand why these activities became intertwined in his thinking. In Burton's writing, a paragraph about male-male sex would often, by some sleight of hand, end with a discussion of cannibalism. Perhaps Burton set them side by side because they were practices seriously tabooed in his world. Or possibly the idea of like consuming like, of taking another's flesh into oneself, seemed to give them a certain kinship. To name his group the Cannibal Club was a way to point to radical "tastes," to refer subtextually to men loving and sharing their kind. These men came together for mutual consumption. In Swinburne's humorous "catechism" for the group, partially quoted earlier, the cannibal wishes that all who do not savor eating humans be "damned" (or "cooked" in hell).

> Oh Lord, thy people know full well
> That all who eat not flesh and fell,
> Who cannot rightly speak or spell
>   Thy various names,
> Shall be for ever boiled in hell
>   Among the flames.

ROSSETTI HAD A taste for setting up house with male companions. He liked putting his artist friends together in the same space—his "most lastingly get-on-ables"—and seeing what kind of work might get made.[19] In October of 1862, not many months after his wife drugged herself into oblivion, Rossetti shacked up with his brother, William Michael, Swinburne, and the writer George Meredith. His initial impulse after Lizzie's death was to gather family around him. When he took the lease on Tudor House, a fine (if slightly decrepit) early eighteenth-century mansion in Chelsea on Cheyne Walk—which he had long coveted—he initially planned to have his sisters and mother move in. But they didn't relish living so far away from friends, Chelsea at the time being an out-of-the-way place. Rossetti swiftly reverted to an older scheme of starting a collective living/working space—with his artist kin—something he had originally envisioned in the Pre-Raphaelite and Hogarth Club days. The results of this establishment would become fodder for legend: a kind of way station or gathering ground for the great artist eccentrics of the day. If a movement can be said to have a location, early Aestheticism emerged from Tudor House.

Swinburne and William Michael moved in a few days after Rossetti. Meredith gleefully reported, "I am to have a bedroom there, for my once-a-week visits" from Surrey. Tudor House struck Meredith as "strange, quaint, grand . . . a palace. We shall have nice evenings there."[20] Crammed with rooms, some dark, others illuminated with light from the river, the house had wooden, spiral staircases and, below ground, a series of odd vaults, which once led to the Thames (perhaps for secret purposes like smuggling). Mirrors were everywhere. The long drawing room with its seven lofty windows worked well for meals. Rossetti took the ground floor dining room for his studio, which had steps leading directly to the garden. So close to the Thames stood the house that tides sometimes flooded the cellars (this was before the completion of the Chelsea embankment), and its elegant atmosphere intermingled incongruously with "all the boating bustle and longshore litter."[21] The garden covered more than an acre, with lime trees and a mulberry tree dating back to Elizabethan times. It eventually became the site of Rossetti's menagerie (wombat, barn owls, rabbits, armadillos, and more) and an outdoor studio for warm seasons. (Lewis Carroll took his pictures of the Rossetti family here.) Swinburne had two ground floor rooms—a study and a bedroom—which he filled with boxes of books, not to be unpacked until sometime later. (William had to go rooting around in them for books on Blake, which Gabriel needed when completing the Blake biography started by his friend Alex Gilchrist, who had died.) Rossetti, with an eye for the exotic and richly colored so apparent in his paintings, began rummaging markets and out-of-the-way curiosity shops in London, Amsterdam, and Paris in order to build up an interior space that would reflect his evolving aesthetic: lacquered or velvet surfaces, painted mirrors, Indian and Japanese ornamentation. On a visit Arthur Munby walked around the house in dreamy admiration, finding it steeped in "the aroma of its manifold romance."[22] Henry James, who came a few years later, touted it as "the most delicious melancholy old house at Chelsea on the river."[23]

"I have reclaimed my studio from the general wilderness and got to work," a relieved Rossetti announced to Madox Brown, soon after Rossetti had moved in.[24] Swinburne dove into his pile of projects: he had his critical piece on Blake to research; he began drafting the novel *Lesbia Brandon* and finished off the last songs for *Poems and Ballads*. The Greek tragedy *Atalanta in Calydon* also commenced its lugubrious life during his tenure on Cheyne Walk. Meredith, an athletic and energetic fellow who wore flannel shirts, went on walking tours in the country. His svelte beauty is memorably displayed in Wallis's *Death of Chatterton* (after Meredith modeled for this painting, Wallis, in true Pre-Raphaelite style, ran off with Meredith's wife). High-spirited and sharply witty, Meredith was nothing like Rossetti with his languor (Rossetti didn't sit, for instance, but rather would fling himself down and immediately relax with his hands behind his head and his gaze intent) or Swinburne with his flighty, nervous hysteria. Meredith had just brought out his tendentious poem *Modern Love* (the *Saturday Review* called it "a great moral mistake"), which details the decay of a marriage, largely based on the "blunder" that was his own union with the daughter of the novelist Thomas Love Peacock. Meredith's subversive works (he would complete fifteen full-length novels and piles of other writing) often dealt with feminist themes: the limited opportunities for women, the stifling box that marriage could sometimes be. William, calm as milk in comparison, quietly went along with his editing work.

For a time, Rossetti shaped a productive space with these men. Male domesticity, by Rossetti's lights, interwove friendship, love, and creative production. Its rhythm was modeled after the way the women in his life (Christina, Maria, and their mother) inhabited the domestic space with reading aloud, embroidery, and conversations forming an intimate circle. Rossetti set up long stretches of time and configured the space so that each would become absorbed in his own task, with occasional glances, sharing of ideas, or commentary on the others' projects (painting, poem, essay). Subtle influences passed from work to work. A form of silent support, a willingness to devote oneself to a task as a form of *being with* another, sharing space came as a deep pleasure for him. He needed to hold fast to a network of colleagues, disciples, and admirers because this kept him invested, paradoxically, in being an outsider. Both self-exiled rebelliousness and the romance of collaboration were building blocks for Rossetti's aesthetic productions. Having a theater for rebellion could be almost as important as the rebellion itself; in other words, what's the point of being an outsider, if no one sees the brilliance in the rejection of convention?

Pockets of tenderness, interspersed with rivalry and brawls, opened up the house. Everyone dropped by. Ruskin sauntered in and was photographed in the garden with Gabriel. Ned and Topsy came and went regularly along with many painters: Frederick Sandys (who moved in for a while, a couple of years later), Millais, Holman Hunt, and Madox Brown. Frederick Leighton stopped in for dinner. (He saw Rossetti in the 1860s as "a considerable influence in the world's art.")[25] Richard Monckton Milnes was a repeat visitor although, surprisingly, Burton never did make it. (Rossetti and Burton did know each other, however, later corresponding about their shared interest of translation.) Rossetti had a bearish physical love for his compatriots. A characteristic gesture: Gabriel slowly passing his paintbrush through Holman Hunt's beard. He called up intense devotion among this clan. "Rossetti was the planet around whom we revolved," Val Prinsep recollected. "We copied his very way of speaking. All beautiful women were 'stunners' with us . . . we sank our individuality in the strong personality of our adored Gabriel."[26]

James McNeill Whistler, the flamboyant American painter, moved in down the way at 7 Lindsey Row, in 1863, with his Irish mistress, model, and businesswoman, Joanna Hiffernan, the pale red-haired girl in so many of his paintings. Whistler, recently transplanted from the Paris art scene, had a dandified arrogance and an acid wit that made him charming and infuriating by turns. These traits speedily cleared a place for him in this clan of individualists. Whistler's mother came and doted on the childlike and sickly Swinburne (Jo had to be carted off when the mother came, not being "respectable," because of her working-class origins and the lack of a ring on her finger). Heavy foot traffic passed between Tudor and Lindsey.

At times Rossetti took the role of the generous father. He helped Whistler sell his work and persuaded him to change the large scrawl of a signature on his canvases to something smaller and more coded: first "J.M.W" and then a butterfly. The two shared a love for pure color. Whistler's *Symphony in White, No. 1: The White Girl*, of 1862, has much in common with Rossetti's *Ecce Ancilla Domini!* of 1850. But the art influences moved both ways. Whistler brought with him the winds from Paris: "art for art's sake." It's no coincidence that Rossetti's painting became Aesthetic in the 1860s, pushing toward dreamy artifice and overripe, slightly sinister, eroticism. The ruckus caused by the first stirrings of decadence in France held the attention of the British painters and poets. In the late 1850s, they followed the obscenity trial of Gustave Flaubert's *Madame Bovary* and then the successful prosecution of Charles Baudelaire's "unwholesome" *Les Fleurs du Mal*. In 1863 Edouard Manet's *Olympia*, his unromanticized depiction of a nude prostitute, was rejected from the official Paris Salon. Even though Gustave Courbet's *The Origin of the World* (1866), his graphic painting of female genitalia, immediately went underground, it still managed to become mythic in the Paris art world. Whistler, friends with all these men, took first Swinburne over to Paris (to meet Baudelaire) and then Rossetti, who visited Courbet's studio. Both Brits met Manet. Rossetti, with a British suspicion of all things French, remained unmoved: Manet's "pictures were for the most part mere scrawls."[27] Certainly some enviousness was mixed into this attitude, and it didn't preclude Rossetti's absorbing the spirit of the times.

"A Prince among his fellows" Whistler found Rossetti. "Well do I remember with strong affection the barbaric court in which he reigned with joyous simple ingenious superiority as he throned it in Chelsea."[28] The "barbarous" or decadent touches of Rossetti's court included dinners that often lasted until five in the morning, great quantities of alcohol seasoning the hours toward dawn. "An emancipated ménage," friend William Bell Scott called the gatherings.[29] Whist was played after dinner, the Thames in a flood of moonlight. Swinburne spouted lines from *Leaves of Grass*, his "Fragoletta," or some parody of Robert Browning. Others brought out their current projects or conversed on what was new in the worlds of art and literature. The wombat was let onto the table, and it chewed the cigars. Swinburne and Solomon got rowdy, nude, and gloriously drunk. One story has them sliding down the banisters with shrieks of joy. "A silver thread of lunacy" ran, the writer and caricaturist Max Beerbohm later wrote, "in the rich golden fabric of 16 Cheyne Walk."[30]

Rossetti required a measure of intimacy with men, but too much intensity wore him out. The warm closeness that could shoot through to the bottom of two selves had a brief life, and it was then replaced with a tangle of pulling toward and pushing away. The two motions consisted of kindred elements: the warmth came from collaboration, the coldness from competitiveness in art or love. It didn't help that Rossetti seemed temperamentally drawn toward those like himself: pains in the neck (falling for difficult people was another way of guaranteeing built-in distance). Quarrels broke out speedily on Cheyne Walk. Swinburne's drinking spun out of control. "Describing geometrical curves on the pavement" was Rossetti's illustration of Swinburne's endeavors to get home when smashed.[31] Ruskin reported watching him, one night, successively drink three bottles of port. Swinburne's sloshed shenanigans began to interrupt Gabriel's painting; Swinburne irritated him by, for instance, "dancing all over the studio like a wild cat."[32] Rossetti wasn't thrilled with Swinburne's walking through the house nude. At three one morning the police pounded on the door, holding up Swinburne, who had been "out on a spree."[33] A jeering group of gutter boys followed the proceedings. Gabriel had the chore of dragging him to bed, with Swinburne all the while "screaming and splashing about."[34] Worse, Morris got pushed into a cabinet by a rowdy Swinburne, and some of Rossetti's precious blue-and-white china shattered. Fanny moved in after a bit, and Algernon, who had been close friends with Lizzie and couldn't bear to see her supplanted so soon, called her "the Bitch." (Later he would compare the two: "as a clot of dung in the gutter at nightfall to the splendour of the evening star.")[35]

Trouble developed with Meredith, whose wit was a little too cutting for Rossetti's fragile ego. When Meredith made fun of Rossetti's paintings in front of patrons and friends, Rossetti fumed. He splashed a glass of milk in Meredith's face after being called a fool. Meredith also got a poached egg thrown at him by Swinburne, when he dared jest about Victor Hugo.

Dante Gabriel Rossetti's *Beata Beatrix*, a painting of Lizzie Siddall, finished after her death. Rossetti captures the moment Dante's Beatrice dies.

Edward Burne-Jones's *King Cophetua and the Beggar Maid*, with the maid's eyes full of an inward-directed melancholy.

John Everett Millais's *Ophelia*, modeled by Lizzie Siddal.
He pictures Ophelia's death as orgasmic.

Dante Gabriel Rossetti's *Ecce Ancilla Domini!*, an annunciation scene modeled by a young Christina Rossetti as the virgin Mary.

Dante Gabriel Rossetti's *Astarte Syriaca*, modeled by Jane Morris, who was given an androgynous body.

Simeon Solomon's *The Mystery of Faith*, with a beautiful man carrying a reliquary containing the host.

Dante Gabriel Rossetti's *The Blue Bower*, modeled by Fanny Cornforth, who appears to be sitting inside a blue-and-white Chinese porcelain pot.

Richard Francis Burton in 1864, looking worthy of Swinburne's crush. *Hulton Archive, Getty.*

Oscar Wilde, around 1894, when he wrote *The Importance of Being Earnest* and was busy feasting with panthers. *Popperfoto Collection, Getty.*

Doing his part in the brawling, Meredith threatened to kick Algernon down the stairs. Whistler got caught in the middle of the volatility over meals—getting hot soup splashed in his face when Gabriel slammed down a spoon in a full tureen, furious at something George had said. Meredith moved out first, later complaining about Rossetti's "bad habits," especially his disgusting dinners and self-destructive schedule: "Eleven a.m. plates of small-shop ham, thick cut, grisly with brine: four smashed eggs on it: work till dusk: dead tired on sofa till 10 p.m. Then to Evans' to dine off raw meat and stout . . . . The poor fellow never sleeps at night. His nervous system is knocked to pieces. It's melancholy."[36] Algernon got kicked out, via letter.

At heart, Whistler, too, was a troublemaker, pugilistic and litigious. Arrested for striking a black man on his way back from Valparaiso, Whistler, a bitter racist, bragged about it over dinner with the Rossettis. Gabriel laughed at "Jemmy," while William took issue. (During the American Civil War, Whistler sided with the slave states, to the discomfort of Gabriel, Swinburne, Burne-Jones, and William, who were decidedly on the side of the North.) Jimmy knocked down his friend the French artist Alphonse Legros (later to become Slade Professor of Art) in a quarrel. Asked to mediate, Rossetti stood with Jemmy, while Burne-Jones crowed that he wanted to take Whistler on. Then the famous libel suit unfolded with Ruskin, who called Whistler, in print, an impudent coxcomb who dared "to ask two hundred guineas for flinging a pot of paint in the public's face"—a description of a key Aesthetic masterpiece, *Nocturne in Black and Gold: The Falling Rocket*. Burne-Jones testified on the side of Ruskin (he agreed that what Whistler did wasn't art), William for Whistler. In the event, Whistler won, but Ruskin was asked to pay only one farthing rather than the £1,000 Whistler sued for.

Despite the fisticuffs, Rossetti remained friends with all. A Rossetti group always fell apart after a short period, then a reshuffling occurred, with a dash of new admirers, and another set would be configured. A functioning balance seemed to have a rather short life: six months to a year. Rossetti was not a practicing sodomite, or in any way a "homosexual" as we would define that term today. Gabriel had little interest in the male-male couple; he wanted larger configurations to bustle around him. This was another way of tempering intimacy—and therefore holding on to it—having it in threes, fours, or more. The Tudor House setup wasn't two, for instance, but four. When Rossetti became Burne-Jones's teacher, Morris mediated, tertiarily. Rossetti and Swinburne would be reading aloud together, and Boyce would drop in. Whistler called, loud and blustery, when Ruskin tried to merge with Rossetti. The Pre-Raphaelite Brotherhood, the Portfolio Society, the Hogarth Club, the Aesthetes, and other configurations are all testaments to the uses of the art fellowship, a circle suffused with shared work passions and shaken into action by troubled love.

OUT OF ARTISTIC collaboration emerged the wonder that was Red House. When he first moved in, Morris brought with him a bulky, "intensely medieval" settle.[37] He had designed the enormous mahogany piece himself, along with other furniture, a few years before. Made up of a long bench with three deep cupboards above, it was given by Morris a central spot in the lofty drawing room. A beautiful and unusual object already, the settle took on at Red House an enchanted life, passing through the hands of four artists. It is an early example of the many later objects that would glow with ideals, become solidly expressive of relationships. First Webb started in on it, caught up in his emotional sympathy with Morris—in his devotion and need to please—making of it both a stage and an odd passageway, something like the wardrobe in C. S. Lewis's novel *The Lion, the Witch, and the Wardrobe*. So sturdy and enormous was this block of furniture that Webb was able to add a ladder to the side, leading up to the top. He built onto the upper layer so that it formed a walkable gallery, to be used by the group for Christmas concerts. They lobbed apples from up here, and Charley Faulkner once came tumbling down from it, hitting the floor with a hard thump. A secret little door sat on top, cleverly opening onto the roof.

Ned wanted to get involved in this romance of wood and paint. He and Topsy sketched scenes on two of the settle doors from the *Nibelungenlied*, the ancient Germanic tale of bloody revenge and cruel sexuality that Rossetti had started to translate years back. Then, on a visit to Red House, Rossetti got fired up by the settle, perhaps because of its ingenious multiple uses or a sense of creative rivalry with Morris. Rossetti's long love for Janey almost certainly had much to do with the fact that she was Morris's wife, which speaks of a desire to compete, itself a kind of erotic attraction and repulsion to Morris. (And Morris's willingness to continue to love and support Janey, even though he knew about this affair, came right out of socialist and proto-feminist ideals: people cannot be possessed.) Rossetti started a painting on the central cupboard door. It would become one of his finest works (and would later be removed, framed, and displayed at Tate Britain, where it still is today).

Gleaming with gold and silver leaf, the scene in deep blues pierced with stars is from the love story of Dante and Beatrice. The central figure, an angel with red wings, has a stocky, androgynous (indeed Rossettian) build and represents Love itself. Two little faces hang in the corners: a dreamy Christ set in a small sun with wavy rays shooting down and Beatrice in her crescent moon. Beatrice, already dead, can still see the love that fills up the universe, a love more important than even Christ's. Love stands there, as a strange man/woman, keeping emotion alive between three.

Making art, writing poems, and doing research were often gifts of gratitude and tenderness. So much pleasure could be found in the work of one's fellow artist or writer, such felt and actionable inspiration, that it became an impetus for one's own work. Burne-Jones, deeply thrilled by Rossetti's sensual poem of the death of a "stunner," "The Blessed Damozel," decided to paint her, in two watercolor panels, in an act of worshipping reverse ekphrasis. So moved was Morris by Rossetti's painting *The Blue Closet* that he not only bought it but also wrote a verse representation of it ("He watch'd the snow melting, it ran through my hair, / Ran over my shoulder, white shoulders and bare").[38] And Rossetti, in turn, took Morris's heavy oak furniture with odd medieval embellishments as essential props in the background of his paintings of the late 1850s. The startling white buckram binding that holds Swinburne's *Atalanta in Calydon* was a Rossetti design. Swinburne penned a poem inspired by Rossetti's *The Christmas Carol*. Entranced by Whistler's *The Little White Girl*, Swinburne wrote some lines to accompany it. "Come snow, come wind or thunder, / High up in air, / I watch my face, and wonder / At my bright hair . . . ."[39] Whistler, whom Swinburne addressed in letters as "*mon pere*," had the poem printed on gold paper and attached to the frame. Burton gave a paper on hermaphroditism at a meeting of the Anthropological Society (on April 17, 1866, "Notes on a Hermaphrodite") soon after Swinburne had written two poems on the topic. Swinburne not only dedicated *Poems and Ballads* to Burne-Jones; he also wrote a poem entitled "Dedication," which appeared at the end of the volume. In it he imagines his poems as a gift to Ned, erotic offerings like kisses or the warmth of breath. He hopes their delicacy will find succour in Ned's art studio, among the "more gracious" world of his hands, be received in his "palace of painting" and "clothed round by sweet art."

Collaboration became deeply rooted in the set. Making things together developed into a philosophy and a politics, one that would have a profound influence on twentieth-century art and identity politics. Much of this emerged from Morris. Clamoring to fill Red House with singular objects, made by hand to adorn this particular space at this exact moment in time, he began to think about all that was wrong with Victorian ideas about art, design, and living (in the twentieth century, Frank Lloyd Wright learned from Morris about the aesthetic whole—every detail of an interior part of its organic life). Why couldn't everyone live among furnishings simply and sincerely constructed out of good materials and sound workmanship? Morris decried the ornate, delicate, luxurious housewares popular at this time as "costly rubbish," elitist and next to useless for the simple art of living: "It is a shoddy age."[40]

As Rossetti tells it, one evening in 1861 a bunch of friends were sitting around talking about the medieval workshop as a place where artists felt inspired to branch out from painting to constructing decorative things. Someone suggested, as a joke more than anything else, that they form such a shop. This band of brothers came to be labeled "the Firm," but officially they called themselves "Morris, Marshall, Faulkner, & Co., Fine Art Workmen in Painting, Carving, Furniture, and the Metals" (later just Morris & Co.). The other four partners who had a stake, as designers and financial backers, were Rossetti, Webb, Burne-Jones, and Ford Madox Brown. While Morris's ideas for this workshop were always deeply serious, such pleasure came from craft fellowships that even he started the endeavor with a jocular, convivial attitude. These first gatherings were conducted something "like a picnic," in Webb's estimation, or, in Faulkner's words, they had "rather the character of a meeting of the 'Jolly Masons' or the jolly something elses than of a meeting to discuss business."[41] Anecdotes were told, the relative merits of certain styles of thirteenth-century furniture were debated, and finally the affairs of the shop would be discussed in a furious rush until late in the night. Started with almost no capital, the Firm moved into premises at no. 8 Red Lion Square amid the cheap lodgings of writers and artists in bohemian Bloomsbury. Setting up shop was no small thing for these middle-class men. To be artists and artisans was to daringly mix classes, painting a canvas and painting a chair having drastically different class connotations. Morris plunging his hands into a dye vat, coming out blue to the shoulder, constituted a radical class rebellion, to his great satisfaction on all fronts.

The first floor held their offices and showroom. Workshops were housed in the attic, and the basement lodged a kiln for firing glass and tiles. Red House became a second work space. Simeon Solomon, William De Morgan, and others joined up. Helpers were taken on and trained from the Industrial Home for Destitute Boys. A record of what it was like to visit the shop in its early days was left by a Mrs. Richmond Ritchie, who was brought there by Val Prinsep on a foggy morning.

> We came into an empty ground floor room, and Val Prinsep called "Topsy" very loud, and some one came from above with hair on end and in a nonchalant way began to show one or two of his curious, and to my uninitiated soul, bewildering treasures. I think Morris said the glasses would stand firm when he put them on the table. I bought two tumblers . . . . I came away . . . with a general impression of sympathetic shyness and shadows and dim green glass.[42]

The circular sent out to advertise their opening functioned also as a manifesto, decrying the "crude and fragmentary" state of the decorative arts. Other design firms were offended. Yet the Firm would become a byword for sophisticated taste in the later 1860s and would eventually enjoy a great commercial success. Hand-painted tiles, embroidery, tapestry, carpets, furniture, metalwork like candlesticks and bedsteads, and even jewelry were among their wares. Morris began developing his remarkable wallpaper patterns, friezes of luxuriant growth. At first Morris himself printed those labyrinthine daisies, lush pomegranates, rose trellises, expectant rabbits, still coveted today. The simple, black-framed, old English elbow chair with its adjustable back, which would come to be the celebrated "Morris chair," had its birth around this time, a joint effort of Webb and Morris.

It was in stained glass that the Firm first made its real mark. One early commission was for a little gem of a church at Selsley. Webb and Morris did a "Creation" window with water, lions, and strange planets. Three figures kneel and watch the Ascension in another Morris window. Brown did the Crucifixion; in it Mary is holding a red handkerchief, her nimbus full of stars. In Burne-Jones's Resurrection, Christ waves a white flag. For his Adam and Eve, he used Brown and his wife for models, and the snake has a human face. In Rossetti's *Sermon on the Mount*, Saint Peter has a recognizable countenance; there stands a young, handsome William Morris.

Stained glass came to be manufactured on this system that involved shaping by numerous hands. As above, a Tristram and Isolde stained-glass series, for instance, included panels by Burne-Jones, Ford Madox Brown, and William Morris. Or Burne-Jones would make a "cartoon" for a window narrative, Morris deal with the color, and Phil Webb arrange the panels. Burne-Jones compared this kind of work, which he called "fettered"—being forced to follow the lead of others, or to give them their head to change his work—with his painting ("open air"), which was done alone: "I love to work in that fettered way, and am better in a prison than in the open air always."[43]

Making things among and with friends—with its sensuality, sympathy, and openhandedness—fueled Morris's growing socialism. Through handwork, he began to see that the vast majority of the people of England toiled at ugly and repetitive jobs that didn't utilize their best selves: their higher mind or their creative impulses. They made objects for others to use, and the objects themselves were often unshapely and truly unneeded, merely symbols of status. What if the simple work of making household wares could call on the creative mind, on carefully developed craft skills? And then what if the people who made these beautiful items of everyday use got to keep and appreciate them themselves? He imagined a world enlightened by "art made by the people and for the people, a joy to the maker and the user."[44] Tight bourgeois houses could open up into free communities of non-possessiveness. Morris's bringing together of design and radical social ideas marked the beginning of the Arts and Crafts movement with its antimachine and pro-workingman aesthetic. Out of Morris's philosophy and activities grew utopian craft communities like Charles Robert Ashbee's Guild and School of Handicraft, founded in 1888 and set up in the Cotswolds. Another was Byrdcliffe Arts Colony in Woodstock, New York, founded in 1903. The Bloomsbury Group took much from Morris: Red House became a model for Charleston, Vanessa Bell and Duncan Grant's farmhouse in Sussex, decorated by themselves, their friends, and colleagues when they moved there in 1916. The idea for Virginia and Leonard Woolf's Hogarth Press came primarily from Morris's much earlier Kelmscott Press, founded upon preindustrial principles and with the sense that books could be art objects expressive of a personal aesthetic. Roger Fry's Omega Workshops of 1913 took up the banner of the Firm: that life should be lived, at all turns and in every detail, poetically.

IN THRALL TO their stout, bearded hero, a circle of shining youths gathered around Morris in the 1880s and 1890s. Pulling at a thread buried in the warp and weft of all these brotherhoods—Red House, Bertolini's, Tudor House, the Firm—a few of these young men championed their sexual relationships with other men. Socialist politics manifested in art communities led, in their thinking, to the open-hearted love of the bodies of comrades. Being committed to the *materials* of life—to the very skin and surface of living—came to mean, in a logical progression, an attentiveness to flesh close at hand and caught up in the same collaborative work. Certainly this sometimes led to sex with women. (There were few women at the center of these later groups, two notable exceptions being May Morris, William's daughter, and Eleanor Marx, Karl's daughter.) But for political freethinkers, excited by transgression, to couple with men constituted another powerful protest against the fabric of a society all wrong.

The most successful and bold of these young turks and hero worshippers was Edward Carpenter. An extraordinarily beautiful man, with a refined and open countenance, Carpenter was attracted to muscled laborers, such as "the thick-thighed hot coarse-fleshed young bricklayer with the strap round his waist."[45] The courage to admit such things, even to himself, came from a hard-won struggle. Carpenter was a clergyman at Oxford, and sex between men constituted a serious sin not only to Christians but to Victorian society at large. Indeed, buggery was considered criminal and was punishable by death up until 1861, when sentences were "lightened" to between ten years and life imprisonment. After 1830, however, the death penalty was generally not applied, and, for the most part, if one was private about it, one could do what one would with one's body. That would change in 1885, when the Labouchère amendment to the Criminal Law Act made "acts of gross indecency" between men punishable by up to two years of hard labor. With this, a large range of same-sex activity became criminalized, not just the single act, and thus to do anything "homosexual" was to be marked as a criminal.

The demons Carpenter wrestled with were more moral than criminal, though. How could he overcome the fact that what called up his deepest emotions was considered an unspeakable abomination? Fighting through a fog of guilt and self-loathing, Carpenter was able to reconcile himself to his passions only by linking them to other causes for justice and reasons for rebellion. Experiencing an epiphany in 1873—"a vibration through [his] whole body"—he made the decision to leave the church and make his life with "the mass of people and the manual workers."[46] Carpenter felt deeply the injustice of modern life, where idle people lived "on the labour of those whom with an elegant contempt they term the lower classes."[47] On principles drawn from Whitman and Morris, Carpenter would not be the effete intellectual, the rentier who watched others produce the necessities of his living. In the 1880s, he bought farmland in Millthorpe and carved out a frugal existence growing his own food, and cultivating vegetarianism, socialism, and a dash even of Buddhism. Carpenter spent enormous amounts of time, energy, and money fighting for social causes—for the workers, for women's rights, for animal rights. Why shouldn't "homogenic love" (one of his many terms) also have its rightful place in a world made new? Carpenter integrated his love of men carefully with his other moral acts. He made his call in a poem heavily influenced by Whitman's *Leaves of Grass*: "Lovers of all handicrafts and of labor in the open air, confessed passionate lovers of your own sex, Arise!" [48] Indeed, he was able to see his spirituality, something in the manner of Dante Gabriel Rossetti, as shot through with the erotic love of men. Why must, he lamented in an early sermon, Christianity be "a blind worship of the ascetic principle, a blind hatred of the body?"[49] Carpenter eventually settled down with a man bred in the Sheffield slums, George Merrill, his "Georgette," who had a fondness for house chores. These were simple acts—living with a workingman on equal footing, loving him as other men might a woman—but they had the weight and significance of revolutionary gestures.

Carpenter was in the vanguard of a movement to make same-sex love more visible by constructing it as a way of life, an identity, the desires of a type of person who had rights. To go visit Carpenter in Millthorpe became a spiritual pilgrimage. C. R. Ashbee arrived and helped Edward dig and replant raspberries. In love with Carpenter's way of life, he set up his Guild and School of Handicraft. The writers Siegfried Sassoon and Robert Graves made the trip to the "prophet," the "seer." E. M. Forster's visit gave him the courage to write his gay novel *Maurice.* Edward and George "combined to make a profound impression on me," Forster remembered. "George Merrill also touched my backside—gently and just above the buttocks. I believe he touched most people's. The sensation was unusual and I still remember it, as I remember the position of a long vanished tooth."[50] D. H. Lawrence constructed his spiritual philosophy around sexuality under the influence of Carpenter. The sexologist Havelock Ellis studied and conversed with Carpenter when researching his landmark book on homosexuality, *Sexual Inversion.*

Carpenter was one of the first to develop what was, for the time, a startling and wholly new idea. In his essays, like the pamphlet *Homogenic Love* (published by the Labor Press in 1895) and *Intermediate Sex* of 1908, he crafted a defense for homosexuality by seeing it as a way of being, a group of legitimate practices that made up a person. This idea that one's sexuality could make up one's identity—a basic foundation of the 1960s gay rights movement—began to take shape only in the 1880s and 1890s. Before this, a man might be interested in having sex with men, and only men, yet this didn't define him—rather, he was, say, a working-class carpenter, an aristocratic MP, or an atheist writer and artist. He wasn't a homosexual. Using labels like "urning," "uranian," and the "intermediate sex," Carpenter carved out a theory that same-sex desire came as a "natural" characteristic for certain types of people. With a female "soul" caught in a male body, the Urning had common traits with other Urnings, such as a more refined and sensitive nature and a propensity to be highly gifted in the fine arts. For Carpenter, this identity served as a way of normalizing same-sex love and laying to rest the judgment that it was "depraved."

The productive brotherhoods that grew out of Red House, Bertolini's, Tudor House, and the Firm lived and moved in a time "just before." In the 1860s these men could use the erotic frisson stirred up between them to fuel their creative endeavors, without earning any kind of label, such as "homoeroticism." Were some of these men "homosexuals"? Contemporary biographers have argued yes for Swinburne, Burton, Milnes, and Solomon. They fell into no such categories in their time, though, and it's possible this fluidity of identity left them with a richer continuum of options. Their erotic impulses ranged widely—becoming threaded together with socialism, flagellation, ekphrasis, crafts, anthropology, Christianity, and more. Physicality was part of the fabric, certainly, but a larger field of play opened up than simply genitals meeting. Things had changed by the late 1870s. What it meant to be a "homosexual" became more visible and hence more and more violently suppressed as criminal and deviant. Male lovers of men had no choice but to band together and define themselves clearly, in order to fight this push to make them disappear.

IN THE WANING years of the nineteenth century, Carpenter was able to feel his love of men to be part of his larger spiritual, even Christian, self. (The deep hatred between the two had not become ingrained yet.) When Carpenter was in his eighties, in the 1920s, a young American man came to visit. Carpenter made expert love to him, "gazing at [his] body rapturously between kisses and growling ecstatically." The young man recalled, "I had the distinct feeling that he felt my coming as if he were coming himself—that in that moment he was me. Afterwards, he said 'When I was a clergyman I thought at Communion I was at one with God. But I realize now that this is a much more intimate communion—for is not Man made in the image of God?' "[51]

CHAPTER SIX

Feasting with Panthers

We are all in the gutter,
but some of us are looking at the stars.

—OSCAR WILDE,
Lady Windermere's Fan

OVEMBER 1869: AFTER penning a letter to Swinburne at the Arts Club on Hanover Square, twenty-nine-year-old Simeon Solomon stepped out into the heavy air of an autumn evening. Mist soon enfolded him, and as he strolled along in his slouching way faces swam up out of the fog. A dream from a few nights before, described in his letter to Swinburne, hung in his mind. In it, he watched a cat and sheep couple. Minutes later the offspring appeared to him: "a little black creature with long nails of wire."[1] To his horror, the creature fastened onto him with its piercing claws, and as he pulled the wires out they grew alive like worms. Perhaps this nightmare speaks, in some unfathomable dream logic, of Solomon's fears about the dangers of his own outlawed desire for other men. Most dangerous of all was the perception by the majority of his contemporaries that his favorite sexual acts were monstrous, begetting disease and moral corruption.

On nights like these, Solomon would go cruising for workingmen. His favorite hunting ground was a few minutes' stroll away: Leicester Square, where he also went for Cannibal Club meetings. Once he picked out his man, he would often take him to a public urinal—the nearby Stratford Place mews, for instance—and enjoy a bit of fellatio and buggery. Men who visited such places for sexual encounters called them "cottages" or "tearooms." Come-ons could be quite open. A lustful and blatant fellow might stand over a urinal masturbating and turn to show his erection. The most efficient activity—a session of mutual masturbation—could be brought off right there at the urinals. Those who fancied being watched found this particularly piquant. For more privacy, couples could retire to the cubicles and practice whatever pleased them. The pissoirs held many dangers. Syphilis could be picked up, of course, as could an arrest for buggery. This may have been the secret to their appeal, for some—throwing oneself in harm's way could be shot through with sensuality. Assaulting and stealing from "sods" (short for "sodomite") became common practice among felonious types, their marks unable to report them, as they themselves were pursuing criminal acts.

Cold tiles, a smell of rank effluvium, the sharp splash of hot piss hitting porcelain assaulted the senses of the cottage haunter and became part and parcel, one imagines, of the tremble of the semipublic orgasm. Sodomy is an act that can call to mind ordure, the cloacal. This was one reason so many found it disgusting. But this was also a motive for cherishing it, as a means to descend into the earthy muck of life.

One didn't have to head to public urinals, however, as street cruising was a vigorous sport. Lingering around the statue of Apollo in Hyde Park was one possibility. Or one could eye the male prostitutes on Fleet Street, Holborn, and the Strand. In 1865, the writer and later sexologist John Addington Symonds (a Burton associate), who struggled with deep self-loathing because of his attraction to men and hadn't yet made love to one, was cruised by a young grenadier in an alley leading from Trafalgar Square to Leicester Square.

> I was too innocent, strange as this may seem, to guess what he meant. But I . . . felt drawn toward him, and did not refuse his company. So there I was, the slight nervous man of fashion in my dress clothes, walking side by side with a strapping fellow in scarlet uniform, strongly attracted by his physical magnetism. . . . He broke abruptly into proposals, mentioned a house we could go to, and made it quite plain for what purpose. I quickened my pace, and hurrying through the passage broke away from him with a passionate mixture of repulsion and fascination.[2]

Symonds's dalliance here proves how easy it could be to pick a man up on the streets of London, if only one was open to it.

An amusing tableau of sexual angling unfolds in the pornographic novel *Teleny; or, The Reverse of the Medal*, published in 1893. Drawn from the lives of its anonymous authors (all part of Oscar Wilde's literary circle and written in a round-robin style, with Wilde himself probably penning parts), its picture of the London street scene appears to be mostly accurate, with the usual literary embellishments. The narrator, a neophyte in the world of same-sex desire, has his eyes opened to the proclivities of "night-walkers" when he follows the erotically mesmerizing Teleny through lonely parts of London. A man in close-fitting trousers and a short, black velvet jacket begins to walk alongside him, humming, coughing, clearing his throat, and scraping his feet. Then the man walks on, turns around, and stares at him in a pointed manner. Another fellow gazing at him either does up or undoes the buttons on his pants. All of this merely puzzles the narrator. What do these men want of him? Then a "mary-anne" (an effeminate "sodomite"), eyes smudged with kohl and cheeks daubed in rouge, tries him. Mincing by in a maidenly way, he shakes his buttocks at the astonished and still confused hero. Next comes a brawny workman who, as he passes, "clenched his powerful fist, doubled his muscular arm at the elbow, and then moved it vertically hither and thither for a few times, like a piston-rod in action, as it slipped in and out of the cylinder."[3] At this, the narrator thinks to himself, "Ah ha!" And then, eventually, "Why not?"

Once a man began to dabble, he discovered speedily that there were brothels where men and boys could be hired. This thriving underground world burst onto a rapt public when arrests were made at a whorehouse at 19 Cleveland Street, in July 1889. The police stumbled onto the establishment in a kind of haphazard, pell-mell manner. It all started with an investigation into thefts at the central post office. A nineteen-year-old telegraph messenger boy, Charles Swinscow, was questioned by the police because he was spending more money than he could possibly earn as a messenger (these were the days before credit cards). Swinscow admitted quite openly that he and a number of other boys (including the wonderfully named Ernest Thickbroom) had been recruited by Harry Newlove (!), a former messenger, to perform all manner of sex acts with middle- and upper-class men at Cleveland Street. Most of these boys had started in on this life with some sexual fun in the lavatory at the central post office, with Newlove and others.

The story took on huge proportions when Newlove named among his clients Lord Arthur Somerset, son of the Duke of Beaufort (soon caricatured in the press as "my lord Gomorrah") and the Earl of Euston, heir to the Duke of Grafton. Rumors went even so far as to touch Prince Albert Victor, second in line to the throne. The newspapers ran with the story, although they avoided mention of sex acts in print. Many felt that detailed facts could be dangerous to the morality of readers, reasoning, it would seem, that if the people discovered that such things as sodomy existed, they might try it themselves. Lord Halsbury, the lord chancellor, argued initially that charges shouldn't be brought at all, because the sensational nature of the case "will give very wide publicity and consequently will spread very extensively written matter of the most revolting and mischievous kind, the spread of which . . . will produce enormous evil."[4] For instance, most of what the witness John Saul, who called himself a "professional sodomite," had to say at trial didn't make it into print. His description of Lord Euston as not an actual sodomite, but rather the type who "likes to play with you and then 'spend' on your belly" appeared in print as "saying what we cannot report."[5] In the event, only Newlove and his associate came out of the affair with convictions, pleading guilty to "gross indecency" in exchange for light sentences. Despite cries in the press of the upper classes corrupting working boys and accusations of two different laws for the different classes (true, of course), none of the titled men were brought to trial. Somerset fled to France and lived in exile for the rest of his life. Euston stayed and sued for libel against the *North London Press*, claiming that he went to Cleveland Street only once, thinking *poses plastiques* were to be had there. He won, largely because the man who accused him was a sodomite and he, apparently, wasn't.

Lord Euston by all accounts did not commit that one act that so many Victorians could not stomach: anal coition. Other relations between men that we today would understand as homosexual—passionate friendships involving intimacies such as kisses and caresses—were deemed by Victorians as shining examples of chivalry and manly purity. Tennyson could, in *In Memoriam*, call himself a widow upon his friend Arthur Hallam's death. This yearning for his dead friend's touch, voice, and body won him the laureate. Even many men who championed same-sex love, as Symonds would later in his life, could not condone this "vice," as he himself called it. (When Oscar Wilde was on trial for sodomy in 1895, the magistrate denied him bail, since "no worse crime than this" existed).[6] As he became more accepting of his desires, Symonds visited male brothels. There he savored the pleasures of brawny young soldiers but "instead of yielding to any brutal impulse, [he] thoroughly enjoyed the close vicinity of that splendid naked piece of manhood."[7] What remained brutal in his eyes is the desire to penetrate another man, a craving he can never lay to rest, but can also never indulge. For some, though, such a demonized act took on the glamour of the holy grail. Deep taboos could call up profound desires.

Walter, the narrator of *My Secret Life*, willing to try every carnal "letch," tests this one out, too. Any sex act seen as an outrage by his fellows would interest him, if for that reason only. As a young man, Walter can't believe a prostitute when she tells him about a man "putting his prick up her bum." Feverishly curious, he sodomizes a woman and feels a strong mixture of "almost mad" sexual desire and then, following immediately, a sense of being shocked at himself. How could he do such a thing? As he becomes slowly indoctrinated into ever more sophisticated fleshly pleasures, he meets a "sod" who tells him that some men are "fond of a bit of brown."[8] When the working-class fellow talks of dildos, Walter shudders and thinks to himself, "Fancy two men together in a stable, one shoving a pestle up the other's bum!"[9]

Walter comes to quietly acclimate himself to this new world, one in which his obsessive craving for sexual contact with women begins to share space with a persistent "strange desire" to handle, "frig," and, eventually, suck another man's penis. With the assistance of Sarah, one of his regular prostitutes, he becomes acquainted with a svelte young house painter who has no sexual experience with men. The poor youth falls into the situation because he's been out of work for some time and is becoming thin from want of nourishment. At first Walter has lurking suspicions. What if he is "an overfrigged bugger, who could no longer come"? For Walter has heard that men who "let themselves out for that work at last got so used up that it was difficult for them to do anything with their own pricks, and that all they could do was to permit men to feel their cocks, whilst they plugged their arse-holes."[10] What Walter fears is that the man might have the dreaded Victorian "illness" of spermatorrhea, that weakness, enervation, and morbidity caused by expending too much sperm. Many prominent doctors, such as William Acton, a popular writer about sexuality, felt that the sperm expended in nonprocreative acts like masturbation and sodomy especially drew out the life force, causing real illness. Yet, somehow, heterosexual orgasm could strengthen the system (when done with a wife), a manly act that built up the blood, like eating raw beef.

Being assured of the painter's sexual innocence, Walter

indulges, without yet even considering buggery. Afterward, he goes home and lies in bed, amazed and exhilarated at what he has dared: "I could not sleep for having frigged a man." He goes over, in loving detail, the minutiae of the other man's sexual self. Despite an uneasiness with these acts he can't shake, Walter continues to see the man. He relishes watching the other man's face as he has an orgasm and dresses him up in silk stockings. After their liaison has gone on for many weeks and a sense of intimacy and trust has been constructed, Walter finds himself maddeningly pursued by the idea of buggering the painter. One night, the unbelievable happens. As Walter pleasures himself with the lad, he "placed him bending over the bed." Overcome by a hunger that whirls through his brain, "like lightening," Walter speaks, as the other man "almost shivered with desire."

"Let me put my prick up your bum."

"That I won't. . . . That I won't."

After some more coaxing, the painter exclaims, "It will hurt—I'm frightened, but will you give me ten pounds really?"[11]

Walter then

> pulled his bum to the level of my prick, I locked the door, I trembled, we whispered. I slabbered my prick and his hole with spittle. . . . I closed on him half mad . . . my brain whirled . . . I wished not to do what I was doing, but some ungovernable impulse drove me on. . . . My rod with one or two lunges buried itself up him. . . . He gave a low moan. "Ohoo I shall faint," he cried. "Ho, pull it out." "It's in—don't move or I won't pay you."[12]

Afterward, Walter rushes out, fiercely loathing himself and the other man, caught up in terrible fears. But it is this very emotion—this heady terror—that keeps Walter's thoughts circling, with "bloody minded baudiness," around this one act. Irretrievably enthralled and, simultaneously, abhorring, for a long time after Walter's "mind ran on anus and nothing else." Even the libertine Walter can't escape the sense that sodomy has a sinful taint, that it's a pushing through into an impenetrable darkness. To commit it is to, momentarily, lose one's mind and jump into an abyss.

BY 1869 SIMEON Solomon felt that he had, at long last, arrived. His paintings hung at the Royal Academy. Rich patrons solicited his work. To his "evenings" at his studio at 12 Fitzroy Street came the cream of the avant-garde: Swinburne, Rossetti, Burne-Jones, Burton. Of all the men in his circle, Solomon had struggled the hardest and come the farthest. Not a Cambridge or Oxford man, he couldn't smoothly fall into the right set. Simeon scrambled his way up, working for every inch of recognition he got. This was because he came into this world an outsider of an indelible stamp. Solomon was Jewish, at a time when the British not only tolerated anti-Semitism but institutionalized it.

At the beginning of the 1800s, avowed Jews could not hold public office or follow most professions, such as teaching, medicine, and the law. Change came slowly over the course of the century, but a solid distrust of what many saw as a foreign and inferior race still loomed. Solomon's father, a London hat maker and paper embosser, became the first Jewish tradesman to legally set up shop within the City of London, under an act passed in 1830. To succeed despite this thick wall of prejudice,

Solomon grew a glittering but thick social skin, willfully pushing through the pall of hate by fierce wit, a shining bohemian glamour, and sheer talent developed through working harder than everyone else.

The Solomons were a family of artists. Irrepressible, the entire clan moved through the air of sophisticated London as cultured intellectuals. A convivial open house became a policy with them: regular salons, dances, impromptu concerts, and amateur dramatics. Sometimes these occasions drew two hundred people. Simeon's elder brother Abraham established himself as a painter with a literary style. Simeon was especially fortunate in his sister. One of his best friends, Rebecca became yet another artist of some repute, working for a time in Millais's studio. Rebecca cut herself loose from stifling philistine conventions, as Simeon would in his different way, and lived the kind of bohemian life Rossetti favored—late nights of talk and drink and sexual revelry as an inspiration for her art. She and Simeon posed stiff competition for each other. A friend wrote in 1865 that she hoped Rebecca "won't have such a wildly incongruous party as she does sometimes. But they say hers are nothing to Simeon's in that respect."[13]

Solomon relished playing roles; a fine impersonator, he often spun out some tomfoolery. He gave spoof lectures on astronomy and chemistry. Showing up in flowing green drapery and sandals became a habit one season. Playing the Greek at first, he would solemnly declaim in a sonorous voice long passages from Jewish rituals. William Richmond, a friend from the Royal Academy Schools, found Solomon "wise and witty," if slightly mad. "He twisted ideas, had a genius for paradox, and . . . convulsed his friends with laughter by his strange weird imagination."[14] Richmond declared him "the greatest genius of our set."[15] De facto social outcasts, Simeon and Rebecca saw no reason not to break those rules of respectability that barely applied to them anyway. Not to take risks was not to live. Why not rage through life on the margins?

Still, the two were careful artists. Simeon's genius earned him a place, when he was just fifteen, in the Royal Academy Schools—required training for artists who would go on to make a profession of it. Like Ned and Topsy, Solomon fell under the spell of late Pre-Raphaelitism in the 1850s and initially took up its creed: a historicized style with a Ruskinian attention to detail. A trim, small, but well-made man, Solomon had a swarthy, mischievous countenance. "A fair little Hebrew," a friend called him.[16] At some gathering or other, he managed to meet that famed introducer and Cannibal, Richard Monckton Milnes, who furthered his career by inviting him to Fryston (and later bought at least two of his paintings). At the chilly, gaunt mansion, dark with books, Simeon found a lover: Oscar Browning, a classics teacher at Eton. Browning helped Solomon catch up with everyone else—all those gentlemen educated in Greek and Roman studies at Oxford or Cambridge. Dear to his painting would be such subjects as Sappho and Bacchus (the hedonist), who were classically decorous but could also be used to depict deviant sexual practices. By painting such figures, Solomon could both sell his pictures and continue an exploration into outlawed desires.

The other man Solomon met at Fryston was Swinburne. Solomon was overwhelmed by him. Seduced, the painter would follow the poet down any road of extravagance. They giggled about sodomy, in loud voices, at the Arts Club. Rumor has them running naked through Tudor House, shrieking, and causing a welcome ruckus with their lecherous talk at Cannibal

Club gatherings. Lording it over Simeon, Swinburne pushed the younger painter to fawn. Simeon seemed never quite able to escape the role of acolyte. Whether because of his Jewishness or his sexual orientation—or even, perhaps, his particular way of being in the world—Simeon stood forever just outside where he wanted to be. Sometimes he set up his relationships so that he'd have the outsider role. More often prejudice forced him out. Either way, he looked into the bright window of the coveted place, caught out in the cold, gazing and longing.

Because of his perennial outsider status, Solomon swiftly became a rising star in both the Cannibal and the Aesthetic clans during the early 1860s. These were men who admired the deviant (and even the criminal, at least up until the point where arrests were made). Swinburne introduced him to Burton, who took little Solomon under his manly wing and made him a Cannibal. He met Topsy and designed stained glass and tiles for the Firm. Ned, who called him the "Jewjube," became a fast friend and strong admirer of his work. The two would sometimes draw pornography together and present it to Swinburne. He held off the delicious pleasure of meeting Rossetti at first because, as he wrote flirtatiously in a letter to a mutual friend: "I am only just turned 17 and am very small and not advanced enough in manners to become the guest of grown up gentlemen at such a late hour."[17] Soon he was in and out of Rossetti's studio, along with those of Holman Hunt, Madox Brown, and Whistler. Sharing produced pictures—ideas about color, costumes for historical works, favored models. Janey Morris may have been the model for Sappho in Solomon's watercolor about lesbian love of 1864, *Sappho and Erinna in a Garden at Mytilene*. Solomon trolled the streets and public places for male working-class models in the same way the others picked up female ones. He discovered one beautiful Greek boy, Gaetano Meo, playing a small harp for coins on a thoroughfare of London. Persuading Meo to sit for him, Solomon lent the boy out as a model to everyone. Perhaps modeling blended smoothly into other intimacies, as with Rossetti, but such stories haven't survived in Solomon's case. Simeon was not a sexual predator, though. Others reported him as always warmly kind. He caressed these boys and leaned on them affectionately, draping himself over their shoulders, "much in the manner of Julius Caesar when in the company of favorite courtiers of tender years."[18]

Simeon burned brightly within this sphere by embracing, even flaunting, those parts of his life that kept him marginalized. Boldly, given the prevailing prejudice, Simeon began as a self-consciously Jewish painter, often using Jewish models and adhering to Old Testament subjects. Just as he tried to figure out what it meant to be an Anglo-Jewish artist—he had no prototypes for this identity—he also had to work out what it meant to be an artist who sexually desired men. At least he didn't have to hide his sexuality from his avant-garde friends; indeed, he was encouraged to try on whatever hankerings met his fancy. Swinburne read Whitman to him, and while Swinburne worked on drafts of his Sappho monologue "Anactoria," Simeon painted his own watercolor of her, forcing her caresses on Erinna. Burton had a lively interest in lesbianism, brought the topic to Cannibal meetings, and would later discuss the practice in his "Terminal Essay" to his translation of *The Arabian Nights* (it's quite possible he introduced the subject to both younger men, although they were also reading French writers such as Baudelaire and Gautier on the topic).

Interest in the hermaphrodite or androgyne also spread like wildfire among the set. Burton studied the phenomena as an anthropologist and a historian, arguing that in both the Bible and ancient Greek mythology "the first creation of humans was hermaphrodite."[19] Swinburne scribbled poems about creatures with plantlike genitals. The women in Rossetti and Burne-Jones canvases grew thick necks, male musculature, beetling brows. Solomon did with men what the other painters did with women. His men had a Rossettian erotic "femininity" about them: swollen, finely carved lips; floating clouds of hair; sensitive, abstracted eyes. As he matured as an artist, his figures gained a "supersexual beauty," Swinburne enthused in a review, "in which the lineaments of woman and of man seem blended as the lines of sky and landscape melt in the burning mist of heat and light." Creatures free of the usual humdrum of earthbound strictures—of needing to fit into one box or the other—they have an ethereal dreaminess, as if about to be pulled up into heaven, or down into the underworld. Swinburne remarked that they had souls "enamoured of soft light and clear water, of leaves and flowers and limbs more lovely than these."[20]

Since Solomon never went to swank prep schools like Eton, he learned to love flagellation from Swinburne (and Milnes and other Cannibals). A flurry of stories about boys being punished by men passed between the two (and between Solomon and Oscar Browning). At Algernon's request, Simeon illustrated some of his birching stories, including a series for his lewd epic *The Flogging Block*. Simeon also created flagellant drawings for himself, based on ancient Greek anecdotes, with titles like *Spartan Boys About to be Scourged at the Altar of Diana* and *Mastigophorus, the Whip Bearer*. Talk of dildos, "swishings," and the works of Sade litter their correspondence. His letters about his erotic cravings hold a rare honesty for their time, a need, no matter how risky, to proclaim his sexual difference. Like a true Cannibal, Simeon even penned some male-male pornography, none of which has survived (although some speculate he co-wrote *Sins of the Cities of the Plain* with the Cannibal James Campbell Reddie). Tantalizingly, extracts appear in a letter to Swinburne. Solomon's narrator has "affections [that] are divided between the boy and the birch." Mixed with a burning for the "rod" is an inexpressible pleasure in the company and confidence of handsome boys. This rod has an unstable identity: an instrument for beating? A dildo? Could it also be an erect penis? Unlike Swinburne's flagellation writings, Solomon's don't resonate darkly, with a lingering on pain and the emptiness of existence. In a letter to Browning, Solomon described a pupil who is beaten "until the wings, which are latent in his shoulder blades, sprout."[21] The painter's rod radiates light, rich in plenitude. It blooms even, "with flowers of Love."

In so many of Solomon's works, reverent young men, with yearning faces, hold enchanted staffs. These long implements, grasped in the hand as support for the body, or gently presented in a ceremony, can be seen in image after image. Sometimes they are walking sticks, other times a sprig of myrtle or birch, or occasionally religious paraphernalia such as a scroll, censer, or candle. The type of tool follows the overall theme of the work. Throughout his career, Solomon's art fell into two categories—the pagan (ancient Greek), or the sacred (either Jewish or Roman Catholic). Not especially religious, Solomon became fascinated by ritual, by the rich robes, gold chalices, heavy scents, solemn rites of Catholicism. He even toyed with converting to Catholicism, not so much for reasons of belief, but rather because it was, to his mind, a more materially sumptuous practice. In one of his most celebrated paintings, *The Mystery of Faith* of 1870, a beautiful man with pale gray eyes holds aloft a tall, narrow monstrance—an elaborate gold and rock crystal reliquary. Not quite a staff but yet echoing one, this case holds the host, a piece of the body of Christ (if one follows the doctrine of the Real Presence). Done almost entirely in gold and white, this glittering watercolor descends directly from Rossetti and Whistler's experiments in white—*Ecce Ancilla Domini!* and *Symphony in White No. 1*.

The image plays on opposing elements. First the viewer is struck by the solidly material, such as the shimmering pigment of the surface itself. Is this a study in pure color? And then the problem of Christ's "body," held there in that container, becomes cause for musing. What does it mean for the spiritual (Christ) to enter the physical (bread or body)? But then the viewer gets caught up in the title of the piece and its most obvious theme: the mystery of faith, which is precisely what transcends the realm of the physical senses. Is this a painting about the sensuousness of ritualized religion or how strange it is that belief has so much truck with physical beauty? Swinburne found such works of Solomon's "suggestive of things hidden in secret places of spiritual reserve."[22] As with almost every image of a man in Simeon's oeuvre, a thread of inexplicable pining runs through its rich fabric, giving the image a touch of eroticized melancholy. Something caught in that heavy crystal scepter calls up deep desire, of the kind stirred by the unobtainable. Like so many of Solomon's paintings, this one stages the bereft inwardness of the one who stands outside.

Staves, lanterns, and twigs appear also in his pagan works. In his most controversial watercolor, *Sacramentum Amoris* of 1868, an almost nude figure with the wide shoulders and chest of a man takes an effeminate stance, hip cocked, one leg bent at the knee. His mouth and cheeks appear rouged, his eyes darkened with kohl, his long hair garlanded with tiny flowers. Loins barely covered by a brief patch of animal fur, with another bit over one arm, the figure feels intensely pagan, perhaps a god of some drunken ritual devoted to the coming of spring (Solomon painted a number of Dionysian images). The eroticism of this work diffuses over the whole, with a languid decadence, unlike the intense focus of the wide-open gray eyes of the churchman in *Mystery*. Here, the hooded, empty eyes of a furred creature stare out of a face formed for nighttime pleasures. In one hand he carries a lantern, which mirrors the monstrance in *The Mystery of Faith*, and in the other a staff taller than he. This wooden stick (a thyrsus or Aaron's rod) blooms, in an enchanted moment, with a lick of fire coming around from the back. Solomon explains this epiphanic symbol as a barren rod until it is looked on by "Love" and then bursts forth in flower and becomes "Very Love." Perhaps an ejaculation, but one not procreative in the usual sense, here orgasm comes as the tender opening of flowers. Staff, rod, dildo, penis (body and blood of Christ, semen): they all illuminate the power of the intimate caress.

Simeon created *Sacramentum Amoris* for his patron, the shipping magnate Frederick Leyland, a major collector of Pre-Raphaelite and Aesthetic work. Leyland saw an early study of it, where the "Amoris," clothed chastely in drapery, looks like a pretty, wistful boy. When he laid eyes on the final watercolor, he vehemently disapproved of its "indelicate" nature. He ordered Simeon to make the figure less androgynous. Solomon refused. In a letter explaining why, he tells how he meant the picture to represent "Love in the highest and most spiritual form." Such love, Simeon argues, has no gender. It "is above and beyond consideration of sex, which would at once limit and animalise it."[23] Leyland couldn't accept this. Not long after it was completed and delivered to Leyland, the painting disappeared for good. All we have left of it now (as is true, tragically, of so many of Solomon's paintings) is a photograph taken just after its completion. It's quite possible Leyland had it destroyed, in a fit of fear and uneasiness stirred by a work that evoked that criminal class: the sodomite.

While Solomon obtained a large measure of critical acclaim, he was haunted always by suspicions of his "perversity." In retrospect, we could say he became more and more reckless, courting disaster in both his art and his personal life. Or more, that running afoul of the law stimulated his art. Solomon developed a life philosophy to which many later artists owe much—Oscar Wilde, Jean Genet—of seeing the artist as a divine malefactor. Illicit longings were aroused when he tried to pull from life more than it could offer. When the freehanded permissiveness that ran through certain sophisticated sectors of society in the 1860s retreated, a new restrictiveness darkened the cityscape. The Society for the Suppression of Vice gained strength, and the police, who generally turned a blind eye to such matters, became more vigilant in arresting men who were sexually involved with other men. Solomon's works were studied with an increasingly suspicious and disapproving eye. The *Illustrated London News* found, in 1869, a "perverted fancy" in his images, whose obscure meaning, whatever it was, must be unwholesome.[24] Then, in 1870, it dismissed his canvases as "effeminate insanity."[25] Initially admiring, the *Guardian* changed its tune in 1871: "He has taken to draw sickly dreams which can give no healthy pleasure, and his imagination feeds on itself instead of gaining tone and strength by vigorous contact with the facts of nature."[26] Such strong words don't surprise us when we realize that Solomon was, arguably, the first to represent same-sex desire pictorially, and show these works in major public venues. To use modern parlance: Solomon was our first gay painter.

IN JANUARY OF 1893, the thirty-nine-year-old Oscar Wilde was perfecting the art of "feasting with panthers."[27] Like all true arts, this one involved complicated preparations. He kept rooms at London's Albemarle Hotel, as a space away from the domesticity of Tite Street in Chelsea, where he resided with his wife, Constance, and his two boys. He was passionately in love with someone new. If Constance worked a calming presence in his life, giving him roots and stability, the twenty-three-year-old slim, blond Lord Alfred Douglas came on as a storm that would ultimately devastate Wilde. Violently moody, swept by narcissism, Douglas taught Wilde a larger promiscuity. From Douglas he learned the decadent enchantment of taking beautiful young men (often introduced to him by Douglas and sometimes shared by the two) out for expensive dinners, then back to his rooms for sex. Money and lavish gifts for the boys followed. Blackmail often came next, with Wilde succumbing to the threats of the "panthers" to go to the police with incriminating evidence like love letters. Already experts at this form of backhanded prostitution, these youths were then rewarded with more cash. Rather than disgust, Wilde felt an admiration for such greed: "their poison was part of their perfection."[28] Corruption and criminality had become aesthetic interests. Art, he felt, required pushing past ideals of good and evil: "Aesthetics are higher than ethics."[29]

But to feast also meant to make art emerge out of the rot of decadence ("Vice and virtue are to the artist materials for an art").[30] The rooms he took in various hotels throughout 1893 and 1894 served both as places to carry on his secret sexual life and as work spaces. And work he did: writing one brilliant play after another in those two years, culminating in his masterpiece *The Importance of Being Earnest* in the early fall of 1894. (So productive was he that he could no longer say, as he did to a friend a few years earlier, "I was working on the proof of one of my poems all the morning and took out a comma." "And in the afternoon?" "In the afternoon? Well, I put it back again.")[31] Wilde mined his transgressions for all the art he could get. Space for creative brilliance opened up between his conventional life as husband, father, famed writer, and leader of Aestheticism and his shadow movements as a lover of teens and frequenter of rough trade. To risk exposure, arrest even, fired his imagination on all fronts. And his doings *were* a risk because of the 1885 passing of the previously mentioned Labouchère amendment to the Criminal Law Act, nicknamed the "Blackmailer's Charter." Wilde lacked discretion. Hotel managers often asked him to move out when dubious characters were seen coming in and out of his rooms at all hours. "He looked like one," Max Beerbohm remarked to a friend when he spotted Wilde and Douglas from a cab in 1893, "whose soul had swooned in sin."[32]

But Wilde built his career on his fabulous self, replete with excess. His genius went into his life, he told the French Symbolist writer André Gide, and only his talent into his works. Newly arrived in London in 1879, not long out of Oxford and without a publication to his name, he shot up to the pinnacle of social success when the Prince of Wales came to a thought-reading séance at his house. (The prince even mustered a Wildean witticism for the occasion: "I do not know Mr. Wilde, and not to know Mr. Wilde is not to be known.")[33] Wilde made himself irresistible by becoming the best raconteur society had to offer—replacing Milnes, many said—and the most shocking wit. His apparel, along with his epigrams, became legendary. A coat shaped like a cello earned him early sartorial fame. A day sculling on the river called for a pale-blue shirt, a light pink silk tie, and a white-lilac perfume. Wilde could not be described as a handsome man; his physique tended toward fleshy ungainliness. His countenance, kind and soft, garnered varied descriptions. Edith Cooper, of the lesbian writing couple Michael Field, described his face as "a rich yet ungainly fruit."[34] A less friendly construction of its pliability came from a fellow writer, H. W. Nevinson, who felt he had "a mouth like a shark's in formlessness and appetite."[35] Being Wilde meant having a limitless appetite, wanting to "eat of the fruit of all the trees in the garden of the world," he explained in *De Profundis*. He denied himself nothing; indeed, he felt that self-denial arrested one's progress. Wilde reveled in pushing against limits, or even past them, up to the point that the possibility of dissolving, self-destructing, opened up. How far can one go, before it's too late? All along, Wilde knew that "the artistic life is a long and lovely suicide."[36]

Wilde turned living itself into an art. He set himself to music, as he has Dorian do in his novel *The Picture of Dorian Gray*, and made his days his sonnets. He learned much of this art from one of his early idols: Swinburne. At Oxford, Wilde couldn't get enough of Swinburne's poetry. Wilde felt that Swinburne exemplified a "passionate humanity" that came from his "effeminacy and languor and voluptuousness."[37] They met each other at one of Milnes's literary "crushes," Wilde the large exotic bird and Swinburne the aging little boy-man with the halo of red hair. Swinburne found him "a harmless young nobody."[38] Yet they later corresponded about—what else?—Whitman. When still forming his character, Wilde consumed anything from the hands of Rossetti, Morris, and Burne-Jones, taking from them a relish of beauty for beauty's sake. On his walls he had Morris wallpaper (when dying in a dingy Paris hotel, he exclaimed, "My wallpaper and I are fighting a duel to the death. One or the other of us has to go").[39] Wilde cherished the few Solomon watercolors he managed to acquire, taking Solomon as the perfect homosexual rebel (although it seems they never met). In conscious imitation of the Aesthetes before him, he began collecting blue-and-white Nankin china. From Wilde come the lines "I find it harder and harder every day to live up to my blue china."[40] When he first moved to London, it was to Chelsea that he went; Rossetti and then Whistler after him had made it bohemian. Wilde would make it stylish among the set of men who loved other men. When Wilde agreed to do a lecture tour in America on Aestheticism because he needed the money, it was on the art of Rossetti and the whole set that he spoke. Whistler, who became both friend and foe of Wilde—as was his way—commented acidly (and enviously, perhaps) of the voyage to America, "If you get sea-sick, throw up Burne-Jones."[41]

Wilde took the sexual radicalism of the Aesthetes and Cannibals and propelled it even further, making it more perilous, more blatantly illegal, and more—as it would be called in the twentieth century—gay. The movement had always flirted with male-male sexuality. There were Burton's writings on sodomy (and sapphism). Morris and Rossetti loved their collaborations with men. Swinburne, throughout the 1860s, seemed to have sodomy always on his mind. (Rossetti remarked that Swinburne talked often, even among women, of "the relations—not exactly of the sexes—but of each sex with itself.")[42] Many speculated that Swinburne was himself a "sodomite"; in America, Ralph Waldo Emerson called him one in print. In reviews of the set, especially Robert Buchanan's notorious 1871 "The Fleshly School of Poetry" in the *Contemporary Review*, which led to Rossetti's mental and physical collapse, the effeminate and emasculating qualities of their work were scorned. And Solomon was Wilde before Wilde. Other lovers of men also found allies and mentors here. Indeed, the most important homosexuals, or writers about homosexuality, of the turn of the century modeled themselves on members of the Cannibals and Aesthetes: the Arts and Crafts leader Charles R. Ashbee on Whistler, Rossetti, Morris; Carpenter on Morris; John Addington Symonds (writer of two key end-of-century texts on homosexuality: *A Problem in Greek Ethics* and *A Problem in Modern Ethics*) on Burton. But it was Wilde, their flashiest champion, who made the Cannibal and Aesthetic sets early beacons in the history of homosexuality.

His fame assured by his writings, Wilde's notoriety as a sodomite emerged from the tragedy at the end of his life. In his consuming passion for Douglas, he got caught in the middle of the combative relationship Douglas had with his violent and cruel father, the Marquess of Queensberry. The father suspected the two had a sexual relationship and hounded Wilde to stop seeing his son. Queensberry left a card at Wilde's club inscribed with "To Oscar Wilde posing Somdomite [*sic*]." Goaded on by Douglas, who loved a fight, Wilde took a fatal step in 1895. He sued Queensberry for libel and lost. The evidence that Queensberry uncovered to substantiate his reasons for calling Wilde a sodomite, proved sufficient for Wilde to be tried under the Labouchère act, for "gross indecency." To the stand came those gorgeous blackmailing panthers. Testimony from maids at the Savoy Hotel, where Wilde and Douglas had rooms the year before, included details about sheets with fecal stains and "traces of Vaseline, soil and semen."[43] Love letters between Wilde and Douglas became exhibits. *The Picture of Dorian Gray* was brought in as evidence that Wilde was like the character Lord Henry Wotton, a cultivated society man who savors corrupting youth—in Wotton's case Dorian, in Wilde's Douglas. Even with all this evidence, the first trial ended in a hung jury, largely because of Wilde's eloquence on the stand. But he lost the second trial, and the judge handed down the severest punishment possible under the law: two years' imprisonment with hard labor. After completing his sentence in 1897, Wilde went into exile on the Continent. His health ruined, he died—probably of complications from late-stage syphilis—in poverty three years later. On his tombstone were inscribed lines from his poem written in prison:

> And alien tears will fill for him
> Pity's long-broken urn,
> For his mourners will be outcast men,
> And outcasts always mourn.

Wilde's trials, covered extensively and sensationally in the papers, brought blatant homosexual practices, for the first time, into the public eye. In the ensuing outrage, condemnation of this "evil vice" came on most fronts. Some, however, wrote cuttingly on the hypocrisy of it all, including the journalist W. T. Stead, who remarked, "If all persons guilty of Oscar Wilde's offences were to be clapped into gaol, there would be a very surprising exodus from Eton and Harrow . . . to Pentonville and Holloway."[44] And some wrote eloquent defenses. A French writer, Hugues Rebell, published a "Défense d'Oscar Wilde" in the *Mercure de France*: "With what joy should I see Pentonville [where Wilde was imprisoned at the time] in flames! And not only in Wilde's behalf, but in behalf of all us pagan artists and writers who are by rights honorary prisoners."[45] The visibility of the sexual lifestyle of such a brilliant writer caused a slow groundswell. Men who had similar desires could look to this martyr as one like them. In E. M. Forster's *Maurice*, the hero calls himself "an unspeakable of the Oscar Wilde sort."[46] Forster, who feared publication of the book, saw Wilde as standing for an embattled community. Increasingly, homosexuals felt a strong sense of belonging to a group with an identity. Havelock Ellis, in his *Studies in the Psychology of Sex* (the first volume published in 1897), noted that "no doubt the celebrity of Oscar Wilde and the universal publicity given to the facts of the case may have brought conviction of their perversion" to homosexuals but also, "paradoxically though it may seem, have imparted greater courage to others."[47] But Wilde had elegantly prefigured this years before, in conversation with William Butler Yeats: "I think a man should invent his own myth."[48]

AROUND SEVEN ON the chill, gloomy evening of February 11, 1873, Solomon went out for a predinner adventure. He made his way along dark lanes to the public urinal in Stratford Place Mews. Men passed in and out, some of them stopping in for a leak, others lingering for a bit, looking at others, hoping to catch a discreet sign. Solomon found himself a fellow cottager—a stranger. This partner, George Roberts, was a much older man (sixty to Solomon's thirty-three), who worked in a stable and could "read but not write."[49] Perhaps Solomon wanted (given his absorption in flagellation) to be roughed up a bit, pushed against a wall, face against hard, damp stone, and penetrated—possessed—while others watched. He could thus shed the accessories of self for a moment, become an object to be used, wanted only for his meat. Here there would be no need to keep up appearances, for the sometimes wearying work of fitting in with privileged circles and their round of educated talk. He could act out in full honesty his sexual yearnings, live freely in his sensual body. This was one of myriad ways Solomon (and others like him) enjoyed the cityscape and the strangers who peopled it, taking a little further a common occurrence: that fleeting glance of two people passing on a street, that meaningful pause, before both disappeared into the crowd. This ephemeral moment could be made to last some minutes more, spun out into anonymous bodies intertwining, new skin touching new skin. And then the two would part for good, as if the city yawned open for an enchanted space of time and then closed up behind them.

Out of this encounter—two men fulfilling consensual wants—unfolded the tragic fall of Solomon's life. At seven-ten, Police Constable William Mitchell caught Solomon and Roberts in the act and arrested them for an attempt to "commit the abominable Crime of Buggery."[50] They were thrown into jail for twelve days and then tried at the Sessions House at Clerkenwell Green. Solomon was then released on bail of £200, posted by his cousin Myer Salaman. Roberts got eighteen months of hard labor, while Solomon had to pay a "surety" of £100 and was set free. The unequal sentencing of the two was purely class-based—Solomon, while Jewish, was still a gentleman. Despite the seemingly light punishment, the arrest turned Solomon into a pariah, even among his bohemian friends. Rumor has him fleeing London and then spending time in an insane asylum. It became difficult for him to show his work publicly, which made it hard to earn a living. Thus began his lost years, when he almost completely slipped out of view. Wilde, after his spectacular fall, lived only a few years more, in poverty and obscurity. Solomon lived thirty-two. His "indecent" act blacked out his fame for good.

At first his set showed some sympathy for his plight. Swinburne, writing to George Powell—another friend of Solomon's—found Solomon's activities a form of insanity. This was rather rich coming from the lover of the birch. "I suppose there is no doubt the unhappy little fellow has really been out of his mind and done things amenable to law," he asked Powell. "I have been seriously unhappy about it for I had a real affection and regard for him—and besides his genius he had such genuinely amiable qualities. It is the simple truth that the distress of it has haunted and broken my sleep," he added.[51] Rossetti lamented, in a letter to Ford Madox Brown, about the "poor devil! What will become of him?" On the bottom of the letter, fearful of being associated with Solomon, he wrote, "BURN THIS."[52] As the moral climate changed, the danger of being associated with such a notorious figure increased. Swinburne especially had fears, having been so close to "a person who has deliberately chosen to do what makes a man and all who associate with him infamous in the eyes of the world."[53] Swinburne turned completely against him, after Solomon, driven by dire poverty, began to sell off some of Swinburne's more salacious letters. Solomon was to him then "a thing unmentionable alike by men or women, as equally abhorrent to either—nay, to the very beasts."[54] Despite an increasing hatred for homosexuals, which Swinburne began to express not only in private letters but also in print, putting him in step with his times, in 1879 he moved in with Theodore Watts, a solicitor and man of letters who became a kind of wife to him, nursing him back to health after drinking almost killed him. In a dedication to Watts, Swinburne celebrated this partner who "cleaves closer than a brother."

Before his fall, Solomon felt presages of coming disaster. With a growing sense of disquietude and apprehension, he wrote to Swinburne in 1871, "My designs and pictures executed during the last three or four years have been looked upon with suspicion." Already by 1870 he had some brush with the law (the details remain obscure). He escaped to Italy with Oscar Browning until things cooled off. Yet he continued to live at the top of his bent; or, as his great friend the Oxford don Walter Pater (also Wilde's most important mentor) wrote in an immensely influential essay, he didn't stop burning "always with this hard, gem-like flame." Almost all of his work before the fall comes imbued with a sense of loss already sustained, of melancholy thwartedness. Swinburne discovered in Solomon's paintings an eternal question, in the face of "the might and ravage of time and 'sad mortality'": "How with this rage," Swinburne quotes Shakespeare, "shall beauty hold a plea, whose action is no stronger than a flower?"[55] Solomon's "beauty" could not hold out against fierce time, against *his* time's killingly narrow view of the body and its freedoms.

We know so little of Solomon today because many of his paintings and letters were destroyed after the disaster, occluding his earlier life. Some brief facts glimmer out of the obscurity of these later years. Deep in the dirt and hunger of street life, with hardly anything left to lose, Solomon could keep open a free space to be his sexual self. His arrest didn't cow him but made him gloriously careless. Other arrests followed. With money from a rich relation, he traveled to Paris, where his fun got interrupted by another collaring, for "obscene touching" in a urinal near the Bourse, with one Henri Lefranc, a nineteen-year-old wine clerk. He spent three months in a French jail. All throughout these years, Solomon never stopped making art. He refined a Symbolist style so personal and modern that it became a kind of secret that hardly anyone at the time could fathom (except for a sophisticated group of Oxford undergraduates, who loved these weird images). But then, why did the public matter anymore, when he couldn't exhibit his work? Now he made paintings only for himself or occasionally for a few coins when he could get them. At various times throughout these years, he maintained relationships with minor dealers. Supple adolescent androgynes with lost eyes stand in forlorn landscapes, their desire turned fully inward. These late works so often took gothic themes and titles: *The Blossoming of the Thorn*, *The Crucifixion*, *Tormented Soul*, *Winter*, *Death Awaiting Sleep*. Boys who have the sorrow of living in a world not made after their pattern, as the Symbolist poet Arthur Symons explained them, people these watercolors. With faces that have brooded "among ghosts of passions till they have become the ghosts of themselves," they "hang in space, dry, rattling, the husks of desire."[56]

Solomon lived in extreme poverty and was often homeless. Rossetti reports, in an 1880 letter to Jane Morris, that Solomon arrived ill at a hospital "not only ragged, but actually without shoes." Others give accounts of spotting him selling matches in the Mile End Road or touting simple drawings on the street, amid vagabonds and ruffians. Periodically his family took him in and gave him money and clothing, but he always ended up back on the street, seemingly unredeemable.

To be an artist increasingly meant to be an outlaw. Solomon chose deliberately during these years to live outside "respectability," giving up all pretense of gentility (although his alcoholism surely played some role in this). He made concrete the weaving together of the illegal and the aesthetic when he broke into a warehouse with a friend to steal gold leaf—an ornament he could no longer afford—for the background of a painting. Solomon roamed in a kind of twilight existence, embracing exile as the result of being unapologetically himself. His friend Robbie Ross (also Wilde's best friend) explained that Solomon "enjoyed his drink, his overpowering dirt, and his vicious life."[57] His sense of humor remained intact. He described himself in a letter as one "whose domicile no man knoweth even unto this day" and who "hath mingled with the ungodly. He hath done things which he ought not to have done . . . ."[58] The last years of his life were spent at the St. Giles Workhouse—a soul-crushing last stop for the destitute. When a rich cousin wanted to take him from the workhouse, Solomon quipped, "Thank you, but I like it here, it's so central."[59] He died there of heart failure, aggravated by alcoholism, in 1905.

While yet alive, Solomon had moved into the realm of myth. Unlike Wilde, he founded no schools, started no movements. He never became a saintly icon of gay identity, celebrated for his bold fall. Rather, Solomon became another forgotten martyr, his art and life a disappearing act perpetuated by his intolerant times.

COLLECTORS AND PORNOGRAPHERS

CHAPTER SEVEN

The Science of Sex

"And what is the medicine of passion, O nurse mine?"
"The medicine of passion is enjoyment."

—*Arabian Nights*

EBRUARY 1876: REVIVED by the soft night breeze of the desert, which spoke to Richard Burton with "a voice of melancholy meaning," he and his wife, Isabel, boarded a pilgrim ship for the last leg of their trip to Bombay.[1] On a foray from Trieste, where Richard had held the consulship for the last four years, the couple traced the itinerary of many of Richard's travels of the 1850s, including his celebrated pilgrimage to Mecca. When Isabel wasn't taking dictation from Richard, who began his autobiography in this way—by "speaking" it to Isabel—they tended the wretchedly poor and sick pilgrims, many dying of "opium, vermin, and misery."[2] When they arrived in the city, Richard's old friend Frederick Foster Arbuthnot, a conventional bachelor whom Burton had been luring into another one of his erotic partnerships, picked them up and drove them through the city in his bold "four-in-hand" style. He took them all around: to the Bhendi Bazar, swarming with buyers and sellers from many lands, the air heavy with such rich scents as that of the heated coats of tethered camels; to the Parsee charnel house, vultures wheeling overhead; to the many-chambered caves on Gharapuri Island (now called Elephanta Island) with their ancient shrines and stone sculptures of the god Shiva. An expedition to the diamond mines of Golconda inspired Richard to write a brief history of the egg-sized Koh-I-Noor diamond (Mountain-of-Light), telling of all the fierce rulers who came to grief over it, cursed by its legendary fatal light.

Although new to Isabel, the wondrous sights and myths of India acted as a kind of review for Burton, who had not only experienced them before but found them spread across the pages of the ancient Eastern texts he was currently translating. The erotic acrobatics and twining limbs of the *Kama Sutra* echo the frozen energy of the three-faced statue of Shiva at the Elephanta. The glittering stone wrenched out of the dark cavern in the earth, blessing its finder with magic that often went awry, has the ring of a tale from the *Arabian Nights*. Like all the texts that passed through his hands, these took on a decidedly Burtonesque hue. Translating often spilled over into reinterpreting in a Burton production. Burton braided, more than most, living and writing inextricably. It's easy to imagine Burton strolling into these ancient texts, as an expert lover in the *Kama Sutra*, say, or a mischievous king, disguised and playing tricks with his subjects, in the *Arabian Nights*. With Burton, living had always unfurled into myth. But it's equally true that, even today, these legendary texts come to English speakers steeped in Burton. When we read the *Kama Sutra*, we do not find ancient India unmediated. We experience it filtered, at all turns, through the meshes of Burton's brimming mind, his peculiar brand of Victorianism.

Richard and "Bunny" Arbuthnot (Burton came up with the nickname in the 1860s) probably first met when Burton visited Bombay in 1854. Bunny, "the merriest of boys," as Burton fondly called him, seized the role, as many young men had before him, of an infatuated disciple to the flamboyant genius. Letters flew back and forth between the two, generally their only means of keeping heated a long-distance friendship since Bunny, born near Bombay in 1833, resided in India until his retirement in 1879. Following his father's profession in the Bombay civil service, Arbuthnot rose to the powerful position of "collector," giving him the wealth and leisure to read broadly. He picked up Richard's hobby of studying and amassing Eastern erotic manuscripts—some have said Burton "corrupted" him, as they believe he did Swinburne, Solomon, and many others. When Bunny enthused to Richard about his discovery of the *Ananga Ranga* ("stages of love," also called the *Kama Shastra*, or "love doctrine"), an Indian sex manual written in the fifteenth or sixteenth century by the poet Kalyan Mall in order to enable a husband to find pleasure in his wife "as with thirty-two different women . . . rendering satiety impossible," Burton cheerfully nudged him into translating it, starting a sort of sexual mentorship between the two.[3]

Arbuthnot took the Sanskrit text to various friends for help with a rough English copy, which he then polished and sent off to Burton in Trieste for finishing. Finding Bunny's creation "rather dull," Richard reworked it, not only giving it a bright grace but subtly infusing it with his own thoughts on sex and love, especially in evidence in the introduction, conclusion, and annotations. This was the early 1870s, and Burton, feeling consistently bolstered by the support of his Cannibal comrades, began to speak out even more boldly, *in print*, than he had before about his fellow Britons' paltry sexual knowledge. In the *Ananga Ranga*, a few wry comments sufficed. For instance, in a list of the kinds of women who can be easily seduced, Burton annotated "the woman who has never learned the real delights of carnal copulation" with the droll "which, allow us to state, is the case of most Englishwomen and a case to be remedied only by constant and intelligent study of the Ananga-Ranga Scripture."[4] A small opening gambit this, in what would become a full-scale political combat. Burton would set himself in the center of a maelstrom, publishing his most sexually explicit work from 1883 to 1890 with the devotion of one who loved to kick up furor around him. Potentially dangerous enterprises, these printings would require much cloak-and-dagger secretiveness, but also put him permanently on the map as an early force for open-eyed acceptance of diverse sexualities.

But how does one get a sexual education manual printed and published in Victorian England? Burton and Arbuthnot took years to pick their way through this conundrum. Even though the names of the genitals in *Ananga Ranga* went untranslated as yoni (female) and linga (male) and the general intent of the book was clearly instructive—in truth, the numerous lists, tables, and charts make for monotonous reading—such subject matter struck most of their contemporaries as patently obscene. Particularly explicit were the five main "postures of congress" and their numerous subdivisions, such as "Saumya-bandha," which was, apparently, "much in vogue amongst the artful students." "The wife lies supine, and the husband . . . sits; he places both hands under her back, closely embracing her, which she returns by tightly grasping his neck."[5] (Burton felt the need to comment that this position was "impossible to Europeans."[6]) And the rather surprising amount of biting, chewing, and scratching prescribed left most British readers bewildered. In an attempt to skirt obscenity laws, Burton and Arbuthnot planned a small print run, for private circulation. Only identifying themselves by their initials reversed—the title page names the translators as A.F.F. and B.F.R.—would guard them from prosecution. But, in any event, the venture had to be scuttled from the very start when the printers first read the proofs. They refused to continue, knowing they could be prosecuted under the Obscene Publications Act. It wasn't too difficult, however, to set the book aside for a time, since Richard and Bunny had already turned to an even more thrilling text, well under way by the time of the Burtons' trip to Bombay.

"Boy Bunny, who has been behaving like a trump," Burton wrote to Milnes in a breezy letter dated March 2, 1875, from "purgatory" (Trieste), "and giving up his mind (as I, his Pa, have ever advised) to the study pure and simply of Hindu erotic literature." The "two ruffians who sign themselves A.F.F. and B.F.R." were trying their hand at a book by "the Holy Sage Vatsyayana [*sic*] Muni." "One of his chapters treats of courtesans," Burton explains, "another of managing one's own wife and the 3rd of managing other men's wives. It is *the* standard book."[7] This was Vatsayana's *Kama Sutra* ("aphorisms on love"), another, earlier Sanskrit classic, written sometime around the third century A.D. This book, which would become one of the most famous in history and always be linked to Burton's name, had never been translated into English and was completely unknown in the West. Arbuthnot carried on an extensive search throughout India for multiple copies, since many were incomplete or corrupted, settling finally on three from Benares, Calcutta, and Jaipur. Using the same process as with the *Ananga Ranga*, Bunny had an English version ready for Burton to peruse when he arrived in Bombay with Isabel. Poring over it together with great delight, they marveled at the inevitable clash of culture and language: How could they close the vast divide between the sexual philosophy of Victorian England and the one presented in this frank explication of the art of Eros?

As with the *Ananga Ranga*, Burton took Bunny's clunky job and gave it his vigorous, elegant touch, adding not only an introduction and notes but his own overall flavor. The task of translation—especially texts with erotic content—flowed seamlessly into arguing with, pushing against, and jesting with his friends. A large measure of the joy in handling amatory writing came from moving through the process in collusion with another fellow: manuscripts shared out, talk of tasty words over dinner, shared laughter about the more outlandish sexual positions. Working with a scholar friend became a requirement: all of Burton's erotic translations were done in collaboration—*Ananga Ranga*, *Kama Sutra*, and *The Perfumed Garden* with Bunny, the *Arabian Nights* with John Payne, who had already translated his own version, and a couple of volumes of explicit Latin poetry with Leonard Smithers. Such work entailed its own kind of coupling—a melding of interpretive readings, a twining of one's language with another's.

A CANNIBAL CLUB specialty had always been the production of sexual texts as group work. Although it wasn't until the 1870s that Burton started on his career of translating erotica—

before this his works had certainly discussed sexuality, but only as part of larger anthropological projects—the Cannibal Club had obtained ground-zero status in the erotic book trade by the mid-1860s. One Cannibal made this feat possible: James Campbell Reddie, who cut his teeth as a pornographer in the 1840s. At that time, a delicate-faced man in his thirties with intelligent eyes, peering owl-like out of attractively deep hollows, Reddie had recently arrived on the London scene from Scotland. Like Solomon, whom he would meet in the 1860s, Reddie never had the advantages of a gentleman's education. He had to cobble together some Latin, Italian, and French on his own, because they were required skills in the smutty-book trade. Many ancient texts in Latin, written in more sexually lenient times, could be sold in translation on the Victorian market. The French and Italians also had a busy trade in bawdy books that could be tapped by an enterprising translator. France, with its more permissive laws, served as something of a capital for the trade, and the French language worked as a kind of lingua franca of the porn world, making its mastery a requirement for an aspiring pornographer.

Reddie originally had higher ambitions. He started his career as a writer. Not able to make the more serious stuff pay, he began penning stories about fornication (his most popular was *Amorous Experiences of a Surgeon*, and some scholars argue that Reddie was the author of *My Secret Life*). Once sucked into the lucrative and thrillingly dangerous profession, he never looked back. Reddie started working for the biggest publisher of pornography and subversive literature of the time, William Dugdale. Dominating the London trade from 1825 to 1868, Dugdale (who went under various aliases, including Henry Smith, H. Young, and J. Turner) kept a shop on Hollywell Street, the Strand (later expanding with more shops), where he sold his own printings of politically radical titles like *For General Circulation: A Plea for the Poor* and seamier works like the serial *Exquisite*, the novels *Adventures of a Bedstead*, *The Spreeish Spouter; or, Flash Cove's Slap-Up Reciter*, and the always popular *The Memoirs of a Woman of Pleasure* (otherwise known as *Fanny Hill*). Reddie soon had a steady job with Dugdale, supplementing his own original work with translations. To supply the seemingly bottomless market for bawdy books, he began bringing his friends' writing to Dugdale. Before long, the first fellow to go to if one wanted anything having to do with erotica was Reddie.

Reddie came to know just about everyone in the business, as author, supplier, translator, and scholar. He grew close with Henry Spencer Ashbee (father of the designer Charles Robert Ashbee and another possible author of *My Secret Life*), who provides us with most of the little that is known about Reddie today. Given that Reddie's profession made him a criminal, forcing him to use pseudonyms (James Campbell, C. Vernon Wilson), make sudden changes of address, and take quick flight to the Continent, Reddie disappeared easily into the obscuring folds of time. (The smidgen more we know of Reddie's activities comes from the meticulous research of the twentieth-century scholar of Victorian pornography Peter Mendes.) In the early 1860s, he fell in with the Cannibal coterie after having joined the Anthropological Society. He could be found dining with Swinburne, chatting with Solomon about sodomy (Reddie's sexual desires, it is rumored, ran to teenage boys), discussing editions of rare erotica with Milnes, and worrying about censorship with Burton. Reddie also began supplying Dugdale with the original writings of these new associates. Soon, Reddie found himself squarely in the midst of the collaborative network of the Cannibals.

How might pornography become an activity to be shared among friends? Could it emerge out of conviviality, out of the warmth released when fellow writers came close, as with the Morris craft fellowship? A round-robin style of writing original erotica developed among the set, with manuscripts passed from hand to hand. Among Cannibals, often a dinner party would suffice to stir to life a coauthored text. Out of one such evening grew a number of collaborative efforts. Reddie described, in a letter to Ashbee, a meal in the early 1860s where one diner lamented he didn't know Latin, which meant he had never had the pleasure of reading the racy bits of the ancient Roman poet Martial. This was probably Ashbee's friend Edward Sellon, the Cannibal who was both a pornographer and an occasional anthropologist.[8] A sort of minor Burton, Sellon used his travels around India in the 1840s to collect facts for his anthropological work (including his papers for the Anthropological Society on worship of the phallus and of female power). His research also served to embellish the more indelicate books he wrote and illustrated, many of them accounts of sexual tourism (some scholars speculate that Sellon may be yet another candidate for the authorship of *My Secret Life*, although either Reddie or Ashbee seems more probable, given that Sellon died in 1866). Sellon did put together an erotic memoir—*The Ups and Downs of Life* (published in 1867)—which includes Burtonesque flourishes about "exotic" Indian sexual practices. Sellon, at the age of forty-eight, left this memoir in midsentence and, apparently trapped in a "down" and feeling he would never find another "up," committed suicide by a gunshot to the head.

At Reddie's dinner party, four of the diners took up Sellon's challenge. They collaborated on a translation of the lascivious sections of Martial, published by Dugdale as *Index Expurgatorius* in 1868. The same group worked together on parodies of religious tunes and rituals, collected in *Cythera's Hymnal* and also scribbled scurrilous versions of Christmas pantomimes, for *Harlequin, Prince Cherrytop.* They probably produced much more, but because Victorian pornography was brought out anonymously, we can't be sure what else emerged from their pens. Who else joined this prolific coterie, besides Reddie? Quite likely Swinburne, as well as the Cannibal George Augustus Sala, friend to Ashbee and another possible candidate for the authorship of *My Secret Life.*[9] Sala, a popular journalist and city chronicler, ranged from investigative work like *Gaslight and Daylight with Some London Scenes They Shine Upon* of 1859—which tells of the delight and anguish of a walk through poor London neighborhoods—to fladge writing like *Mysteries of Verbena House: Mrs. Belasis Birched for Thieving*, penned with Sellon's help. Literary impersonation also held its charms for Sala. He once wrote a series of letters to the *Englishwoman's Domestic Magazine* posing as a young female horse rider in Hyde Park. These letters, published in its correspondence column, provided Sala with an opportunity to ruminate on the lovely sensations felt by this lady when the movements of her strong horse caused her tight corset and her soft leather trousers to rub and caress her.

This set of men found great fun in participatory pornography. Most of their productions radiate a lighthearted exuberance, taking as their theme the cheerful absurdity of copulation. For instance, here's Eve about to "eat" of the forbidden fruit, sung to the tune of the nursery rhyme "There was a little man who had a little gun":

It's a strawberry, said Eve, or a carrot, I believe
  Or a cucumber, or something of that breed, breed, breed,
But now I come to scan it, I think it's a pomegranate,
  Because it is so very full of seed, seed, seed.[10]

Here's a stanza from a common hymn of the English country church, transformed by this group of jokers:

See him rise! With pride ascending,
  Oft in favoured sinners lain,
Thousand thousand crabs attending
  Swell the triumph of his train;
      Hallelujah! Hallelujah!
Rises prick to fall again.[11]

A subversive bite underlies these squibs—against church and religion—in true Cannibal style. But mostly the laughter running through the lines resonates with a kind of silly, slaphappy fellowship. This was pornography produced for the sheer joy of doing something scandalous with one's friends. If we compare this mode of production with the way that pornography is usually produced and consumed today, the difference is startling. Contemporary pornography so often gets made and used alone: one woman or man solitary in a room, intent and serious. And how often does our pornography ring with hilarious nuttiness?

SILLINESS ASIDE, PRINTING such works was dangerous. It's not too much to say that it cost some men their lives. Dugdale, after numerous arrests and imprisonments, died in prison in 1868 while serving two years' hard labor for selling obscenity. Into the vacuum left by his demise stepped a mysterious figure who would become the kingpin of the pornographic book trade, publishing the major works of the era, including the renowned serials *The Pearl* and *Cremorne*. Even today, no one knows who this man was. He first took the alias Thomas Judd, then began calling himself William (sometimes Henry) Lazenby. Later his moniker became Duncan (sometimes Donald) Cameron. This latter name happened to belong to a wild friend of Swinburne and Burton, a Cannibal named Charles Duncan Cameron. (Arthur Munby describes in his diary seeing "the disreputable fellow" Cameron and Swinburne at the Arts Club in their cups and making "a scandalous noise . . . and actually—incredible dictu—embraced one another in some indecent fashion."[12]) Was this Cameron the shady publisher? It would seem not, since the real Cameron supposedly died in Geneva in 1870. But the historian Mendes speculates that Cameron's death was rather a skilled performance, a pretend death, so that he could have the perfect front for his new trade. It's impossible, at this juncture, to know the truth.

Whoever he was, he threaded himself into the fabric of the Cannibal clan, knowing most of them personally and publishing their sexually explicit writing. Like Dugdale, "Cameron" eluded arrest for many years by keeping four or more addresses around London and carefully guarding his identity. The authorities did snatch him eventually, in fact numerous times, but he managed always to get off, probably because he had powerful friends (Milnes, otherwise known as Lord Houghton the MP, was certainly one). Finally he did get caught, in 1886, with mountains of concrete evidence against him. The London *Times* reported that "5 cabloads of indecent books" were seized, weighing in total over a ton.[13] Some 140 stereoscopic slides, 16,000 prints, 300 photographs, and other articles, "all of which were of the most indecent character," were also carted off. Under the terrible strain of the two-year sentence with hard labor, "Cameron," it has been speculated, went the way of Dugdale, dying in prison sometime between 1886 and 1888.

While Burton didn't, as far as we know, contribute to the works of the Reddie-Swinburne-Sala clan, he certainly was up on their busy activities. "The prospect of a book which can produce horripilation is refreshing," Burton maintained.[14] With so many friends who were involved in all aspects of the erotic book trade, he asked around for advice about his own projects. Richard, Bunny, and Milnes decided to form a fictitious society in order to bring out their erotic works. They called it the Kama Shastra Society of London and Benares (a Hindu holy city in northern India) and claimed to have printers in Benares or Cosmopoli (ancient name of a city on the island of Elba). "Many a laugh they had over it," Isabel remarks on the bogus society, "for the purpose of puzzling people when they wished to bring out any book that was not for the drawing room table."[15] By having the title page state that the books were printed in other countries, they could protect their London printers from prosecution. They also sold it only through private subscription (advertised through the mail), another way to avoid exposure to the authorities. Using two different printers protected their proofs in case the police closed down one operation. Such precautions were common practice among their pornography-producing friends, and similar fake societies and printing locations covered sub-rosa activities, such as the "Society for Preventing the Propagation of Children in Foreign Parts," located in "Modern Babylon"; "The Phlebotomical Society," in "Cytheria"; the predictable "The

Society of Vice"; and "The Nihilists," who claimed to publish their work in Moscow. The Kama Shastra group brought out the *Kama Sutra* in 1883. "It will make the British Public stare," Burton crowed.[16] In 1885 they succeeded in printing the *Ananga Ranga* the same way. It's hard to gauge the effect of these two books on nineteenth-century readers. The *Ananga Ranga* never became an influential text, probably because it is based on the earlier *Kama Sutra* and repeats many of its ideas. Only two editions of the *Kama Sutra* were printed in Burton's lifetime. But its real impact came when piraters took it up, with great alacrity, printing multiple editions in Brussels, Paris, and probably the English Midlands. Thus it gained a wildly popular following, if all underground, not easily traceable. By the twentieth century, though, it became arguably the most widely published book in history despite the fact that it wasn't until 1962 that it could be published openly. For the sexual revolutionaries of the 1960s, Burton's *Kama Sutra* gained the status of required reading. An easy calculation can be made here: Burton was some eighty years before his time.

While Burton could be as frivolous and jesting as his Cannibal fellows, his intentions in publishing his translations had their more serious side. First there was the obvious anthropological value of such texts in the study of various Eastern societies and their sexual practices. More urgent in the 1870s and 1880s, though, was education about the sexual body. With his broad-minded secularism, Burton thought the ignorance of his Victorian contemporaries about sexual manners injurious, and this was nowhere more true than when it came to women. He castigated the men of the West for not studying all ways and means to call up sensual passion. Most Eastern societies, Burton reports, teach their male youth the "art and mystery of satisfying the physical woman," whereas Europeans neglect any such tuition, thus "entailing untold miseries upon individuals, families and generation."[17] In footnotes to the *Kama Sutra*, he fulminates about how Western men "never pay the slightest attention to the passion" of women. Recognize the female orgasm, Burton proclaimed. Such a statement constituted a political act, in a time when prominent doctors believed that "the majority of women . . . are not very much troubled with sexual feeling of any kind."[18] While most Victorians obviously knew that women could be well "troubled" by the delights of the flesh and enjoyed orgasms of at least equal intensity as men's, the idea that their natures had less sexual heat than men—that evangelically minded women, upright and pure, found sex to be a duty done out of love—held a kind of official status. The female orgasm deserved demystification, Burton insisted: learn how it works!

A refreshing practicality runs through Burton's *Kama Sutra*. The last paragraph of the work sums it up: "In short, an intelligent and prudent person . . . attending to Kama, without becoming the slave of his passions, obtains success in everything that he may undertake."[19] The full text centers on advice to the reader on how to find the maximum benefit for the individual, whether in the realm of sexual bliss, financial increase, or religious merit. It points out that Kama—"the enjoyment of appropriate objects by the senses of hearing, feeling, seeing, tasting, and smelling, assisted by the mind together with the soul"—is as necessary for the existence and well-being of the body as food.[20] Speaking out boldly and straightforwardly about matters the majority of Victorians kept clouded in ignorance and shame, the *Kama Sutra* advocates careful and clear explanation about the sexual act. One part tells of "the means of attracting others to yourself" and opens extensive lists of recipes for charms, love philters, and aphrodisiacs. To make a man, for instance, "lovely in the eyes of other people," tie the gilded bone of a peacock or hyena to the right hand.[21] Burton felt that many of these prescriptions should be studied for their efficacy, and he derided European skepticism. "But Easterns know better," Burton wrote; "they affect the fancy, that is, the brain; and often succeed in temporarily relieving impotence."[22]

The chapters that give counsel to "courtesans" read as downright feminist and modern. The section lays out a kind of business plan for sex workers (as they would be called today) to follow in order to "obtain sexual pleasure, as well as their own maintenance."[23] No judgments about the profession are found here. Rather, it is presented as a legitimate occupation for women, one that requires skill and intelligence. Hoodwinking men in order to obtain the most money and security from them plays a key role in most of these tips. Pretending to be in love with the man comes high on the list of do's as does entertaining men in long conversations. Here can be found useful instructions for getting rid of a lover, like "speaking on a subject with which he is not acquainted," and hints about which ones to avoid ("one whose mouth contains worms").[24] And if she should fall in love with one of her clients, the courtesan is referred to earlier chapters, which deal with acquiring Kama.

ALTHOUGH HE WASN'T to bring out his major translations of erotica (the *Kama Sutra* and the *Ananga Ranga*) and his most important sexology work (the notes and essays that are part of his translation of the *Arabian Nights*) until the 1880s, it was on his travels in the 1850s and 1860s that Burton gathered the rich details that gave his later work the texture of observed life. In June of 1853, Burton stepped out of his hotel in the Greek quarter, losing himself in a throng of good-humored strollers, savoring Cairo at night. The stalls stayed open late, and sauntering about with a pipe in hand or sitting at a coffeehouse chatting and listening to storytellers, singers, and itinerant preachers was the way to spin out the hours until bedtime. A barefooted girl trilled and quavered a tune to a saint, accompanied by a tambourine and a discordant scrannel pipe. The prostitutes, wearing burkas, streamed by. Street criers drowned out the excited talk: "Oh chick pease! O pips!" sang the grain vender, rattling them in his basket. The blind woman begged by rapping two sticks together and intoning, "The grave is darkness, and good deeds are its lamp!"[25] Meeting up with a Moslem friend, Burton walked to the citadel and sat upon a high wall. "There are certain scenes," Burton remarked, "which print themselves upon Memory, and which endure as long as Memory lasts."[26] Old Cairo under moonlight was one. "The whole view is so strange, so fantastic, so ghostly, that it seems preposterous to imagine that in such places human beings like ourselves can be born, and live through life, and carry out the command 'increase and multiply,' and die."[27]

Burton, moving through the city in disguise, liked to watch. True, unsullied observation, he believed, depended on dissimulation. His goal to penetrate the mysteries of Arab life required playing the part of a native, he was convinced, since as a European he wouldn't be able to "see people face to face."[28] From long experience, he knew that Europeans could know only the "worst specimens" of the culture. In long flowing robes, his skin dyed with walnut oil, his beard long and head shaven, Burton played the role of a dervish and Sufi. It had taken him months to perfect this impersonation. With his gift for languages, speaking the requisite Arabic, Persian, and Hindustani came easily. Rather, the difficulty lay in the most mundane minutiae. In the simplest gestures loomed the dangers of discovery. He had to imitate the way Moslems drank a glass of water, sat in a chair, walked down the street, and even urinated and defecated—all so different from the European way. Burton found merging with the Arabs thrilling. "It is impossible to ignore the dear delights of fraud and deception," he wrote, "the hourly pleasure taken . . . in playing a part till by habit it becomes a nature."[29] Smoking hashish with his friends, sleeping with prostitutes (this was before his marriage), he practiced *Kayf* for a time. A kind of intoxication with being alive itself, *Kayf* is untranslatable into English. Burton found it a respite from his unceasing drive and ambition. Being not Burton, throwing off the sense of himself as an English explorer, he reveled in a "savouring of animal existence; the passive enjoyment of mere sense" that came with cultivating an exquisite sensibility.[30]

But this dissolving of self never lasted for long. To facilitate his secret research, he added to his other roles the practice of medicine, which really meant being something of a magician, utilizing potions, charms, and incantations. The beauty of the role of doctor lay in the access it gained him to the entire range of the social hierarchy. Thus, in the persona of Shaykh Abdullah, as he called himself, he learned that when writing out a prescription for a patient of rank an impression of his ring seal must be affixed to the beginning and end of it, so that the patient's enemies wouldn't attempt poisoning. Of more interest to him, though, were those least privileged. Misfortune made for stories to tell. The humble classes, often more easily persuaded to spin tales, have some of the best roles in the *Arabian Nights*. Burton, who at this time had already memorized his favorite *Nights* tales, knew it was the porter, the fisherman, and the lowly slave girl he would need to study to undertake his momentous translation. ("The translation," Burton writes in his preface to the *Nights*, "is a natural outcome of my Pilgrimage to Al-Medinah and Meccah.")[31] Across his hotel hallway lived an Arab slave dealer. Burton found ample opportunity to study the Abyssinian slave girls, first by watching them through open doorways. Then the dealer asked the new doctor to cure some of them from the "price-lowering" habit of snoring. By mesmerizing each of them separately, he reports, he silenced their nighttime noise. But he also had much to ask them, mostly about sexual practices and customs, and he scribbled prodigious notes. Meanwhile, he flirted with the girls, but found the experience unsatisfying. He would say to one, "How beautiful thou art, O Maryam!—what eyes!—what—." And she would reply, "Then why don't you buy me?"[32] This struck Burton as the "most effectual gag to Cupid's eloquence" and really not so different from England's upper-class marriage market.[33] There, where the women were also "bought," a more subtle type of exchange occurred, without the kind of straightforward haggling found in Cairo.

It took all of Burton's skill and hard work as a spy to hunt out sex between men. Though homosexuality was rife in Cairo, it was kept almost as secret there as in London. Burton shared much with Solomon and Wilde in that he, too, felt the thrill of trolling for sodomy. While historical evidence of Burton's sodomitical activities doesn't exist, as it does in the case of these other two, we can surmise on the basis of hints in the "Terminal Essay" of his translation of the *Arabian Nights* that Burton prowled about Cairo in a way not so different from Solomon's use of the London cityscape. The Egyptians were, he writes, famous for their enjoyment of male-male buggery. Burton also picked up various anecdotes on the practice during late-night conviviality over hashish and *arakí* (a kind of local cognac), with his Arab mates. They chuckled over a tale of one Sa'id Pasha, who, in the early nineteenth century, solemnly advised a European consul general to try sodomy—"to make the experiment, active and passive"—before offering his opinion upon the subject.[34] This seems like reasonable advice; one wonders whether Burton followed it.

The essential difference between Solomon's city haunting and Burton's lay in the way that Solomon threw himself into encounters with strangers. He wanted to caress them, feel the movements of their limbs in the dark. Burton, on the other hand, found his pleasure in beholding. But the amount of distance had to be just right: he relished watching as a native, not a stranger, the latter creating too much apartness. Burton's project involved a complicated way of being with others. Was he just a voyeur and assiduous note taker, or a detached scientist? Where does one stop and the other begin? Observation means making a clear distinction between "self" and "other." Burton's books are all about drawing distinctions between peoples and practices: these "exotic" places were worth visiting because of their foreignness. Burton often saw himself as a member of a superior race who came to study and control the "barbarous savages." (This was especially true in Burton's studies of Africans, where his vicious racism was often indistinguishable from that of his countrymen.) Yet he was never just a dispassionate observer; he always found an opening for engagement. His empathy for most cultures, his willingness to try out their religions, their languages, their everyday being, make his books still valuable and eminently readable. Burton, always in motion between extreme positions, oscillated between, on the one hand, fascination with all aspects of human life and, on the other, universal misanthropy. Hardly ever happy in his own skin, Burton eventually applied all of his most damning observations about humanity to his own culture. His inability to ever be *placed*, to be consistently spiritually homeless, made him peculiarly modern, one of the first inhabitants of an unerring globalism.

Burton's scientific inquiry had a dash of amateurism mixed into it. Indeed, the disciplines of anthropology, ethnography, and sociology were so young that the nineteenth-century practitioners still hadn't figured out institutional rules. In the meantime, Victorian readers had an extraordinary appetite for accounts of faraway places and the people who dwelt there. Travel diaries, studies of new cultures, and books of adventure became best-sellers, as many of Burton's books did. Adventurers garnered celebrity attention. Burton shined for a time, alongside David Livingston, whose reputation as a saintly hero provided a piquant contrast to Burton's satanic one. The warm light of adoration, though, had little to do with the quality of their scholarship. Burton's writings on sexuality titillated, amused, as well as informed. His myth as a man rested not just on his carefully objective work but also on his personal appeal as a libertine, experimenter, and worldly figure who not only had knowledge but had *lived it*.

The Victorian voraciousness for news of other worlds fueled all types of "research." A good deal of this was little more than investigative journalism from reporters whose only motivation was curiosity and fact gathering. One of the most influential of these, the newspaperman Henry Mayhew, wrote an immensely popular series of articles for the *Morning Chronicle* in 1849 and 1850.[35] He ventured into the shambling, grubby "rookeries" of the East End and recorded the experiences of Londoners who barely scraped by, many of them living invisibly on the detritus and refuse of the wasteful city. These honest street sellers, desperate scavengers, and starving and sick indigents could seem, to the middle classes, as alien a people as the Egyptians. Most readers came avidly to his pages because of the strangeness of this chaotic land, which, magically, blustered, limped, and thieved right alongside their own lives. Few queried the motivations behind these articles—no one wondered whether Mayhew had his facts straight, or worried about the exploitation of the misery of others, the schadenfreude and voyeuristic relish. We might call Mayhew an early sociologist or ethnologist, but in his work, as in Burton's, passion and the pure pleasure to be found in voyeurism mixed with the "science." Some did come to Mayhew's accounts with serious intent, though. Dickens found many of his characters in Mayhew's pages and ventured into the East End neighborhoods himself, poking into opium dens and workhouses in order to research his novels, adding to them a heavy measure of social criticism. Christian Socialists like Charles Kingsley and Marxist radicals of the Morris stripe read Mayhew for documentary evidence of rife social injustice and a call for action.

UNLIKE BURTON, THE author of *My Secret Life* proved a sexual voyeur of the English. He started his long career of peeping while still quite young. A fresh-faced eighteen-year-old, Walter traveled to London broke and a little down. Too much masturbation over *Fanny Hill* had, he believed, left him feeling sickly and worried about spermatorrhea. Luckily, his friend Henry provided a means to pull himself out of his funk. Henry's father, a gun manufacturer, owned a large warehouse on the East End, with a vast basement running under a block's worth of houses and shops. A storeroom for boxes of muskets that stood on shelves like coffins, these dark vaults let in glimpses of light through gratings that formed the sidewalks of the streets above. Dozens of women would loiter on these sidewalks, gazing into the row of display windows of a linen draper's shop as they chatted and waited for omnibuses. Walter and his friend could stand below, look up, and spy "a flock of women's legs of all sizes and varieties flashing before [them], thick and thin, in wonderful variety."[36] On brilliant sunny days, and if the woman was in the right position, they could see all that their hearts desired because "in those days even ladies wore no drawers."[37] One of these gratings doubled as a lavatory for working women. Henry and Walter would stand under streams of urine in raptures. Rich in details about what the people above them say and do, these passages take on the quality of street journalism, or of studies of the bodily minutiae of a people.

His scopophilia ever increasing as he matured, Walter filled hundreds of pages with what he saw. Penetrating the secret lives of others became a regular joy. In European hotels he stumbled upon peepholes letting into other rooms, enabling him to observe the intimate acts of strangers. At times he had to work hard to open sightlines between two interiors, even starting to carry a portable gimlet in order to make his own spy holes, eventually staging such scenes in brothels. Walter couldn't get enough of clandestine watching.

The most elemental space Walter needed to plumb, one that

explains all his other needs to survey interiors, was the bodily orifice, most commonly the vagina. Sexual penetration involves crossing a bodily threshold, and Walter's favorite physical gesture was moving from the exterior of another person's body into its interior. In one section of *My Secret Life*, entitled "small entrances, large interiors," the narrator describes his surprise at the way women's genitals appear to hide an unknown spaciousness. Over and over he asks: What do these women *contain*?

Hundreds of pages of *My Secret Life* are devoted to detailing his acts of peering into women's orifices, handling them, wondering (and wandering) about their insides. This need to imagine chambers inside another person implies a desire to step into them. And then stepping inside would necessitate really knowing that person—her interior and exterior self. This is what Walter really hankered after. Usually getting to know someone comes from conversation. Yet, for Walter, knowledge had an odd physical immediacy. It came from the sexual caress, he seemed to think, as if knowing all the ins and outs of another's body were a means of knowing that person. But Walter wants even more than simple knowledge. He desires to dwell in another because he wants *to be* her—to look through her eyes, inhabit her body. Walter aches to experience the openings and gaps of another's being. Throughout the many volumes of his memoir, hundreds of passages have Walter lamenting the impossibility of jumping into a woman's skin and understanding her pleasure. "How I should like to experience a woman's sensations as her cunt heats and moistens," Walter yearns in one section.[38] But like Burton, who wants to look, to touch, *to be*, Walter fails to find the unity he seeks: a radical empathy involved in being inside another person. His essential aloneness comes to be truly felt at the moment—those many moments—

when he tries hardest to break out of the prison house of the self. The orgasm marks both the need for and the ultimate failure of knowledge.

Is there any difference between the voyeurism of Burton and that of the author of *My Secret Life*? Certainly, Walter has some claim to the position of amateur anthropologist, with his excellent observations of the sexual lives of servants, working women, prostitutes, and the middle classes, and his stellar descriptive powers. The historian, sociologist, or anthropologist could pick up both *My Secret Life* and Burton's writings on sexology and find much of value. Also, the reader in search of sexual arousal could find meat for pleasure in both men's writing. What might serve to separate the two is intent. The author of *My Secret Life* wrote his memoir for many reasons—a need to remember, to hold on to his sexual experiences, to reexperience them, perhaps. Even his act of publication involved mixed motivations. But there is no getting around the fact that this book's primary intent is to serve as an aid to masturbation. Although Burton surely wouldn't have minded if his books became one-handed reads, his motivations for publishing his travel books, his sex manuals, and *Arabian Nights* were much more ambitious. Burton yearned to be considered a scholar and scientist, even while he always worked to undermine that reputation, in his sneering, antiestablishment way.

A number of contemporary critics thought his books *were* pornography, of course, not much different from *My Secret Life*. And Burton found this attitude itself worthy of study and interest, even while it also occasionally infuriated him. He liked thinking of his books as radically interdisciplinary. With the Cannibal Club, Burton wanted to keep permeable the boundaries between the sciences and other types of thinking and writing. Swinburne and Solomon, for instance, made their art also do the political work of exploring sexual deviance. Milnes's political labors against obscenity laws cannot be separated from his collection of rare pornography and his own erotic writings. But it wasn't only erotic scholarship that needed to share space with science, Burton felt. Even branches of study that bordered on the magical could create productive discourse.

Burton's views that the sciences should maintain a loose, interdisciplinary continuum, with cross-fertilizations coming from the arts, from Eastern religions, and from superstitions, were so serious that he brought about an institutional schism. When the more conventionally scientific Ethnographic Society merged with the Anthropological Society in 1871, to form the Royal Anthropological Institute, Burton was instrumental in pushing for a splinter group calling itself the new Anthropological Society. Burton objected to the merging of the two, because they had become too "respectable." The more conservative institute no longer cherished the rebelliousness of the original society, which did not "tremble at the idea of 'acquiring an unhappy notoriety.'" The earlier group's intent had been to make room for all kinds of thought, including "the subversive and the conservative; the retrograde equally with the progressive."[39] Especially dear to his mind was the old society's willingness to air ideas about "popular" science, such as phrenology (the reading of character from the lumps and formations on the skull) and spiritualism. Didn't they warrant scientific discussion? The splinter group, like the original one, welcomed papers on the occult: séances, mediums, telepathy, and fairies.

As his work with the *Kama Sutra* and the *Ananga Ranga* makes apparent, more and more Burton came to believe that knowledge about sexuality—including the most straightforward scientific knowledge—should be had not merely for the increase of information but also for the sake of pleasure itself. Indeed, the pursuit of knowledge was a pleasure, and that enjoyment was, perhaps, the final goal of the sciences. Burton worked in the strain of pleasure for pleasure's sake, an *ars erotica*, wherein the ultimate pleasure came from talking and thinking about sex, in *knowing* through celebrating. Bringing sex into the conversation, into language, was a means of relishing, not just studying. Central to the Cannibal Club, and even the more official Anthropological Society, was this sense that knowledge was something to be enjoyed sensually, among fellows, with an exuberant sense of play and performativity. Yes, sexuality was confined by the stymieing rules of a given society, but sometimes these dictates could be parodied, bandied about. Even more, sexuality could perhaps be the means to break out of all such laws and confines.

CHAPTER EIGHT

Burton's Exotica

So he embraced her and she embraced him and that hour was such as maketh a man to forget his father and his mother.

— *Arabian Nights*

ALL 1885: RICHARD and Isabel found themselves under surveillance. "My landlord thinks the house is being watched," Isabel wrote to their publisher; "he has seen two or three strangers hovering about."[1] Was a spy for the Society for the Suppression of Vice shadowing them, in an attempt to build an obscenity case? In London on a six-month leave from his job as consul in Trieste, Burton and his wife felt hemmed in. The streets clanged with people, horses, and conveyances; the air hung heavy with factory smoke. A new restrictiveness could be felt. The two missed the calm sweep of their garden back home. A shady lime tree that spread its branches over a much used writing table stuck, nostalgically, in Burton's mind. "Our tree is out beautifully now," he reminded Isabel in a low voice. "Are you regretting it?" "No," Isabel replied with a remark that could have come out of the *Arabian Nights*, "*my* tree is wherever *you* are."[2]

Burton and Isabel had come to London to bring out the first couple of volumes of his translation of the *Arabian Nights* (called by Burton *The Book of the Thousand Nights and a Night*), the work that would come to be most associated with Burton's name. Over his years of lonely travel, when bouts of melancholy alienation overmastered him, he turned to these stories; they acted as talismans against ennui and despondency. Opening the *Nights* brought instant solace. Transported, as if by genie, from his dull surroundings to the land of his predilection, he stood under the "diaphanous skies, in air glorious as ether, whose every breath raises men's spirits like sparkling wine" and saw, once more, the evening star transforming the scene into a "fairy-land lit with a light which never shines on other soils or seas."[3] These tales, his favorites committed to memory as a young man, marked Burton's thoughts so indelibly that to recall them was to bump into other versions of himself. They had been a means both to bring others closer—reciting them around campfires in the Islamic East worked as a way to reward the hospitality of the shaykhs—and to retreat inward, into the rich rooms of his mind, enchanted spaces something like those gemmed and gold-strewn caves or underground caverns in the tales themselves.

Arabized versions of ancient Persian stories, the oldest probably dating to the eighth century, these interwoven tales of magic lanterns, prophetic dreams, trick doors, and wily slave girls had already been translated into English numerous times but in heavily bowdlerized editions: "castrated," in Burton's estimation. In effect, the *Arabian Nights* well known and loved by so many throughout the nineteenth century were "garbled and mutilated and unsexed and unsouled" versions of the glorious originals. The significance and effect of this cycle of stories—some didactic, others romantic or unvarnishedly bawdy—emerged only when the "gorgeous tints, the elevated morality and the religious tone" were thrown into strong relief by the "wild orgies" and the "Rabelaisian outbreak."[4] Meaning came from the startling juxtaposition of high and low found in all human experience, the fall from the heights of spiritual ecstasy down to the mundane grubbiness of the exigencies of the body, with its fat, flatulence, and decay.

Who better than Burton to restore the warm entrails? He had been working, if fitfully, on this "labour of love"—eventually filling sixteen volumes—since the early 1870s. But he realized that his plan to be the first to bring out the complete tales in English had gone awry, in a typical Burtonesque piece of bad luck, when John Payne, a thirty-nine-year-old poet, scholar, and translator, advertised his unexpurgated edition in 1882. In a characteristically generous gesture, Burton, the more famous "oriental" scholar, contacted Payne to tell him of his own translation, at the same time offering him "precedence and possession of the field."[5] When Payne's version came out, though, Burton found it far too delicate, timid in its approach to themes like homosexuality, birth control, and adultery. Payne had been "obliged to draw it mild," and Burton's version could still hold its own.[6] Not only did the sexual matters still need to be brought prominently to the fore with a frank boldness, but he would include "a vast heterogeneous collection of notes" that was "a marvelous repertory of Eastern wisdom."[7]

Publishing a book containing such explicit sexual material became another risky venture, not so different from that of the *Kama Sutra* and the *Ananga Ranga*. Like these earlier volumes, he brought out the *Nights* for private subscribers only, under the fictive Kama Shastra Society imprint. Unlike the earlier books, though, the *Nights* had Burton's name prominently on the title page. With this act, Burton well knew, he was asking for trouble. Not only did the Society for the Suppression of Vice get busier in the 1880s, but the National Vigilance Association formed in 1884 to investigate "dangerous indecency" such as brothels, ribald theater, and sellers and producers of pornography. That is why Isabel, who did the work of getting Richard's books into print, felt sure she was "dreadfully spied upon" the entire time she was in London.[8] A suspect character, who she thought was a member of the Society for the Suppression of Vice, even took rooms in her lodging. When she insisted to her landlord that she would go if the other party didn't, the "unaccountable person" left.[9] Yet no prosecutions materialized, even though the translation did garner hysterical reviews, not so different from Swinburne's public lashing in 1866. It was "a morally filthy book," the editor of the *Echo* proclaimed.[10] Burton had unloaded on the public "one of the grossest . . . books in the English language," scolded John Morley in the *Pall Mall Gazette*—the critic who had called Swinburne "the libidinous laureate of a pack of satyrs."[11] The influential *Edinburgh Review* scorned "this appalling collection of degrading customs and statistics of vice." So horrible in their estimation was this work that "no decent gentleman will long permit [it] to stand upon his shelves."[12]

Burton had been spoiling for just such a fight. In advance, he hired Sir George Lewis, a solicitor who was an expert in obscenity laws. "I don't care a button about being prosecuted," he fulminated to his wife, "and if the matter comes to a fight, I will walk into court with my Bible and my Shakespeare and my Rabelais under my arm, and prove to them that, before they condemn me, they must cut half of them out, and not allow them to be circulated to the public."[13] Swinburne had used similar arguments to fight the censors of his work, pointing to Sappho's place, for instance, in the classical education of boys in the best schools. Both Burton and Swinburne had, of course, made something of a career out of dodging and reviling prudery. In 1875, Swinburne mocked, in print, Charles Hastings Collette, the secretary of the Society for the Suppression of Vice. In response to Collette's idea that perhaps "the book entitled Rabelais" ought to be suppressed, Swinburne replied gleefully in a letter to the *Athenaeum*, suggesting other titles that should be banned:

> The book entitled Milton is not so immaculate as the virtuous who have never read it may be fain to believe. Of the book entitled Dryden, the book entitled Pope, and the book entitled Swift, I need hardly speak, and should indeed, in the presence of the Society for the Suppression of Vice, prefer to pass them by with a shudder and a blush . . . .[14]

He goes on to toy with the idea that perhaps Shakespeare and even the Bible should be considered indecent by "this wonderful Society." Collette, doltishly missing Swinburne's irony, wrote a response emphatically stating that the society had no future plans to suppress Shakespeare and the Bible.

The two giggled over these matters when Burton was in London for these six months, the still-adoring Swinburne periodically punctuating their meetings with his wild laughter, Burton interrupting with his dry cynicism. Other entertainments brought out the bracing Cannibal camaraderie, such as dinner parties with Milnes and company, Burton chaffing his friend across the table. Burton also made a significant new friend in a perennial Cannibal hanger-on. Henry Spencer Ashbee, who had been clamoring to meet Burton for many years, held the distinction of being the most consequential collector and scholar of erotica in Britain. Moreover, Ashbee, a man out for Burton's heart, is another candidate for the authorship of *My Secret Life*. Ashbee would not only come to be an active supporter of Burton's erotic publishing ventures; he also provided a good deal of the scholarship for Burton's history of homosexuality in the "Terminal Essay" of the *Arabian Nights*. Just after meeting him, Burton toured Ashbee's immense erotic library, kept in private rooms at 4 Gray's Inn Square, and both the Burtons attended his Tuesday evenings. Ashbee's son Charles, making Burton's acquaintance on these Tuesdays, never got over the explorer's electrifying effect. Still an undergraduate at Cambridge, Charles would become a leader in the Arts and Crafts movement and, as a follower of Carpenter and Morris, a vocal proponent of the "Whitmanic love of comrades" or "the freer, more direct, relationship between men."[15] (If Charles's father was indeed the author of *My Secret Life*, he had an even more subversive and farsighted view than his son: "A man had as much right to use his anus as he liked, as a man to use his penis—that was the conclusion I came to.")[16] Young Charles got Burton, "a grim splendor of a man," permanently on the mind. He remembered these evenings in Burton's company:

> Oriental stories, creepy, and if uttered so that we children could not quite hear, went up to heaven unexpurgated with the wine and the tobacco smoke. I always associated him with the drawings of my Dalziel's *Arabian Nights*, he was the Djinn who

> brought the hatchet and the cord, he was Agib losing his eye, the Barber extracting the bone from the hunch-back's throat . . . King of the Djinns—there was no end to the possible transformations of that appalling beard of his.[17]

Burton's erotic allure came from his dangerousness, his esoteric—even evil—knowledge. C. R. Ashbee learned on these Tuesdays that male-male desire meant risk, that it somehow signified the mystery of traveling to unknown lands to find fulfillment, or finding those unknown lands inside oneself.

IN THE *Arabian Nights* characters will do anything for love or lust. With the help of genies, who haunt enchanted seal rings, lanterns, saddlebags, or "cucumber-shaped jars of yellow copper," astounding riches or powers might be obtained in order to win a woman or man whose beauty "was as the full moon when at fullest on fourteenth night."[18] The lovelorn waste away, go insane, or approach the edge of death. Then drastic measures must be taken, including the invocation of the supernatural creatures called afreets, who often meddle in the affairs of humans, bringing together or sundering lovers. In one of the most affecting tales of redeemed love in the *Nights*, the intricately wrought "Tale of Nur al-Din Ali and His Son Badr al-Din Hasan," a genie and an afreet decide to bring to bed two of the loveliest youths of the land. Badr al-Din Hasan, who has just lost his riches, falls asleep on the grave of his father in Bassorah. While he's asleep the genie and afreet carry him through the air to the bed chamber, in Cairo, of the captivating daughter of a vizier (a sultan or king's right-hand man), Sitt al-Husn, who only has to set eyes on him to love him. Calling him "O my little dark-haired darling," she presses him to her bosom.[19] "He took her to his embrace and found her a pearl unpierced; and he abated her virginity and had joyance of her youth in his virility."[20] Falling asleep in her arms, Badr al-Din is taken up again by an afreet. Through a mishap, he is left outside the city gates of Damascus and, being poor and unknown, is forced to become a lowly cook. Ten years pass, during which time the father of Sitt al-Husn comes to suspect the identity of the father of his daughter's son. In order to prove it, he replays the magical night. Badr al-Din is once again in the room of his lover, as if the ten years had fallen away or those moments of bliss had, somehow, stretched themselves into ten years. "Surely I am in the mazes of some dream," Badr al-Din exclaims.[21]

Everywhere in Burton's *Arabian Nights* can be encountered a deep, unashamed delight in the body: a young man takes the feet of the woman he adores "and kissed them, finding them like fresh cream, pressed his face on them." Burton compares this aspect of the *Nights* (what he calls its "turpiloquium") with the European novelist who "marries off his hero and heroine and leaves them to consummate marriage in privacy." But the Eastern storyteller must "usher you, with a flourish, into the bridal chamber and narrate to you, with infinite gusto, everything he sees and hears."[22] Not so different from the frolicking tone of much of the Cannibal-produced pornography, a good deal of indecorous humor enlivens the *Nights*. In "How Abu Hasan Brake Wind," a wealthy man at his wedding feast "let fly a fart, great and terrible."[23] So ashamed is he that he flees the country. After ten years away, he finds himself seized with homesickness. Under disguise he returns to his city and overhears a young girl ask her mother to tell her about the day she was born.

The mother replies, "Thou wast born, O my daughter, on the very night when Abu Hasan farted." Finding that his "fart hath become a date," Hasan goes back into exile.[24]

Burton loved the way these narratives made the "most fantastic flights of fantasy, the wildest improbabilities, the most impossible of impossibilities appear . . . utterly natural, mere matters of every-day occurrence."[25] In many of the tales, obscure toilers grimed by poverty suddenly have the chance to be utterly redeemed. Those replete with wealth, power, and personal beauty can, in a stroke, take a tumble and become instantly starved, loathed, and ugly. Space especially has charmed abilities, able to contract or expand. In any field or patch might be found a metal ring set in a trapdoor, which opens on a cavern underground, full of riches or a magic lantern to bring forth a genie to work one's wildest desire. In one especially appealing tale, "The Ruined Man Who Became Rich Again through a Dream," a Baghdad merchant down on his luck dreams of a "speaker" who instructs him to go to Cairo to find his fortune. Once there, the chief of police, a capricious and cruel man, has him beaten and thrown in jail. When he tells the chief of his dream, the chief laughs at him, calling him "o man of little wit." The chief has had a similar dream calling him to Baghdad to find a treasure, buried in the yard of a particular house. When freed, the Baghdadi wends his way home, knowing that he will find riches buried by the fountain in his own yard. Invoking buried treasure in these tales alludes to a more subtle idea: that one has unplumbed depths of great value in one's own self or body. A kind of autoerotic urge comes up repeatedly. Magic discloses the secret hoard, what was already there to begin with, or what was always meant to be. Just as in Christina Rossetti's gemlike poems, here stepping into secret chambers opens many rooms of bounty, the riches and joys of the lone self.

One treasure that Burton gives open play to his translation is the wit and intelligence of women. The women in the *Nights* astonished English readers because they are more decisive, active, and "manly" than the men. Victorian Britons "are wonderstruck by their masterful attitude," Burton found, "and by the supreme influence they exercise upon public and private life."[26] While some of these tales clearly come from worlds where women have few rights and are treated generally as possessions, many of the female characters' agency, cleverness, and authority beat anything found in Victorian novels. Irresistible heroines save the day in numerous vignettes. In "Ali Baba and the Forty Thieves," it is Morgiana, the brave slave girl, who delivers Ali Baba from those many thieves.

As narrated in the frame structure of the *Nights*, the tales themselves all come from the teeming imagination of Scheherazade, a young woman who had "perused the books, annals, and legends . . . the stories, examples and instances of by-gone men and things. She had studied philosophy and the sciences, arts and accomplishments."[27] The stories are told by Scheherazade in order to save the women of her land from further acts of misogynistic violence. King Shahryar believes that all women are constitutionally unfaithful. Therefore, he decides he will take a different woman to bed each night and then have her head struck off in the morning, because "there never was nor is there one chaste woman upon the face of earth."[28] He runs through most of the women in the area until Scheherazade decides she must put a stop to it. She gives herself up as the king's next victim, yet she staves off death by spinning 1,001 interwoven tales. These, then, are bedroom tales, told between the sheets, punctuated by sexual delights. The pleasures of the body feed right into the relish for storytelling.

Yet what truly put Burton on the map as a sexologist, a proponent for emancipation, were the footnotes and essays that embellished the *Nights*. Decades of obsessive observation and study of all things related to the body came into his service here (an anthropologist, Burton felt, "took for his domain everything that concerns man and woman").[29] Crammed with odd and fascinating observations, facts, and obscure esoterica, the annotations adorn the tales with their own charmed erudition, their sometimes satirical wealth. These notes and the notorious "Terminal Essay" in volume 10 would be Burton's most significant contribution to the field of sexology. Many seemingly chosen for maximum offensiveness to Victorian mores, Burton's comments still have the capacity to startle. In one footnote, he ruminates on incest and how it is "viable and healthy" for certain cultures. Chatting with women friends about losing their virginity, he hears that the pain resembles "the drawing of a tooth."[30] Burton speculates that women in harems get bored and try out lesbianism. A dissertation on why "debauched women" enjoyed negroes—stereotypically, on account of the size of their parts—takes up a good chunk of the bottom of one page. Other notes gloss brief histories: on the condom (made of sheep's gut, India rubber, fish bladder), sexually transmitted diseases, and flatulence. He queries why exceptionally gorgeous women will often fall for ugly men and details how various Eastern peoples urinate and wipe after "evacuation" (using sand and sometimes pebbles); he gives recipes for aphrodisiacs he has found effective for prolonging pleasure (burning "a candle of frog's fat and fibre" holds back a man's semen until the wax burns down).[31] Witty sayings enliven the scholarly mastery. For instance, Burton expounds on the truth of a bit of verse: "A maiden's mouth shows what's the make of her *chose*; / And a man's *metule* one knows by the length of his nose . . . And the eyebrows disclose how the lower wig grows."[32] Curses get translated, such as a variation on the English "mother fucker": "Oh sucker of thy mother's clitoris."[33] Cross-dressing, eunuch making, bestiality, dildos, masturbation, merkins ("counterfeit hair for a woman's privy parts"), and artificial vaginas (stuffed with cotton and lashed to a chair) warrant careful historical exegesis.[34]

And this is all before the 200-page "Terminal Essay." Its discussion of pornography cleverly defends the *Nights* against charges of indecency. "Theirs is a coarseness of language, not of idea; they are indecent, not depraved; and the pure and perfect naturalness of their nudity seems almost to purify it, showing that the matter is rather of manners than morals."[35] The longest portion of the essay, entitled "pederasty"—which meant at the time sex between men of any age—stands as the first (more or less) objective study of homosexual practices published publicly in English. (The only earlier one was John Addington Symonds's *A Problem in Greek Ethics*, but Symonds limited it to one hundred copies privately circulated among friends and acquaintances.)

Was such a work ethnography and anthropology or only the rankest pornography? This was an especially interesting query to pose in the nineteenth century, since the Victorians themselves were so befuddled about what should be deemed "indecent" and what "serious." A number of scientific works were published by pornographers, since they couldn't be published elsewhere, such as *Discourse on the Worship of Priapus* and *Aphrodisiacs and Anti-Aphrodisiacs*. And many works of pornography took scientific-sounding titles, in order to evade the censors, like *A History of the Rod*, *Dissertation on the Advantages of Flagellation* and *Curiositates Eroticae Physiologiae*. Works that were prosecuted for obscenity were often anything but. An example was the notorious arrest of Cannibal Club member Charles Bradlaugh and Annie Besant in 1877 for publishing and selling a booklet teaching couples about various methods of birth control, entitled *Fruits of Philosophy; or, The Private Companion of Young Married Couples*. The work was meant primarily for the benefit of working-class women, to provide a means of wresting control of their lives, so often taken over by childbearing. Bradlaugh and Besant were found guilty but won on appeal. The British publisher Henry Vizetelly spent three years in prison for translating and publishing Émile Zola's novels in 1889 (Burton was furious at this verdict, commenting, "What can we expect from their absurd ideas of morality?")[36] When Havelock Ellis brought out his scientific study of homosexuality, *Sexual Inversion*, in 1898, the London bookseller George Bedborough was prosecuted for selling it. (After a difficult trial, he was let off with a fine of £100.)

As for the *Nights*—and all of Burton's books—even today the question remains open. Some of the notes in the *Nights* have the seriousness of scientific inquiry. Others feel like randy locker-room gossip. Readers came to these notes, as they still do today, with varied stances. Earnest scholars of human sexuality like Havelock Ellis, Freud, and Alfred Kinsey found them an extraordinary repository of historical and cultural knowledge. Others gathered from them different degrees of stirring pleasure (somewhat how adolescents today approach the nudity in *National Geographic*). Wilde's lover, Alfred Lord Douglas, for example, found himself so enthralled by a passage he found in Burton's *Nights* that he wrote a sonnet "on purpose to bring it out."[37] This was about a boy's "sugar lips," sweet for kissing but also, one imagines, for other types of oral skill. Surely some readers milked the *Nights* for both.

The *Nights* worked as an act of defiance. Burton's ire had been roused by the increasing intolerance of sexual expression. He must have heard about Solomon's fate from their many mutual friends, adding fuel to his fury. While Burton couldn't have intended it as such, his "Terminal Essay" stood as a forceful gesture of protest against the silencing tactics of the Labouchère amendment—passed that same year—the law that would bring down Wilde a decade later. Homosexuality should be discussed openly, the *Nights* states, by itself starting this open discussion. Burton wanted to present the subject "in decent nudity not in suggestive fig-leaf or *feuille de vigne*."[38] Yet, while this text makes an important political statement, Burton, in his usual disconcerting way, expresses contradictory opinions on male-male sexuality. While he calls it "le vice," an "erotic perversion," and a "depravity of taste," he also treats it with humorous affection, dubbing it "love *à posteriori*" and making statements like this one: "Easterns add that the devotion of the moth to the taper is purer and more fervent than the Bulbul's love for the Rose."[39] He argues that buggery should not be criminalized but rather should fall under "the pitiful care of the physician and the study of the psychologist."[40] While such a view is clearly wrongheaded, for its time it stands as a leap toward acceptance. Of deepest value is Burton's serious care in enumerating the long history of sex between men, proving that most cultures had practiced it. He exhorts us, in reference to the ancient Greeks, to "not forget that the love of boys has its noble sentimental side."[41]

Despite the cries of censors, the volumes of the *Nights* sold so well that they made the Burtons well off and remain to this day the standard translation. Surprisingly, given their raciness, Burton believed that women especially would find pleasure in the volumes and would want to consume them greedily. Richard and Isabel maintained the fiction that Isabel had never read an unexpurgated copy, although that impossibility is manifestly clear. Indeed, she edited it. Popular newspapers passed around a little piece of verse on the Englishwomen's insatiable yearning for Burton's *Nights*: "What did he say to you, dear aunt? / That's what I want to know . . . / An Arabian old man, a Nights old man, / As Burton as Burton can be; / Will you ask my papa to tell mamma / The exact words and tell them to me?"[42] With his usual dark, often bitter humor, Burton commented to his wife about the surprising amount of cash earned for the *Nights*: "I have struggled for forty-seven years, distinguishing myself honorably in every way that I possibly could. I never had a compliment, not a 'thank you,' nor a single farthing. I translate a doubtful book in my old age, and I immediately make sixteen thousand guineas. Now that I know the tastes of England, we need never be without money."[43]

IN TRIESTE IN the 1880s, while they were publishing the volumes of the *Nights*, the Burtons settled into the stuccoed villa Palazzo Gossleth, perched on a wooded overlook, which commanded views of the city, mountains, woods, and the Adriatic. The entrance to their home yawned so wide that a carriage could be driven into it, and a marble staircase led up to twenty rooms. Burton's writing space was a sizable room, facing north and receiving the full force of the gusty bora wind. He acquired long plank desks, one each devoted to his separate writing and translating projects. He usually kept eleven desks active, each strewn with reams of paper, heaps of manuscript, and high-stacked books. A magpie scholar, Burton kept afloat at any given time vastly different topics, from the history of swordplay to the gold mines of Midian. From about 1885 to 1890 (when he died in this house of a heart attack), Burton's tables slowly began to list toward one topic.

After the *Nights*, Burton still didn't feel finished with the study of homosexuality. He never would. When Richard and Bunny, under the Kama Shastra imprint, brought out Muhammed al-Nafzawi's fifteenth-century *The Perfumed Garden* in 1886, they used a French translation of the original Arabic text. The most fluidly readable of the three "pillow" books Burton "Englished," *The Garden* couches its sexual advice in amusing stories, full of infectious gaiety, something like the *Arabian Nights* but more explicitly carnal. Whimsical monikers for the male and female sexual organs, for instance, take up many pages, such as, for men, the "Smith's bellows," the "Swimmer," and the "Funny-head," while women might have "Starlings," "Annexers," or "Delicious ones." Around the time they published the book, Burton heard rumors that the original Arabic text contained more material, excised from the French version because of its homosexual nature. He manned a hunt for a complete Arabic manuscript. Traveling with Isabel to North Africa, he scoured bookshops and markets in Algeria and Tunisia; he called on all the French and Arabic scholars and archivists he or his friends knew. Burton never would find this elusive chapter. While searching, though, he started a revision, changing the title to *The Scented Garden* and using the project as an excuse to discourse lengthily on male-male sexuality in extensive annotations.[44] He included some history on the practice, as he did in the "Terminal Essay," but he also began to take note of more recent scholars. Here he brought in commentary, for instance, on the ideas of the nineteenth-century German scholar Karl Heinrich Ulrichs, known for his term "Urning" for homosexuals, a word favored by many homosexual rights activists of Burton's time. What this fat manuscript, rumored to have numbered over a thousand pages, finally contained is all hearsay, however, since no one has read it. Isabel, not wanting Burton's name to be associated forever with this "perversity," burned it after he died.

Not only did "his special study" engross him more and more; he introduced into his circle other scholars of love between men. While he was working on *The Scented Garden* revision, in the late 1880s, Burton kept up a correspondence with the poet and scholar John Addington Symonds, the author of two consequential end-of-century histories on "sexual inversion" (a term for homosexuality, referring to a reversal of gender traits), *A Problem in Greek Ethics*—which Burton admired and felt should be read in conjunction with his work—and *A Problem in Modern Ethics*. Symonds, who struggled throughout his life with his sexual attraction to men (calling it in a poem "the soul-commingling friendship passion-fraught"), had always been a peripheral member of the Cannibal coterie, meeting Burton and Swinburne when he became a fellow of the Anthropological Society in 1865.[45] Insatiably curious about which men slept with men, Symonds would quiz Swinburne, just as he did Walt Whitman, trying to figure out what they were up to behind closed doors. (Swinburne eventually turned on Symonds, attacking him as "the Platonic amorist of blue-breeched gondoliers" and, when he died, as "the late Mr. Soddington Symonds.")

The Burton-Symonds letters about male-male sexuality became intimate enough for Burton to admit to Symonds that he was working on a general history of "le vice."

Burton was just one writer in a network of friends Symonds used to keep open a dialogue about "inverts"—"a passion which is inherent in human nature."[46] Symonds believed that criminalization led to a dampening, distorting repression and silence that "convert it from a healthy outlet of the sexual nature into a morbid monomania."[47] Another of Symonds's friends was Havelock Ellis, the eminent British sexologist and confrere of Freud. It was Symonds who persuaded Ellis to collaborate with him on what would become the groundbreaking study of homosexuality *Sexual Inversion*. With the "Terminal Essay," which Ellis and Symonds had read, Burton had cleared a certain amount of the way. Could *Sexual Inversion* have been written in the 1890s if the "Terminal Essay" hadn't been published in the 1880s? It's unlikely. *Sexual Inversion* keeps up a steady stream of dialogue—and some refutation—with Burton and the writers and artists associated with Cannibal and Aesthetic circles. Whitman finds an airing here, and the Wilde trials come up in a slightly later edition. Symonds and Edward Carpenter submitted their personal sexual histories, which appear in the work anonymously. (Ellis's lesbian wife, Edith, the other impetus for Ellis's interest in the subject, submitted her own story). While Simeon Solomon is never mentioned by name, it's difficult to read the appendix, entitled "Homosexuality among Tramps," without being haunted by a sorrowful picture of the painter in his later years.

Another man thoroughly smitten with Burton's *Arabian Nights*, and probably also admiring *Kama Sutra* and the other sex manuals, was Leonard Smithers, an ambitious Sheffield solicitor, who wrote Burton awed letters in the 1880s. Pulled into Burton's charmed circle, Smithers immersed himself—headlong—in a career in erotic books. Following the lead of the Kama Shastra Society, Smithers created the Erotika Biblion Society with Harry Sidney Nichols (an already established printer of "sub-rosa" literature). Smithers, aspiring to bring Burton into a collaborative dance, asked his mentor to render Smithers's prose translation of ancient Latin poems on Priapus, the Greek god of virility, into verse. And so he did.

Priapeia; or, The Sportive Epigrams of Divers Poets on Priapus is the most explicit book about sodomy published in Victorian Britain. To bring out such a dangerous book, the two hid behind pseudonyms. Burton took the name Outidanos, Greek for "worthless," and Smithers Neaniskos, "young man." Caught up in their zeal for role-playing and disguises, they began to sign their correspondence with these monikers. Behind the masks of these names and the Erotika Biblion imprint, Burton and Smithers published this series of little poems or epigrams. Under Burton's translations of each poem, sits a prose translation by Smithers, followed by Burton's scholarly glosses. Each page attests to the sway and countersway of the men's interleaved words; the layout of the book itself speaks of their intimacy. The rhythm, not so different from the act described in the poems, lays one man's translation over the other's—Burton's masterful scholarly frame pressing down on the body of the whole.

In most of these poems, the "Rigid God," the "standing prickle," chatters to us directly. With fate working in its bathetic way, Burton's last literary speaker is a penis itself. What does this "pillar perking from the groin of me" have to say to us?[48] In his frolics in the "gardens" of girls and boys, he speaks out with immediacy, telling us, "I am sodomizing you."[49] Here again we find Burton's fascination with male-male rape. The "mentule" (a Burton favorite for penis) guards his sacred garden, and anyone who tries to steal fruit will find the god opening, or "cleaving," their bowels. One typical warning: "Pierced with a foot-long pole thy skin shall be stretched in such fashion / Thou shalt be fain to believe ne'er had a wrinkle thine arse."[50] Nowhere in Victorian pornography can be found such detail about the mechanics of these acts, nor the strange vocabulary that comes out of rendering ancient Latin into an English that is then veiled slightly by French. An example of how complicated these coinages can become is this statement: "the mentule of a sodomist is smerdalea," with "smerdalea" containing the French *merde* and the English "smeared."[51] In *Priapeia,* Burton's rage, turned, as usual, into cynical, bawdy jests, erupts. The most visceral and shocking reaction to purity campaigns and the Labouchère amendment, *Priapeia* is a product of a long festering.

In the midst of another collaborative translation of Latin erotic writing, Catullus's *Carmina*, Burton had his fatal heart attack. It was Isabel who was left to deal with Scotland Yard when it began investigating the publishing activities of the two men. Smithers, served with a search warrant, had to destroy *Priapeia* manuscripts and hide correspondence and page proofs. So vehement had the pursuit of the men who published this work become that Smithers was forced to flee to Paris. Isabel found her husband's risky fascination with the subject of homosexuality vexing. Writing to Smithers after Burton's death, she asked him frankly about it. "I wish you would counsel me on one point. Why did he wish the subject of unnatural crime to be so largely aired and expounded? . . . I never asked him this question *unfortunately*."[52] She was never to puzzle her way through this enigma.

Trying to fill Burton's shoes, Smithers devoted his life to the publication of sexually radical work. He quickly found himself stepping into the void left when the mysterious pornography overlord who called himself Cameron was imprisoned and then died. While some of what Smithers printed can only be called smut pure and simple, he had a strong interest in work that held literary, aesthetic, and political value. He carried on Burton's pet interest, bringing out such homosexual classics as *Teleny* and Symonds's two scholarly works mentioned earlier. Smithers began drinking absinthe with the young avant-garde writers and artists of the mid to late 1890s, those who had entered their adulthood succored by the transgressive genius of the Swinburne-Rossetti-Solomon coterie. Fashioning himself as something of an Aesthete, with his large straw hat, flashy diamond ring, and monocle, Smithers befriended the young poets and writers who would become the biggest names in Decadence, the fin-de-siècle movement that emerged from Aestheticism, bringing to it a stronger tendency toward nihilism, morbidity, and the erotic grotesque.

"His face," Wilde wrote of Smithers, "is wasted and pale—not with poetry, but with poets, who, he says, have wrecked his life by insisting on publishing with him . . . . He is the most learned erotomaniac in Europe."[53] When the great illustrator and Decadent Aubrey Beardsley—whose gorgeous, sinuous ink drawings of sickly orgasms, freakish bodily functions, and cruel women were already notorious—was fired (because of his association with Wilde, the convicted "sodomite") from the editorship of the celebrated Aesthetic organ the *Yellow Book*, Smithers established a rival journal, the *Savoy*, which featured the works of Beardsley, Ernest Dowson, Arthur Symons, William Butler Yeats, and Joseph Conrad. Smithers handed out much needed paychecks and moral support to these young, struggling writers and artists. He also published Wilde, after he came out of jail, when all other publishers turned their back on him—the loathed homosexual. The two became great friends.

Smithers's willingness to publish the incendiary work of the Decadents made him a conduit. Through his efforts flowed the experimentalism that would feed directly into the Modernism of James Joyce, T. S. Eliot, Virginia Woolf, and the Bloomsbury circle. Thus did he carry on Burton's bluff, unblushing, courageous work, his motto echoing Burton's own flaying of philistinism: "I'll publish anything the others are afraid of."[54]

CHAPTER NINE

Cabinets of Curiosity

I described them [my sexual experiences] as they had occurred at the time, and the pleasure of doing so was nearly the same, even had I done them twenty times, and described them twenty times.

—ANONYMOUS,
My Secret Life

ARLY 1870S: ONE crisp winter night the narrator of *My Secret Life* took himself off to the Argyll Rooms, the nightspot favored by Rossetti and his friend George Boyce. Paying the extra shilling to ascend the gallery, he looked down over the gin-drinking dancers below—hoi polloi to those who could afford the second floor. The glow of gas jets from the chandeliers warmed the tipsy waltzers. Upstairs, women in silk and satin gowns with long trains called for "fizz" (champagne) and cooled themselves with delicate fans. In a paneled alcove, painted with classical scenes such as "Europa and the Bull," "Leda," and "Bacchus and Silenus," Walter sat with a prostitute who charged rather a lot, which he would find out when they left together in a cab. Helen M., as he called her, thought sex with him distasteful for some reason, perhaps because he couldn't really afford her and gave her half fare (all that he had in his pocket). Despite her rush to get it over with, Walter still found her the most delicious woman imaginable. When she undressed, "the sweetest smell as if of new milk, or of almonds escaped from her."[1] Walter felt an irresistible compulsion—"as if it were my destiny"—to pour into her ear all his amatory secrets, everything that he had done with women and men. "I emptied myself body and soul into her."[2]

Look at the diversity of the amusements I've planned and executed, he seemed to say; marvel at the manifold assortment of positions the body can enjoy. *My Secret Life* also says this to its readers. The book has the exhaustive (and exhausting, in this case) qualities of an encyclopedia. It's as if the author had set himself the obsessive task of recording (and doing) every possible sexual act he had it in him to imagine. What implements might have erotic uses? Walter experiments with them all (not leaving out toothbrush, foolscap paper, kid gloves, umbrella handle, doormat, and blowpipe). Which spaces can be inhabited while copulating? Walter tries out most—cowhouse, privy, rickyard, game preserve, glover's shop, fair, grotto, and cemetery. What are the various sensations that can be enjoyed with different kinds of men and women? Most forms come under his hands, including a bricklayer's woman, a costermonger, an equestrian, a grand duchess, a "dwarf," a "donkey-pricked" man, and a woman with two chambers to her vagina (as a lover of interiors, Walter enthuses about this one). Casting up his accounts and exhibiting notches in his bedpost have their seductions for Walter, whether it happens in the ear of a mistress or on the pages of his memoir. These lists can seem endless. One of these compendiums impresses even the most jaundiced eye with its multicultural attentiveness:

> I find that I have had women of twenty-seven different empires, kingdoms, or countries, and eighty or more different nationalities, including every one in Europe except a Laplander. I have stroked Negress, Mulatto, Creole, Indian half-breeds, Greek, Armenian, Turk, Egyptian, Hindu . . . and squaws of the wild American and Canadian races.[3]

Why the Laplander missed out will forever remain a mystery.

A fear that strikes many a journal keeper drives our narrator: if I don't write it out, will it be forgotten? Worse: if it's not inscribed, did it really happen? Shoring himself up against oblivion, Walter puts it all down, as if his thoroughness could finally wrest experience from the chaos of being and bring it into a tidy and finished form. Reading over his manuscript, Walter realizes the capacity of it "to explain myself, even to myself." All diaries do this, of course. They assist in confirming: so *this* is who I am, after all. But Walter has a special compulsion to take the messiness of the life of the body and arrange it into an ordered packet of pages. So strong is his urge that he falls into creating taxonomies and fussy categories. For one long stretch, for instance, he claims to describe every type of vagina that exists. He likes to think he has "in fact become a connoisseur in cunts."[4] Six types, apparently, occur in this rich world. The one that is to him "the most delicate, the most refined, handsomest, and most exciting" is the "straight cut" variety, "with stripes." These pretty gadgets feature "the nymphae . . . slightly more developed, as well as the clitoris," creating "a visible red stripe between."[5] Woe to those older women who have spent far too many hours "frigging" themselves over the years and thus find themselves in the unenviable position of having "lipped cunts with flappers," one of Walter's least favorite kinds, often found among "French gay women in the baudy house."[6]

Needless to say, Walter's breaking out into classifications and charts is unusual for a work of pornography. Even stranger is the massive index he compiles, a kind of scholarly apparatus or last-ditch effort to organize the disorderly world. Certain passages in these final forty-five pages read like a "things to do list" poem from one of the twentieth-century New York School poets (like James Schuyler). Here is a section from the *r*'s (page numbers excised):

Reckless whoring
Reciprocating enjoyments of man and woman
Recherché eroticisms
Recurrent lusts
Recondite lustful expressions
Refined fucking and sucking of a harlot
Reflexions: on sexual matters; on being clapped;
  miscellaneous
Relations, about mine
Reminiscences on sexual matters
Repentance
Revenge, a woman's fucking for
Rickety, a sofa
Road harlots
Robing room, woman fucked in
Robbery of a pen
Ropes, amatory exercises with
Ruined, I am

Runaway girl, Rosa W***e
Rumps (*See arse, backside, buttocks*)

Such care would have made the author of *My Secret Life* a man out for Burton's heart (and probably did, since it's likely they knew each other). Both men fall into the scholarly mania of trying to fit people (and places and things) into categories. And somehow their nutty inventories can slip into erotic exercises. What are the sensual pleasures to be found in such obsessive orderliness? Rather than the rapture that can come with abandonment—the erotic dissolving of the self so loved by Swinburne—these are tamped-down delights. Mastery and containment bring arousal here. The recording of his exploits brought its own weight of "secret pleasure": "I reveled in the detail as I wrote it, for in doing so I almost had my sexual treats over again."[7] Walter turns, through words, a singular physical event into an abstraction. With a will to bring all under their dominion, Walter and Burton got turned on by Adamic posturing, by being the ones to name, label, and identify their surroundings. Such are the pleasures of the scientist, the historian, *and* the pornographer.

Rather than keeping these experiences at the level of abstraction, Walter wants to plug them back into lived experience. He went on to keep up a regular liaison with Helen, an inventive, unrestrained companion who could understand the sophisticated refinements of desire. He relied on her as a kind of vessel he could fill with his tales, something like Scheherazade and her king. Storytelling became foreplay. She, too, "had great pleasure in talking of her former tricks."[8] To milk more pleasure out of the process of doing, writing about doing, and then doing again, he had Helen read the manuscript—of what he had done with others and what he had just done with her. Reading his memoir became part of their sex life. He would "read it to her whilst in bed and she laid quietly feeling my prick."[9] Or she would read aloud, while he frisked about her body. This was having your sex diary and eating it too.

IT WAS A sweltering day that August 9, 1869, when Burton and Swinburne scaled Puy-de-Dôme, a dormant volcano in Vichy, France. At the summit they found themselves wrapped in a "rolling and rushing sea of mist."[10] Clothed in heather this time of year, the mountain meadows provided Swinburne with white blossoms to press in letters to his sister and mother. Burton collected purple ones for Isabel. Always the scientist, Burton compared the crater with the many he had studied all over the world (geology being another one of his many interests). Since they couldn't get much of a view from up there, Burton used his "glasses for taking measurements and longitudes and other professional and scientific things," as Swinburne vaguely described them, in order to find a spot that would give them a prospect of the Auvergne countryside.[11] Added to his work in cartography (this was the man who made an important effort toward discovering the source of the Nile) and geography, Burton also became attentive to climate and general weather patterns. How could he fold together these enthusiasms with the overriding one of sexology? More precisely, could same-sex love be mappable? Already in the late 1860s a theory germinated, one that would become a centerpiece of his "Terminal Essay" of the 1880s.

Laid up with fatigue when they got down from the mountaintop, Swinburne delighted in Burton's nursing: the older man waited on the poet and brought him books to read in bed. Swinburne found it a great treat "at last to have him to myself" for a month, not forced "to share him with the world and his wife."[12] Enthusing about his love for his companion in letters to his mother and sister—"so good, so true, kind, noble, and brave"—Swinburne expressed some despair at the arrival of Mrs. Burton ("though we are excellent friends").[13] He later wrote about this trip in a poem. He ponders the way that being with Burton transformed the landscape ("her"). For him, Burton's "eyes made bright / The splendour of her beauty, lit by day / Or soothed and softened and redeemed by night."[14]

At Vichy to undergo the "water cure" (their second time there together), both men hoped to restore shattered health and spirits. Heavy drinking had undermined their constitutions. Swinburne had been fast on his way to a total breakdown; he had recently fainted in the reading room of the British Museum. Falling, he cut his forehead on the iron staple of a desk and created a big stir (his later friend and biographer Edmund Gosse saw the famous man being carried out in a chair, "red hair dabbled in blood," and thought he was dead).[15] More spectacular collapses would follow in the early 1870s, culminating in another fond friend and nurse, Watts, taking him in for good. For his part, Burton had been drinking his way around South America, in a black depression over his career. For all his work for the military and scientific elite of his country—despite his extraordinary accomplishments and his abilities as a linguist and explorer—he continued to be rewarded with minor consul posts, in unimportant, forgotten places.

Burton had an incredible knack for being the perennial outsider. Often without even realizing what he was doing, he found a way to offend those who had power over him. He had a surprising ability to make enemies (and friends, too, but often they were outsiders as well). The last low-level post he had been given was in Santos, Brazil. Settling with Isabel in São Paulo, Burton had sunk into a funk, born of boredom with tedious work. Trying his usual remedy, he had set out into the wilds. No one heard from him for many months. This was his dark era when Wilfrid Scawen Blunt encountered him, describing his appearance as that of a "released convict" who "seldom went to bed sober." "I have sat up many nights with him, talking all things in Heaven and Earth, or rather listening while he talked till he grew dangerous in his cups."[16] Meanwhile, Isabel was back in England, working on his behalf. She got him a coveted consulship in Damascus (which would last for two years, then came the Trieste post). This trip to Vichy with Swinburne worked as a way station for recovering his powers, before he took up the new job.

No matter where he was and what state of mind he happened to be in, Burton found some meat for his theories. He wanted to convert all countries, cultures, and peoples from life into language. Then he wanted to bind those words up into many volumes, stamped with his name. His time in South America, France, and elsewhere helped him fill in the gaps in what would be his grand theory: his sexual cartography. Burton worked out that there was a "Sotadic Zone" (named after the ancient Greek poet Sotades, who wrote of love between men). Within this zone, same-sex liaisons are "popular and endemic, held at the worst to be a mere peccadillo."[17] Outside it, the practice happens "only sporadically amid the opprobrium of their fellows."[18] The zone, Burton explains, is a band that runs along the northern and southern shores of the Mediterranean, taking in southern France, all of Spain, Italy, and Greece, and the coastal regions of Africa from Morocco to Egypt. As it runs eastward, it narrows to embrace an area that includes Asia Minor, Mesopotamia, Afghanistan, and a slice of India. Here the belt broadens, enfolding China, Japan, and, rather incredibly, all of the "New World where, at the time of its discovery, Sotadic love was, with some exceptions, an established racial institution."[19] But Burton didn't feel that homosexuality was "racial"; rather, it emerged out of a natural concatenation of climate and geography. He proposes that somehow within the zone "there is a blending of the masculine and feminine temperaments," arising from the "manifold subtle influences massed together in the word climate."[20] In effect, same-sex desire can be explained by meteorological alchemy. In today's language: you're gay because of the weather.

Burton never draws out all the implications of his theory: Do straight people who travel to Cairo and get worked on by that magical atmosphere become gay for a period? And then do they turn heterosexual again when they go back to the queer-stifling fogs and damps of London? Burton does admit to some major anomalies, three being London, Berlin, and Paris. Here, Burton can't help acknowledging, "the Vice seems subject to periodical outbreaks."[21] One novel means England had of dealing with this problem, he claims, was to send its homosexuals into the zone. Apparently, Italy has an ideal climate for this, especially Naples, "whence originated the term 'Il vizio Inglese,'" since Britain sent so many of its own there.[22]

While the Burton Sotadic Zone strikes us as outlandish, it's no more bizarre than many theories about sexuality touted in his time, like the one that strenuous intellectual work will make women barren. Or another: if women get the vote, they will stop menstruating (wishful thinking on the part of some feminist suffragettes, like Elizabeth Wolstenholme Elmy). So many ideas about sexuality could not escape clouding by religious and moral dictates—such as the belief in the sinfulness (and criminality) of homosexuality—that Burton's zone provided a refreshingly nonjudgmental attitude. If homosexuality is climatic, it's a naturally occurring phenomenon, like sunspots, hot springs, or the northern lights. It can't be helped; one must just put up with it. As a natural force, same-sex desire can't be deemed immoral, or against God's will. While Burton himself didn't take it this far, being ambivalent about homosexuality, his theory became a stepping-stone in the long process, still incomplete today, of realizing that homosexuality is as "normal" as heterosexuality.

To think that one could organize sexuality into a schematic diagram, to squeeze it into a simple schedule, brought Burton gratification. In the "Terminal Essay," he delights in making little lists. One consists of famous men who were homosexuals, which includes Napoleon, Julius Caesar, and Molière. Another gives a sampling of Greek words for same-sex practices and practitioners, like "To live the life of Abron," which means to be the passive receiver of anal sex, or "Thrypsis": "the rubbing," a joy of "sapphists." "Hippias" can be used to describe the situation when the "patient (woman or boy) mounts the agent."[23] Burton moves into Latin or French when he feels his words must be slightly veiled, such as the definition of the term "Phoenicissare," which he construes "cunnilingere in tempore menstruum."[24] One doesn't need to know Latin to figure that one out.

Burton and Walter lived in an era of rabid catalogers, charters, and genealogists. "Subdivision, classification, and elaboration," the Cannibal George Augustus Sala pointed out, "are certainly distinguishing characteristics of the present era of civilization."[25] If it can be named, labeled, and taxonomized, the Victorian thinking went, then it can be controlled and understood. Sexuality, as a potentially dangerous and explosive realm, came under the stern eye of the labeler and has never escaped it since. Starting around 1870, sexologists, doctors, and psychiatrists (a term coined in the nineteenth century) began to organize those practices of the body that were not procreative under a list of "perversions." This movement was, in many ways, part of the larger one away from Christian belief: what used to be a "sin" became a medical category, still demonized (and in some cases criminalized) but now to fall under the aegis of science and thus to be studied and maybe "cured."

To name and group is, in many ways, to call into existence. The lonely fellow who all along, in the quiet of his personal life, found himself excited by feet and shoes, for instance, suddenly fit into the category of the "foot fetishist." Now he had a "pathological" condition with a specialized etiology. Others read about his "sickness" and were struck by their own hankering after feet. Should they run to the doctor and give a full confession? Could something be discovered in their childhoods that might throw light on this "deviance"? Does this desire say something about their basic identity?

Enjoying sexual intimacies with other men didn't call into question men's basic sense of self—except to think, perhaps, that they were sinners—until names came about that made what they did with their genitals involve their *whole identity*. These activities coalesced around an idea of mental illness, labeled sexual "inversion." Sexologists and their cohorts captured unruly individuals and pinned them down, like butterflies in a shadow box, by means of a technical vocabulary, a genus.

One of the most famous sexologists of the nineteenth century, and an influence on all who followed in his footsteps (Havelock Ellis, Freud, and Alfred Kinsey, to name the three most famous), was the Austro-German psychiatrist Richard von Krafft-Ebing. To his 1886 *Psychopathia Sexualis* we owe the labels "sadist" and "masochist." Another lover of the list, Krafft-Ebing attempted to enumerate all the "general pathologies" in his book, including such conditions as coprolagnia (the impulse to engage in disgusting acts, often including excrement), satyriasis (chronic nymphomania that leads to a lecherous delirium), zooerasty (the inability to engage in sex acts unless animals are involved), and fetishism (for hands, bodily defects, hair, handkerchiefs, shoes, fur, silk, velvet, gloves, roses, beasts).

From Krafft-Ebing comes the delight in case histories, which Ellis (who considered *Psychopathia Sexualis* "a great work") and Freud picked up. Krafft-Ebing's work is chock full of tales and confessions of "sufferers" caught up in their "illnesses." These individuals, with a new identity organized around some of their bodily gratifications, found a new way of understanding their place in society, as seen through a newly formed category of perversion. Like many works that started out with serious scientific intent, *Psychopathia Sexualis* quickly became a cult classic, read like a collection of bizarre erotic short stories. Wilde was one of many who found it an amusing read.

What had previously been undifferentiated, amorphous, and hidden fell into the light of discourse. Before categorization, one might argue, sexual practices moved in a large sea of possibility. One could pick from a range of acts—whatever the imagination might cook up—and not feel that it affected one's fundamental identity. Swinburne favored a bit of whipping, but it wasn't until the early 1890s that he might get caught in the meshes of the hard label of "masochist" (or, in the twentieth century, a "closeted homosexual"). With the rise of sexology and medicalization, what Swinburne had was a mental illness that needed treatment, needed to be mastered by someone who had more knowledge and power (by the time of this development, though, Swinburne was too old to be a practicing flagellant).

Yet another argument finds a great deal of good in the rise of sexual categorizing. It was a step toward compassion, rather than merely punishment. Seeing homosexuality as a sin leaves little room for anything but hatred. Also, with labels came, in the twentieth century, identity politics. If one identified as a sexual masochist, one could, eventually, find similar people who could rally around this personhood. When homosexuality became an identity, then it could be deemed a "class" of people who had basic rights, like other classes: gender, race, religion. In the twenty-first century, agitation to loosen these labels has been growing. To be transgender, for instance, is to claim rights as a free person and a citizen, not a person who fits into the rigid box bounded by such words as lesbian, gay, transsexual, or even man and woman.

THE SEXOLOGISTS WERE not the only ones addicted to categorizing. As compulsive hoarders, recorders, and classifiers, the Victorians made gathering and taxonomizing a hobby. Anyone who had the time and leisure might take up the pursuit, considered elegant and even "aristocratic." Thus in George Eliot's *Middlemarch* the charming vicar, Camden Farebrother, has a weakness for entomology. He fits up his study with labeled drawers and shelves, amassing a collection of every insect in the region. Nothing brings him more pleasure than adding rare specimens to his tidy groupings. Parlors or libraries often had "cabinets of curiosity," put together by either the amateur naturalist of the house or the one in the family who had an interest in souvenirs, archaeological artifacts, celebrity relics, or what have you. Home taxidermy became so popular that ladies' craft magazines ran instructional articles. (The *Ladies Manual of Art or Profit and Pastime* of 1890 taught "skinning, preparing, and mounting the mammalian, or quadrupeds.") More than any of their predecessors, the Victorians felt the need, in the midst of their world of rapid change and resulting anxieties, to feel in control of nature, the arts, and the human animal. The upsetting transformations of industrialism that led to their love of nostalgia and their need to mourn the past also brought an eagerness to grasp and fix. Creating carefully tended and labeled collections might contain, at least for a bit, the chaos that time and change could engender.

The nineteenth century was the age of the museum, the collection, and the zoo. London Zoo opened in 1828. The first exhibitions were organized and became immensely popular, especially the Great Exhibition of 1851 and the International Exhibition of 1862. Almost all the major museums in Britain opened in the nineteenth century: the National Gallery in 1824, the Victoria and Albert Museum (initially called the South Kensington Museum) in 1852, the National Portrait Gallery in 1856, the British Natural History Museum in 1881, the National Gallery of British Art (later renamed the Tate, then Tate Britain) in 1897. The Victorians were the ones who taught us to love those little collections of days: the memoir, journal, and diary.

THE ROSSETTI CIRCLE knew the *zing* that came with collecting. A bit of devilish competition, not so far off from their collaborative acts, cropped up when it came to decorating bohemian interiors. Who could amass the most complete set of blue-and-white Nankin china? An unruly saga unfolded between Whistler and Rossetti when Jimmy crowed about his gorgeous plates. This got Gabriel going: "My dear Jimmy, if I take to it, I will beat your collection in a week."[26] Soon a zealot—"I pant and gasp for more"—Gabriel rummaged through antique markets in Paris and Amsterdam, rooted about obscure curiosity shops in London, and bought entire lots of platters, teapots, cups, and lidded pots from auction houses. Covered jars picturing prunus branches became particular favorites. (Rossetti called them "hawthorn pots," Whistler "Long Elizas," an Anglicized version of their Dutch name, "Lange lijsen.") Before long, Gabriel could brag to Ford Madox Brown, "My Pots now baffle description altogether . . . while the imagination which could remotely conceive them would deserve a tercentenary celebration. COME AND SEE THEM."[27] An elaborate tale made the rounds about Gabriel's swiping a prized piece from the collection of the rogue Charles Augustus Howell (exhumer of Lizzy), who then snuck into Tudor House to steal it back, substituting a cracked bit of crockery. "But it seems that in collecting, as in love and war," William Michael sagely reported on his brother's devotion, "everything is fair."[28] Once at a dinner at the painter Albert Moore's place, soup was served out of a particularly enthralling blue-and-white tureen. Rossetti exclaimed, "I say, what a stunning plate!" and then flipped it over to check its mark, in the process pouring soup all over the table. The two kick-started a craze for Chinese porcelain. Wilde took it up as part of an aesthetic attitude, giving it its famous motto: "I find it harder and harder every day to live up to my blue china."

Turning one's home and studio into an extravagant domain became part of the aesthetic way: life itself must be carefully curated. Rossetti made his interiors into wondrous settings in which to place his romantic self, whether the wonder came from squalor, rusticity, or grandiose beauty. One means of making Tudor House a moving fairy tale, praised as such by Munby and Henry James and many others, was to fill it with strange animals. Rossetti purchased peacocks for their iridescent colors and let them strut freely through the thickets of paintings and lovely bric-a-brac. A gazelle cavorted about the large garden. Two barn owls swooped across the grand rooms, one named Jesse and the other Bobby. There was a raccoon who enjoyed slurping raw eggs. The armadillo disappeared and turned up in the neighbor's kitchen fireplace, terrifying the cook. Rossetti fell in love with the wombat (the one that came on the table and chewed the gentlemen's cigars) and, when it died, drew a little picture of himself grieving over the roly-poly creature (with his depiction of himself also looking rather round and rollable). In general, bad things happened to most of the beasts. The puppy named Punch got lost. The white dormice fought and killed each other or died by eating their own tails. A zebu bought at the Cremorne Gardens pulled out the stake it was tied to and chased Gabriel around the garden. Whistler watched the scene, later describing Rossetti "tearing round round and round a tree, a little fat person with coats tails flying, until, at last he managed to rush up the garden stairs and slam the door."[29]

Rossetti and his cohorts were embroiled in the *thingness* of present reality—the heft of furniture, sheen of wallpaper, hang of jewelry, warm radiance of skin. Their collections were, in this sense, a little like Walter's, who was also devoted to physical life—to touch, texture, smell. For these artists, bringing together exquisite and meaningful groupings became part of their creative process. Morris bought up medieval tapestries and textiles in order to work out preindustrial means of weaving and dyeing. His collection of illuminated manuscripts emerged as learning devices when he, with Burne-Jones, started the Kelmscott Press to print hand-painted books. Paintings became themselves cabinets of curiosity or little windows into aesthetic realms.

Whistler, Burne-Jones, and Rossetti made pictures that worked as shadow boxes, full of the bric-a-brac that cluttered their lives and houses. Chinese porcelain ended up in a number of them (along with a huge range of other collected and arranged objects). In Burne-Jones's *Cinderella*, we see the girl just before her spectacular rise, one foot in a glass slipper, with rows of blue-and-white dishes gleaming behind her. In Rossetti's *Girl at a Lattice*, on the window ledge sits a jug from his collection, in its frilly saucer, holding burnt-orange blossoms. The flush of the girl's cheeks, set alongside the smooth blue-and-white, calls to mind the delights of hot flesh against cool porcelain. Will she move to the right an inch and press her face against the vase? (More such jars and vessels shine out of Rossetti's *Woman Combing Her Hair* and *Morning Music*.) Whistler placed a Chinese pot on the fireplace mantle that Jo (his mistress) leans on, in *The Little White Girl*. She also holds, for good measure, a Chinese fan. Looking into these paintings today, we discover maps of materiality. We get a tactile snapshot of the material present of these men's lives as they were being experienced *just then*.

Rossetti's *Blue Bower* is a crowded diorama. When he couldn't decide how to complete the background of this picture—which sort of motif or floral arrangement to use—he decided to do a kind of blowup of the pattern on his "hawthorn pots." The wall behind the girl (modeled by Fanny Cornforth) casts the entire painting in cobalt blue and milky white, making it a tribute to his love for Chinese porcelain. *The Blue Bower* works as a meditation on representation versus reality. The painted blossoms on the porcelain background are mirrored by "real" cornflowers that sit in front of the Japanese instrument, the koto, that Fanny strums. The cornflower poetically echoes Fanny's last name (Cornforth), creating a blurring between person and flower—identity and the inanimate. Here pictured is the fervid collector's dream. Not the dream of Pygmalion, where the artist's statue of a beautiful woman, fetishlike, suddenly breathes and speaks to him, but rather the one where the collector wants to enter into his own collection. In *The Blue Bower*, the woman appears to be sitting *inside* a large vase, as if Rossetti wanted to imagine what it would be like to be contained by one of his treasured pots. This reminds us of Walter's desire to climb inside the dark chamber of the vagina—his enthrallment with the idea of re-enwombment. To disappear into his collection, Rossetti would have to shrink the way Alice does in Lewis Carroll's wonderland and then step into the magical frame of one of his paintings, something like walking through the door of the romance of objects that was Tudor House. For Burton, this would be akin to becoming an item in a list so long that it grows around and subsumes its creator.

THUS THE SENSUAL gratification here emerged by, first, assembling objects from far-flung places, then positioning them strategically as props or backdrop, and, finally, transforming the whole into another exquisite object: the painting. This process resembles Walter's more explicitly sexual one. Both dialectics brought an erotic charge, one that emerged from knitting together the acts of doing and creating. Teased out of the jumble of things and movement that is life, they created a pattern, a consumable arrangement, a tactile system. The loving attentiveness of these artists to the particulars of their beloved things and the placing of them side by side in their collections and paintings arises from a similar controlling desire as Walter's careful tableaux of his lovers' bodies.

HENRY SPENCER ASHBEE, the friend of Burton and Hankey, combined the Victorian love of collecting with the interests of the sexologists. By the 1870s, Ashbee, forty-five years old, bewhiskered, well fed, and with a look of enthusiastic industry, had made such a success as a textile merchant that he could indulge freely the expensive hobby that consumed his life. At the end of November 1879, Ashbee had just returned to London after a hunt in Paris and Brussels for rare and choice volumes to add to his massive collection of erotic books, numbering in the thousands. In Paris, asked to join the Amis des Livres, a prestigious group of bibliophiles, Ashbee had basked in the presence of comrades who shared his collecting passion, fellow bibliomaniacs as they were. Already a member of the Philobiblon, the influential English collector's society established by Milnes, Ashbee could never get enough of such backslapping fellowship. At their dinners, he could show off his newly acquired treasures. While most of his comrades collected books of a less sensual type, Ashbee wasn't the only one who collected pornography. Three of his closest friends were themselves major collectors: Milnes, Frederick Hankey, and James Campbell Reddie. Ashbee would buy up the entire collections of the latter two men; Milnes lost most of his vast library in a fire at Fryston Hall in 1876. The collecting of erotica has always been an important subset of bibliophilia, since the scarce is meat and drink to collectors. Sexually explicit volumes quickly become rarities, subject as they have been to frequent burnings. Usually published clandestinely and in small print runs, these books can dwindle to a few strays or even disappear altogether after a couple of decades of existence. For "the real lover of books for their own sake," Ashbee explains, "these unknown and outcast volumes . . . are infinitely more interesting than their better known and more universally cherished fellows, and acquire additional value for him in proportion to the persecution they have suffered, their scarcity, and the difficulty he experiences in acquiring them."[30] A tender tone pervades Ashbee's words, for the disenfranchised of the book world.

Being a book collector makes for dusty obscurity generally. It is not a profession that leads to celebrity. How could Ashbee broadcast his ardor to more than just a tiny circle of like-minded comrades? He decided not just to accumulate pornography; he also wanted to catalog it. And he would include not just his own books but also every work written about sexuality *ever published*. This would be his life's vocation. That he ultimately admits defeat is no discredit to his zealous work ethic ("I have no hope of ever exhausting my subject").[31] The result of this compulsion came to be an imposing feat of scholarship. His bibliography, started in the 1870s, would eventually run to three volumes and almost two thousand pages. He knew he would have to publish under a moniker, despite his hankering after some measure of recognition for his accomplishments. To admit openly that he'd dabbled so heavily in the illegal trade could get him arrested; at the very least it could ruin his reputation as a respectable merchant and citizen.

So, what should he call himself? As a lover of puns and bawdy jokes, Ashbee made up a pseudonym with a fittingly scatological ring to it: Pisanus Fraxi. With this name, he could include not only "piss" and "anus" but also a play on his last name: "fraxinus" means "ash tree" in Latin. (Other pseudonyms he would hide behind throughout his career of subterfuge: Pensylvan, with its ring of the phallus in the forest, Apis, which is "bee" in Latin, and the Burrower, for queries to bibliophilic journals.) He had the first volume of his bibliography privately printed in 1877, in 250 copies (the only copies ever printed, thus making the tome an eminently collectible item). The unwieldy title involved a further bit of pedant's humor. He called it *Index Librorum Prohibiorum: Being Notes Bio- Biblio- Icono- graphical and Critical on Curious and Uncommon Books*. The Latin—"Index of Books Worthy of Being Prohibited"—was a parody of the Vatican's list created in the sixteenth century. Cherishing the book as object, Ashbee made all the volumes gorgeous things, with different color types and various typefaces, decorative embellishments, all on heavy toned paper. He bound them in red pigskin, stamped in gold. For the second volume, printed in 1879, he came up with another funny, roundabout name: *Centuria Librorum Absconditorum*, or "A Company of a Hundred Hidden Books." In 1885 came the third volume, entitled *Catena Librorum Tacendorum,* "A Chain of Books to Be Passed Over in Silence." An especially ironic title this one, since this is precisely the one thing Ashbee couldn't do: bear to forgo gossiping, in fact being as noisy as possible, about every book in the chain.

Ashbee's bibliography doesn't just enumerate details proper to the discipline—the dates and places of publication, the various editions, the purported and real authors, the physical minutiae of the books, and so on. (Discovering these details was no mean feat, since "everything connected" with the trade, Ashbee explains, is "involved in obscurity, and surrounded with deception.")[32] What makes this work so fascinating, and such a marvelous and strange document, is that Ashbee felt the need to give summaries of the plots and, in many cases, copious extracts of the works themselves. An example of the beginning of one of Ashbee's entries shows the jarring tonal clash between the work of the scholar and that of the pornographer:

> *Letters from a Friend in Paris*. Vol I. London. 1874. 8vo. (counts 4); size of paper 6 3/4 by 4 3/8, of letter-press 4 7/8 by 3 inches; three lines on title-page; 2 vols.; pp. 202 ex titles, and 235 including titles; toned paper; issue 150 copies.
>
> The scene is in France. The writer of the letters and hero of the adventures is a photographic artist, who obtains, through a friend with whom he had sodomitical intercourse, admission into a family, a member of which the said friend is about to marry, our artist having already enjoyed the bride elect. This amiable family consists of father, mother, two daughters, and a son, who live together in a state of the most complete and indiscriminate incest. Our hero goes the round, and has connection with them all, including both father and son, actively and passively. . . . [33]

"Amiable" here strikes exactly the right tone: ironic, expressive of enjoyment. The core of Ashbee's earnest pursuit is lighthearted; he loves being a scholar and literary critic, but he is also stirred by the contents of the books he studies.

Ashbee's bibliography becomes *itself a piece of pornography*. For some entries, he includes ten or more pages of direct quotation. This work thus takes on a tantalizingly confused generic status. On the one hand, Ashbee is deadly earnest about the task of the bibliographer. Scrupulous care goes into his research and the accuracy and precision of his entries. He includes many pages of his "sources consulted"; his indexes rival those of *My Secret Life*; and his footnotes would have impressed even Burton (some of them are strikingly like Burton's: in one on hermaphrodites Ashbee claims to have studied a true one himself; in another, he discourses lengthily on the fact that sodomy was very common in Turkey, Italy, and France). Yet within the tight grid of structured bibliography, the quotations from the erotic works break out with a kind of giddiness, a jumble of bodies and messy secretions. The excerpts are cast in an idle mold—the laziness of masturbation, hack writing, time wasting. Still, Ashbee's textual and bibliographic works, in extreme contrast, have the severity and discipline of the master of his profession, of countless hours of close labor. The two types bumping up against each other startle the reader. Ashbee felt joy from both the industry and sensual languor. "The struggle for knowledge, hath a pleasure in it," Ashbee admits, quoting the Marquis of Halifax, in the preface to the first volume, "like that of wrestling with a fine woman."[34]

Ashbee's scholarly labor held many a sensual pleasure, decidedly of the flesh. It was a matter of scholarly responsibility to him to handle all the books he described, to hold, caress, and open them up. He was compelled to run his fingers over the texture of thick laid paper, let them bump over deckled edges, smooth down the nap of vellum. To clasp the heft of leather and paper, to whiff the peculiar odor of aged books, these were to him life's richest rewards. Before he even cracked them open, Ashbee found heady gratification from their very *thingness*. And then—lo and behold—this was also the subject of their contents. Their plots unfurled life as throbbing tactility, experience as the utopia of gratified orifices: if sex is life, then existence stays at the level of skin and its shudder of pleasure. Everything having to do with books—from their exterior to their interior, from possessing and touching to reading—held erotic usage in the world according to Ashbee.

Ashbee's is a classic Victorian tale: to devote one's life to loving pornography means turning the love into a strict endeavor. Similar to the collections of his fellow collectors—Walter's sexual diary and Rossetti's paintings—Ashbee's chambers at 4 Gray's Inn Square came to contain his truest self. Each book there bound a flurry of activity. The pages marked out days of pleasure, pulled from the tasks of possessing the love object: owning it and then consuming and recording it. His bibliography doubles as a record of his life as collector. This catalog and the books it documents served to explain Ashbee to himself.

The very stuff of Ashbee's identity was contained in those books, their rooms, their listing. No wonder Ashbee began to worry in earnest, when he became ill in 1899, about the fate of his erotic books. How could he ensure they wouldn't be put on a bonfire by some prim hand? He bequeathed them to the British Museum in his will, but to guard against prudish purging, he stipulated that the curators take his complete book collection, or none of it. This ruse to save the some two thousand erotic volumes worked, for the most part. The British Museum could hardly reject the collection outright, since Ashbee had acquired many extremely rare editions of other kinds of books—most notably around four hundred different editions of *Don Quixote*. But the curators certainly had an aversion to bringing into their folds the *kruptadia* (from the Greek for "hidden"). When Ashbee died, in 1900, the curators did take on all the books. The lion's share of the erotic ones went into their "Private Case," established in the 1860s, to be kept under lock and key, and only to be perused by those who could get past many "rigorous restrictions." The archivists did feel justified, despite a clear stipulation in the will to prevent it, in destroying six boxes worth of poorly printed pornography, ephemera that seemed, to them, to have no clear place in any library or collection. This destruction served as extinction: most of the volumes were the only ones in existence.

Since no catalog or list of these books existed—except for Ashbee's own bibliography, which itself was suppressed—his books slipped into invisibility, hidden in the backwaters of the archive. They had to wait to be pulled back into public existence—as if Ashbee himself waited patiently in those volumes, folded up and ready to be unfurled—until 1936, when the first catalog of the "Private Case" was drawn up. The author, taking a page from Ashbee's book, called himself Rolf S. Reade—an anagram for his real name, Alfred Rose—and gave it another of those brutal Latin titles: *Registrum Librorum Eroticorum*. Ashbee would probably not have disapproved, since it was their forbidden, tabooed quality that made these books so cherished by him. "The desire to possess that which is forbidden" Ashbee found inescapable, as it was "as strong in the man as in the child, in the wise as the foolish."[35]

Postscript

EMERGED FROM THESE tales with a desire to soak in more. If only I could, like Burton, slip into a disguise and stroll down a Victorian London street at night. Or learn to be a peeping tom, like Walter, and visit the sumptuous rooms of the Argyll, or sit on a park bench at night and contemplate a cruise. One could ask why this thirst for erotic detail, this almost unseemly need to watch Victorians move through their private sexual lives? Such intimate minutiae are easily accessible in today's world, where one can pick up an erotic memoir that describes a woman's adventures in anonymous sex (such as Catherine Millet's *The Sexual Life of Catherine M.*) or a dancer's love affair with anal sex (Toni Bentley's *The Surrender*). To me, what is fresh and unusual about the people in the pages of this book is how arduous this trying could be in more sexually stifling times. Dampered and curbed at all turns, the art of Swinburne, Solomon, Rossetti, and the rest flowered out of dark, secret places.

But why listen in on anyone's sexual life? It is not too much to say that thinking people—anyone serious about the examined life—feels some personal questioning about sexual identity, whether it is one's own or that of one's family or close friends. Whether a young boy or girl is gay or straight is just the beginning of the adventure. Where does a feminist—male or female, straight or gay—take desires for sexual violence? Who decides what type of surgery should be done, if any, when a baby is born with ambiguous genitals? What should the mother do when her grade-school boy wants to wear dresses to school and use the girls' bathroom? The transgender movement affects all, even if everyone does not realize it yet. If smart, creative people can figure out ways of moving out of gender categories altogether, we must be willing, eventually, to follow them as best we can.

Reading or looking at sexually explicit material was not possible for most Victorians. The people discussed here had few patterns to follow; they had to make their ardent way with only the courage of their desires. But since they felt that sexuality was an important idea to toss around, that working through gender confusions—or creating them—was a worthy practice, they embraced standing on the margins. Despite our, in some ways, more sexually open times, we somehow feel a kinship with these Victorians. Ruminating on one's sexual identity—one's deepest desires—can still feel like stepping into a lonely wilderness. In tracing the works and lives of the people in this book, we can almost see our own dark chaos and confusion, writ boldly and with little shame.

The tendency today is to dissect, endlessly, the dark reaches of our minds—and our societies—in psychotherapy, in talk shows, in self-help books, in magazines and newspapers. Memoirs excavate the layers of the self; they shine a bright light on interiority. We inherited this practice from the Victorians. But what we hear from the Rossettis, Swinburne, and even, sometimes, Burton is that perhaps there is a use in holding on to those shadows, in maintaining the mystery of the self. Can one, these two groups ask with their work, inhabit the demons, cultivate darkness, and draw out its fine strands?

Tread lightly, comes the echo, and keep the *dark core dark*.

Notes

There have been many excellent studies of the individuals and groups discussed here, as well as scholarship on Victorian sexuality and pornography in general. A large body of work by other writers has provided me with general guidance and many insights and references. The following works were especially valuable:

On Burton and his circle: Mary S. Lovell, *A Rage to Live: A Biography of Richard and Isabel Burton* (New York: Norton, 1998); Edward Rice, *Captain Sir Richard Francis Burton* (New York: Scribner's, 1990); Fawn Brodie, *The Devil Drives: A Life of Sir Richard Burton* (New York: Norton, 1967); Dane Kennedy, *The Highly Civilized Man: Richard Burton and the Victorian World* (Cambridge, Mass.: Harvard University Press, 2005); Lisa Z. Sigel, *Governing Pleasures: Pornography and Social Change in England, 1815–1914* (Piscataway, N.J.: Rutgers University Press, 2002); Colette Colligan, *The Traffic in Obscenity from Byron and Beardsley: Sexuality and Exoticism in Nineteenth-Century Print Culture* (New York: Palgrave Macmillan, 2006); Peter Mendes, *Clandestine Erotic Fiction in English 1800–1939* (Aldershot, UK: Scolar Press, 1993); James Pope-Hennessey, *Monckton Milnes: The Years of Promise, 1809–1851*, vol. 1 (New York: Farrar, Straus and Cudahy, 1955) and *Monckton Milnes: The Flight of Youth 1851–1885*, vol. 2 (New York: Farrar, Straus and Cudahy, 1955); Ian Gibson, *The Erotomaniac: The Secret Life of Henry Spencer Ashbee* (Cambridge, Mass.: Da Capo Press, 2001); James Nelson, *Publisher to the Decadents: Leonard Smithers in the Careers of Beardsley, Wilde, Dowson* (University Park, Penn.: Pennsylvania

State University, 2000); Steven Marcus, *The Other Victorians: A Study of Sexuality and Pornography in Mid-Nineteenth-Century England* (New York: Basic Books, 1964).

On the Rossettis and their circle: Jan Marsh, *Dante Gabriel Rossetti: Painter and Poet* (London: Phoenix, 1999) and *Christina Rossetti: A Writer's Life* (New York: Viking, 1995); Jerome McGann, *Dante Gabriel Rossetti and the Game That Must Be Lost* (New Haven: Yale University Press, 2000); Julian Treuherz, Elizabeth Prettejohn, and Edwin Becker, *Dante Gabriel Rossetti* (London: Thames & Hudson, 2003); Rikky Rooksby, *A.C. Swinburne: A Poet's Life* (Aldershot, UK: Scolar Press, 1997); Donald Thomas, *Swinburne: The Poet in His World* (New York: Oxford University Press, 1979); Philip Henderson, *Swinburne: Portrait of a Poet* (New York: Macmillan, 1974); Ian Gibson, *The English Vice: Beating, Sex, and Shame in Victorian England and After* (London: Duckworth, 1978); G.H. Fleming, *Millais: A Biography* (London: Constable, 1998); Penelope Fitzgerald, *Edward Burne-Jones* (London: Penguin, 1975); Stephen Wildman and John Christian, *Edward Burne-Jones: Victorian Artist-Dreamer* (New York: The Metropolitan Museum of Art, 1998); Fiona MacCarthy, *William Morris: A Life for Our Time* (New York: Knopf, 1995); Linda Parry, ed., *William Morris* (New York: Harry N. Abrams, 1996); Stanley Weintraub, *Whistler: A Biography* (New York: Da Capa, 2001); Richard Ellmann, *Oscar Wilde* (New York: Vintage, 1987); Neil McKenna, *The Secret Life of Oscar Wilde* (New York: Basic Books, 2006); Chuschichi Tsuzuki, *Edward Carpenter: 1844–1928, Prophet of Human Fellowship* (London: Cambridge University Press, 1980); Colin Cruise, ed. *Love Revealed: Simeon Solomon and the Pre-Raphaelites* (London: Merrell, 2005); Richard Dellamora, *Masculine Desire: The Sexual Politics of Victorian Aestheticism* (Chapel Hill: University of North Carolina Press, 1990); Wayne Koestenbaum, *Double Talk: The Erotics of Male Literary Collaboration* (New York: Routledge, 1989).

Introduction

1 Letter from Simeon Solomon to Algernon Charles Swinburne, November 1869, in Cecil Lang, ed., *The Swinburne Letters*, vol. 1 (New Haven: Yale University Press, 1959), 48–49.

Chapter 1: Erotic Melancholia

1 Quoted in "Painters behind the Scenes," *Edinburgh Review*, April 1897, p. 499.

2 Letter from D. G. Rossetti to Charles Augustus Howell, August 16, 1869, in William Fredeman, ed., *The Correspondence of Dante Gabriel Rossetti*, 8 vols. (Cambridge, UK: Brewer, 2002–08), 4:235.

3 Letter from D. G. Rossetti to W. M. Rossetti, October 13, 1869, in Fredeman, *Correspondence*, 4:303.

4 Letter from D. G. Rossetti to Ford Madox Brown, October 14, 1869, in Fredeman, *Correspondence*, 4:304.

5 Letter from D. G. Rossetti to W. M. Rossetti, October 13, 1869, in Fredeman, *Correspondence*, 4:302.

6 William Holman Hunt, *Pre-Raphaelitism and the Pre-Raphaelite Brotherhood*, vol. 1 (London: Macmillan, 1905), 198.

7 Quoted in William Michael Rossetti, ed., *Ruskin: Rossetti: Preraphaelitism* (London: George Allen, 1899), 19.

8 Letter from D. G. Rossetti to his mother, April 13, 1860, in Fredeman, *Correspondence*, 2:292.

9 Letter from D. G. Rossetti to Ford Madox Brown, April 22, 1860, in Fredeman, *Correspondence*, 2:294.

10 Quoted in Jan Marsh, *Dante Gabriel Rossetti: Painter and Poet* (London: Phoenix, 1999), 142.

11 Zuzanna Shonfield, *Precariously Privileged: A Professional Family in Victorian London* (New York: Oxford University Press, 1987), 112.

12 W. E. Fredeman, "The Letters of Pictor Ignotus: William Bell Scott's Correspondence with Alice Boyd, 1859–1884," *Bulletin of the John Rylands Library* 58 (1976): 92.

13 Quoted in William Sharp, *Dante Gabriel Rossetti: A Record and a Study* (London: Macmillan, 1882), 184.

14 Virginia Surtees, *Dante Gabriel Rossetti: Paintings and Drawings, a Catalogue Raisonné*, vol. 2 (Oxford: Clarendon Press, 1971), 168.

15 Quoted in Francis Brookfield, *The Cambridge "Apostles"* (London: Pitman, 1907), 268.

16 Quoted in M. H. Abrams, *The Norton Anthology of English Literature*, 7th ed., vol. 2 (New York: Norton, 2000), 1043.

17 Quoted in Penelope Fitzgerald, *Edward Burne-Jones* (London: Penguin, 1975), 50.

18 Quoted in Lady Georgiana Burne-Jones, *Memorials of Edward Burne-Jones* (London: Macmillan, 1904), 167.

19 Malcolm Bell, *Sir Edward Burne-Jones: A Record and Review* (London: Bell and Sons, 1901), 29.

20 Quoted in Fitzgerald, *Burne-Jones*, 224.

21 John Ruskin, *Modern Painters* (New York: John W. Lovell, 1885), 3:624.

22 Quoted in G. H. Fleming, *Millais: A Biography* (London: Constable, 1998), 78.

23 Georges Bataille, *Eroticism: Death and Sensuality* (San Francisco: City Lights, 1986), 11.

24 William Acton, *The Functions and Disorders of the Reproductive Organs* (London: Churchill, 1865), 138.

25 Quoted in Edward Rice, *Captain Sir Richard Francis Burton* (New York: Scribner's, 1990), 392. For more on the Cannibal Club and the pornography they produced, see Lisa Z. Sigel, *Governing Pleasures: Pornography and Social Change in England, 1815–1914* (New Jersey: Rutgers University Press, 2002).

26 Arthur Symons, *Dramatis Personae* (Indianapolis: Bobbs-Merrill, 1923), 249.

27 Georgiana Stisted, *The True Life of Captain Sir Richard F. Burton* (London: Nichols, 1896).

28 Ezra Pound, "Swinburne versus His Biographers," *Literary Essays of Ezra Pound*, ed. T. S. Eliot (New York: New Directions, 1968), 292.

29 Edgar Allan Poe, "Philosophy of Composition," *Graham's Magazine*, April 1846, pp. 163–67.

30 *The Complete Works of Algernon Charles Swinburne*, ed. Edmund Gosse and Thomas J. Wise, vol. 14 (London: W. Heinemann, 1926), 305.

Chapter 2: Erotic Faith

1 Quoted in Jan Marsh, *Dante Gabriel Rossetti: Painter and Poet* (London: Phoenix, 1999), 201.

2 "The Can-Can at Valentino's."

3 William Michael Rossetti, ed., *Dante Gabriel Rossetti: His Family Letters*

with a Memoir by William Michael Rossetti, vol. 1 (London: Ellis and Elvey, 1895), 126.

4 *Athenaeum*, June 1850, pp. 590–91.

5 Angus B. Reach, "Town Talk and Table Talk," *Illustrated London News*, May 4, 1850, p. 306.

6 Charles Dickens, "Old Lamps for New Ones," *Household Words*, June 15, 1850, pp. 1–2.

7 William Rossetti, journal entry, December 25, 1849, in William Michael Rossetti, ed., *Preraphaelite Diaries and Letters* (London: Hurst and Blackett, 1900), 235.

8 Virginia Woolf, "I Am Christina Rossetti," *The Second Common Reader* (New York: Harcourt, 1932), 264.

9 William Michael Rossetti, "Memoir," *The Poetical Works of Christina Georgina Rossetti* (London: Macmillan, 1928), lxviii.

10 Woolf, "I Am Christina Rossetti," 263.

11 Rossetti, "Spring."

12 "Our Camp in the Woodland," *Fraser's Magazine*, July 1864, p. 204.

13 Rossetti, "Winter: My Secret."

14 M. N. Cohen, ed., *The Letters of Lewis Carroll*, vol. 2 (London: Macmillan, 1979), 986.

15 Quoted in Rikky Rooksby, *A. C. Swinburne: A Poet's Life* (Aldershot, UK: Scolar Press, 1997), 166.

16 Henry Adams, *The Education of Henry Adams: An Autobiography* (New York: Houghton Mifflin, 1918), 139–41.

17 Letter to William Rossetti from Barone Kirkup, March 6, 1867, in William Michael Rossetti, ed., *The Rossetti Papers, 1862–70* (London: Sands, 1903), 233.

18 Edmond and Jules De Goncourt, *Pages from the Goncourt Journals* (New York: New York Review of Books, 2007), 284.

19 Algernon Charles Swinburne, *William Blake: A Critical Essay* (London: Chatto and Windus, 1906), 99; Swinburne and William Michael Rossetti, *Notes on the Royal Academy Exhibition of 1868* (London: John Camden Hotten, 1868), 50.

20 Swinburne, *Blake*, 100.

21 Letter from Swinburne to Milnes, July 11, 1865, in Cecil Lang, ed., *The Swinburne Letters*, 6 vols. (New Haven: Yale University Press, 1959–62), 1:124; Swinburne, "To Sir Richard Burton."

22 Edmund Gosse, *The Life of Algernon Charles Swinburne* (London: Macmillan, 1917), 122.

23 Quoted in Dane Kennedy, *The Highly Civilized Man: Richard Burton and the Victorian World* (Cambridge, Mass.: Harvard University Press, 2005), 220.

24 Quoted ibid., 67.

25 Richard F. Burton, *Personal Narrative of a Pilgimage to Al-Madinah and Meccah*, 3d ed., vol. 1 (New York: Dover, 1964), xxiii.

26 Richard F. Burton, *Explorations of the Highlands of the Brazil*, vol. 1 (London: Tinsley Brothers, 1869), 374n.

27 John Morley, *Saturday Review*, August 4, 1866, pp. 145–47.

28 Quoted in Rooksby, *Swinburne*, 141.

29 Gosse, *Life*, 160.

30 Edmund Gosse, *Portraits and Sketches* (London: Scribner's, 1912), 4.

31 Quoted in Donald Thomas, *Swinburne: The Poet in His World* (New York: Oxford University Press, 1979), 131.

32 Letter to George Powell, August 10, 1866, in Lang, *Swinburne*, 1:171.

33 Swinburne, "The Triumph of Time."

34 Quoted in Rooksby, *Swinburne*, 24–25.

35 Gosse, *Life*, 109.

36 Swinburne, *Blake*, 106.

37 Swinburne, "Matthew Arnold's New Poems," *Swinburne as Critic*, ed. Clyde K. Hyder (London: Routledge, 1972), 99.

38 Letter from Swinburne to William Michael Rossetti, August 4, 1870, in Lang, *Swinburne*, 2:115.

39 Anthony Harrison, *The Letters of Christina Rossetti*, vol. 1 (Charlottesville: University Press of Virginia, 1997), 269.

Chapter 3: The Seductress and the Bluestocking

1 *William Allingham: A Diary*, ed. H. Allingham and D. Radford (London: Macmillan, 1907).

2 Albert Smith, *Household Words*, September 12, 1857.

3 Anonymous, *My Secret Life* (New York: Grove Press, 1966), 524–25.

4 Daniel Joseph Kirwan, *Palace and Hovel; or, Phases of London Life* (Hartford, Conn.: Columbian Book Co., 1878), 476.

5 *My Secret Life*, 1738–39.

6 James Beard Talbot, *The Miseries of Prostitution* (London: Madden, 1844), 43.

7 Kirwan, *Palace*, 476.

8 J. Ewing Ritchie, *The Night Side of London* (London: William Tweedie, 1858), 6.

9 Oswald Doughty and J. R. Wahl, eds., *The Letters of Dante Gabriel Rossetti*, vol. 2 (London: Oxford University Press, 1965), 131.

10 Ibid., 254.

11 Edmund Gosse, "An Essay on Swinburne," in Cecil Lang, ed., *The Swinburne Letters*, 6 vols. (New Haven: Yale University Press, 1959–62), 6:245.

12 Algernon Charles Swinburne, "Sappho," *Saturday Review*, February 21, 1914, p. 228.

13 Algernon Charles Swinburne, "Sonnet (with a copy of Mademoiselle de Maupin)."

14 Letter from Swinburne to George Powell, July 29, 1869, in Lang, *Swinburne*, 2:20.

15 Quoted in Rikky Rooksby, *A. C. Swinburne: A Poet's Life* (Aldershot, UK: Scolar Press, 1997), 4.

16 Quoted in Penelope Fitzgerald, *Edward Burne-Jones* (London: Penguin, 1975), 49.

17 Letter from Holman Hunt to Ford Madox Brown, Oct.12, 1862, in Terry Myers, ed., *Uncollected Letters of Algernon Charles Swinburne*, vol. 1 (London: Pickering and Chatto, 2005), 20.

18 Dante Gabriel Rossetti, "The Stealthy School of Criticism," *Athenaeum*, December 1871, pp. 792–94.

19 Letter from Henry James to Alice James, 10 March 1869, in Percy Lubbock, ed., *Letters of Henry James*, vol. 1 (London: Scribner's, 1920), 18.

20 Lady Georgiana Burne-Jones, *Memorials of Edward Burne-Jones* (London: Macmillan, 1904), 231.

21 Quoted in Fiona MacCarthy, *William Morris: A Life for Our Time* (New York: Knopf, 1995), 134.

22 Val Prinsep, "A Chapter from a Painter's Reminiscences: The Oxford Circle: Rossetti, Burne-Jones, and William Morris," *Magazine of Art*, no. 2 (1904): 168.

23 Quoted in MacCarthy, *Morris*, 364, ill. VIII.

24 Letter from D. G. Rossetti to Jane Morris, February 4, 1870, William Fredeman, ed., *The Correspondence of Dante Gabriel Rossetti*, 8 vols. (Cambridge, UK: Brewer, 2002–2008), 4:362.

25 *Letters of Henry James*, 1:17.

26 *Saturday Review*, June 1, 1872.

27 Richard Burton, *Wanderings in West Africa*, vol. 2 (New York: Dover, 1991), 295.

28 Ibid., 286.

29 Richard Burton, *A Mission to Gelele, King of Dahome*, vol. 2 (London: Tylston and Edwards, 1893), 49.

30 Justin McCarthy, *Reminiscences*, vol. 2 (London: Harper, 1899), 285.

31 Isabel Burton, *The Romance of Isabel Lady Burton: The Story of Her Life*, vol. 1 (New York: Dodd Mead, 1897), 166.

32 Wilfrid Scawen Blunt, *My Diaries*, vol. 2 (New York: Knopf, 1921), 130–31.

33 Ibid., 131.

34 Depending on the source, the year is given as 1850, 1851, or 1852.

35 Isabel Burton, *Romance*, 1:52.

36 Ibid., 91.

37 Lord Redesdale, *Memoirs*, vol. 2 (London: Hutchinson, 1915), 562.

38 Isabel Burton, *Romance*, 1:84.

39 Ibid., 91–92.

40 Ibid., 82.

41 Thomas Wright, *The Life of Sir Richard Burton*, vol. 1 (London: Everett, 1906), 142.

42 Quoted in Edward Rice, *Captain Sir Richard Francis Burton* (New York: Scribner's, 1990), 355.

43 Blunt, *My Diaries*, 2:128.

44 Isabel Burton, *The Life of Sir Richard F. Burton*, 2 vols. (London: Chapman and Hall, 1893), 1:450–51.

45 Ibid., 451.

46 Florence Nightingale, *Cassandra: An Essay* (New York: Feminist Press, 1979), 116.

47 Isabel Burton, "Preface," *Explorations of the Highlands of the Brazil*, by Richard Burton, vol. 1 (London: Tinsley, 1869), viii.

48 Quoted in Rice, *Captain*, 178.

49 Isabel Burton, *Inner Life of Syria, Palestine, and the Holy Land*, vol. 1 (London: Henry S. King, 1876), 4.

Chapter 4: The Grove of the Evangelist

1 Letter from Swinburne to Richard Monckton Milnes (Lord Houghton), August 18, 1862, in Cecil Lang, ed., *The Swinburne Letters*, 6 vols. (New Haven: Yale University Press, 1959–62), 1:56.

2 Ibid., 54.

3 Letter from R. F. Burton to Leonard Smithers, February 17, 1889, in David Young, ed., "The Selected Correspondence of Sir Richard Burton, 1848–1890" (Ph.D. diss., University of Nebraska at Lincoln, 1979), 266; quoted in Fawn Brodie, *The Devil Drives: A Life of Sir Richard Burton* (Middlesex, UK: Penguin, 1971), 245–46.

4 Quoted in Lang, *Swinburne*, 1:48n.

5 Letter from Swinburne to Richard Monckton Milnes (Lord Houghton), August 18, 1862, in Lang, *Swinburne*, 1:54–55.

6 Swinburne, "Laus Veneris."

7 Quoted in Ian Gibson, *The English Vice: Beating, Sex, and Shame in Victorian England and After* (London: Duckworth, 1978), 103.

8 Letter from Swinburne to Richard Monckton Milnes, February 10, 1863, quoted ibid., 124.

9 From Milnes's commonplace book, quoted ibid., 125.

10 Letter from Swinburne to George Powell, July 29, 1869, in Lang, *Swinburne*, 2:20.

11 Anonymous, *Miss Coote's Confessions*, in *The Pearl*, no. 2, August 1879 (New York: Blue Moon, 1996), 48.

12 Anonymous, *My Secret Life* (New York: Grove Press, 1966), 2196–98.

13 Quoted in Ronald Pearsall, *The Worm in the Bud: The World of Victorian Sexuality* (Gloucestershire: Sutton, 2003), 340.

14 E. B. Pusey, "The Resurrection of the Body," *Parochial and Plain Sermons*, vol. 1 (Oxford: John Henry Parker, 1852), 275.

15 Quoted in Gibson, *English Vice*, 230.

16 Letter from Algernon Charles Swinburne to Edmund Clarence Stedman, February 21, 1875, in Edmund Gosse, ed., *The Letters of Algernon Charles Swinburne*, vol. 1 (New York: John Lane, 1919), 187.

17 Algernon Charles Swinburne, *Lesbia Brandon* (London: Falcon Press, 1952), 9.

18 Ibid., 18.

19 Edmund Gosse, "An Essay on Swinburne," in Lang, *Swinburne*, 6:246.

20 Letter from Swinburne to George Powell, July 29, 1869, in Lang, *Swinburne*, 2:20.

21 Monckton Milnes's commonplace book, 1860, quoted in Ian Gibson, *Erotomaniac: The Secret Life of Henry Spencer Ashbee* (Cambridge, Mass.: Da Capo, 2001), 31.

22 Richard Burton, trans. and ed., *The Book of the Thousand Nights and a Night*, vol. 10 (Denver: Carson-Harper, 1900), 45n.

23 Richard Burton, "Terminal Essay," in *Nights*, 10:204.

24 Isabel Burton, *The Life of Sir Richard Francis Burton*, vol. 1 (London: Chapman and Hall, 1893), 101.

25 Burton, "Terminal Essay," 206.

26 Ibid., 205n.

27 Ibid., 273.

28 Ibid., 238.

29 Ibid., 235.

30 Ibid.

31 Ibid.

32 Edmond and Jules De Goncourt, *Pages from the Goncourt Journals* (New York: New York Review of Books, 2007), 213.

33 Ibid., 213–14.

34 August 16, 1862, entry, in Virginia Surtees, ed., *The Diaries of George Price Boyce* (Norwich, UK: Real World, 1980), 35.

35 Steven Marcus, *The Other Victorians: A Study of Sexuality and Pornography in Mid-Nineteenth-Century England* (New York: Basic Books, 1966), 260.

36 Swinburne, "Arthur's Flogging."

Chapter 5: Cannibals and Other Lovers of Men

1 D. G. Rossetti to Charles Eliot Norton, January 9, 1862, in William Fredeman, ed., *The Correspondence of Dante Gabriel Rossetti*, 8 vols. (Cambridge, UK: Brewer, 2002–08), 2:441.

2 Quoted in Fiona MacCarthy, *William Morris: A Life for Our Time* (New York: Knopf, 1995), 158.

3 Quoted in John William Mackail, *The Life of William Morris* (London: Longmans, 1899), 1:160.

4 Letter from D. G. Rossetti to William Allingham, September 18, 1860, in Fredeman, *Correspondence*, 2:315.

5 Quoted in Jan Marsh, *Dante Gabriel Rossetti: Painter and Poet* (London: Phoenix, 1999), 221.

6 Quoted in Penelope Fitzgerald, *Edward Burne-Jones* (London: Penguin, 1975), 74.

7 Quoted in Mackail, *Life*, 160.

8 Ibid., 336.

9 William Morris, *News from Nowhere* (London: Longmans, 1912), 107.

10 J. Ewing Ritchie, *The Night Side of London* (London: William Tweedie, 1858), 117.

11 Quoted in James Pope-Hennessy, *Monckton Milnes*, vol. 2, *The Flight of Youth* (New York: Farrar, Straus and Cudahy, 1955), 161.

12 Henry Adams, *The Education of Henry Adams: An Autobiography* (New York: Houghton Mifflin, 1918), 141.

13 Walt Whitman, "We Two Boys Together Clinging."

14 Arthur Munby, diary entry, Dec. 2, 1867, quoted in Derek Hudson, *Munby: Man of Two Worlds: The Life and Diaries of Arthur J. Munby, 1828–1910* (London: Murray, 1972), 246.

15 Algernon Charles Swinburne, *William Blake: A Critical Essay* (London: Chatto and Windus, 1906), 335.

16 Edward Sellon, "On the Phallic Worship of India," *Memoirs Read before the Anthropological Society of London*, vol. 1 (London: Trübner, 1865), 334.

17 Richard F. Burton, "Notes on Certain Matters connected with the Dahoman," *Memoirs Read before the Anthropological Society of London,* vol. 1: 308.

18 Letter from Swinburne to M. D. Conway, November 7, 1866, Cecil Lang, ed., *The Swinburne Letters*, 6 vols. (New Haven: Yale University Press, 1959–62), 1:308.

19 Dante Gabriel Rossetti to George Price Boyce, October 20, 1862, in Fredeman, *Correspondence*, 2:495.

20 Letter from George Meredith to Frederick A. Maxse, June 9, 1862, in C. L. Cline, ed., *Letters of George Meredith*, vol. 1 (London: Oxford University Press, 1970), 149.

21 William Michael Rossetti, *Dante Gabriel Rossetti: His Family-Letters*, vol. 1 (London: Ellis and Elvey, 1895), 229.

22 Arthur Munby, diary entry, May 12, 1863, in Hudson, *Munby*, 160.

23 Letter from Henry James to John LaFarge, June 20, 1869, in Leon Edel, ed., *Henry James: Letters*, vol. 1 (New York: Alexander James, 1975), 120.

24 Letter from D. G. Rossetti to Ford Madox Brown, November 2, 1862, Fredeman, *Correspondence*, 2:501.

25 Quoted in Marsh, *Rossetti*, 319.

26 Quoted in Georgiana Burne-Jones, *Memorials of Edward Burne-Jones* (London: Macmillan, 1906), 164.

27 Letter from D. G. Rossetti to Frances Mary Lavinia Rossetti (his mother), November 12, 1864, in Fredeman, *Correspondence*, 2:209.

28 Quoted in Stanley Weintraub, *Whistler: A Biography* (New York: Da Capo, 2001), 93.

29 Quoted in Marsh, *Rossetti*, 259.

30 Quoted in N. John Hall, *Max Beerbohm: A Kind of Life* (New Haven: Yale University Press, 2002), 149.

31 Quoted in Fitzgerald, *Burne-Jones*, 72.

32 Quoted in Edmund Gosse, *The Life of Algernon Charles Swinburne* (London: Macmillan, 1917), 106.

33 Quoted in Philip Henderson, *Swinburne: Portrait of a Poet* (New York: Macmillan, 1974), 73.

34 Quoted ibid., 73.

35 Quoted in Rikky Rooksby, *A. C. Swinburne: A Poet's Life* (Aldershot, UK: Scolar Press, 1997), 83.

36 Letter from George Meredith to William Hardman, October 1868, in Cline, *Letters*, 1:376.

37 Letter from D. G. Rossetti to William Allingham, December 18, 1856, in Fredeman, *Correspondence*, 2:147.

38 William Morris, "The Blue Closet."

39 Swinburne, "Before the Mirror."

40 William Morris, *Clarion*, November 19, 1892.

41 Letter from Charley Faulkner to Crom Prince, April 1862, quoted in Mackail, *Life*, 157.

42 Quoted in Mackail, *Life*, 155.

43 Lady Georgiana Burne-Jones, *Memorials of Edward Burne-Jones* (London: Macmillan, 1904), 2:159.

44 William Morris, "The Beauty of Life," *Hopes and Fears for Art* (London: Longmans, 1908), 103.

45 Edward Carpenter, *Towards Democracy* (London: Swan Sonnenschein, 1905), 69.

46 Edward Carpenter, *My Days and Dreams* (New York: Scribner, 1916), 77.

47 Quoted in Chushichi Tsuzuki, *Edward Carpenter, 1844–1928: Prophet of Human Fellowship* (London: Cambridge University Press, 1980), 22.

48 Carpenter, *Towards Democracy*, 28–29.

49 Quoted in Tsuzuki, *Carpenter*, 23.

50 E. M. Forster, "Terminal Note," *Maurice* (London: Penguin, 1972).

51 Quoted in Timothy d'Arch Smith, *Love in Earnest* (London: Routledge, 1970), 24.

Chapter 6: Feasting with Panthers

1 Letter from Simeon Solomon to Algernon Charles Swinburne, November 1869, in Cecil Lang, ed., *The Swinburne Letters*, 6 vols. (New Haven: Yale University Press, 1959–62), 2:49.

2 *The Memoirs of John Addington Symonds*, ed. Phyllis Grosskurth (Chicago: Hutchinson, 1984), 186.

3 Anonymous, *Teleny; or, The Reverse of the Medal* (London: Wordsworth, 1995), 80.

4 Quoted in Chester Lewis, David Leitch, and Colin Simpson, *The Cleveland Street Affair* (London: Weidenfeld and Nicolson, 1977), 105.

5 Quoted in Morris Kaplan, *Sodom on the Thames: Sex, Love, and Scandal in Wilde Times* (Ithaca, N.Y.: Cornell University Press, 2005), 189–90, 195.

6 Quoted in Richard Ellmann, *Oscar Wilde* (New York: Knopf, 1988), 460.

7 *Memoirs of Symonds*, 253–54.

8 Anonymous, *My Secret Life* (New York: Grove Press, 1966), 1151.

9 Ibid.

10 Ibid., 1538.

11 Ibid., 1562.

12 Ibid., 1562–63.

13 Quoted in *Solomon: A Family of Painters: Abraham Solomon, 1823–1862, Rebecca Solomon, 1832–1889, Simeon Solomon, 1840–1905* (London: Geffrye Museum, 1985), 22.

14 Quoted in Bernard Falk, *Five Years Dead: A Postscript to "He Laughed in Fleet Street"* (London: Book Club, 1938), 321.

15 Quoted in Colin Cruise, ed., *Love Revealed: Simeon Solomon and the Pre-Raphaelites* (London: Merrell, 2005), 11.

16 Quoted in Falk, *Five Years*, 321.

17 Quoted in Gayle Seymour, "The Life and Work of Simeon Solomon" (Ph.D. diss., University of California at Santa Barbara, 1986), 29.

18 Falk, *Five Years*, 327.

19 Richard Burton, "Terminal Essay," in *The Book of the Thousand Nights and a Night*, vol. 10 (Denver: Carson-Harper, 1900), 209n.

20 Algernon Charles Swinburne, "Simeon Solomon: Notes on his 'Vision of Love' and Other Studies," *A Pilgrimage of Pleasure*, ed. by R. G. Badger (Boston: Gorham Press, 1913), 51.

21 Quoted in *Solomon: A Family of Painters*, 26.

22 Swinburne, "Simeon Solomon," 54.

23 Quoted in Seymour, "Life," 160.

24 *Illustrated London News*, February 6, 1869, p. 135.

25 Ibid., February 12, 1870, p. 182.

26 Quoted in Cruise, *Love*, 155.

27 Letter from Oscar Wilde to Lord Alfred Douglas, January–March 1897, in *The Complete Letters of Oscar Wilde*, ed. Merlin Holland and Rupert Hart-Davis (New York: Henry Holt, 2000), 758.

28 Letter from Wilde to Lord Alfred Douglas, January–March 1897, in *Complete Letters*, 759.

29 Oscar Wilde, *The Critic as Artist* (New York: Mondial, 2007).

30 Oscar Wilde, "Preface," *The Picture of Dorian Gray* (New York: Charterhouse Press, 1904), xiv.

31 Oscar Wilde, *Decorative Art in America*, ed. Richard Butler Glaenzer (New York: Brentano, 1906), 216n.

32 Quoted in N. John Hall, *Max Beerbohm: A Kind of Life* (New Haven: Yale University Press, 2002), 223.

33 Quoted in Joseph Pearce, *The Unmasking of Oscar Wilde* (San Francisco: Ignatius Press, 2004), 129.

34 Quoted in Ellmann, *Oscar Wilde*, 35.

35 Quoted in Pearce, *Unmasking*, 63.

36 Quoted in Ellmann, *Oscar Wilde*, 270.

37 Letter from Wilde to H. C. Marillier, December 12, 1885, in *Collected Letters*, 272.

38 Letter from Swinburne to Clarence Stedman, April 4, 1882, in Lang, *Swinburne*, 4:266.

39 Quoted in Neil McKenna, *The Secret Life of Oscar Wilde* (New York: Basic Books, 2006), 463.

40 Quoted in ibid., 14.

41 Quoted in Ellmann, *Oscar Wilde*, 156.

42 Quoted in Jan Marsh, *Dante Gabriel Rossetti: Painter and Poet* (London: Phoenix, 1999), 259.

43 Quoted in Kaplan, *Sodom*, 245.

44 Quoted in H. Montgomery Hyde, *The Trials of Oscar Wilde* (New York: Dover, 1973), 340–41.

45 Quoted in Ellmann, *Oscar Wilde*, 483.

46 Quoted in Alan Sinfield, *The Wilde Century: Effeminacy, Oscar Wilde and the Queer Moment* (New York: Columbia University Press, 1994), 3.

47 Havelock Ellis, *Studies in the Psychology of Sex*, vol. 2 (Philadelphia: F. A. Davis, 1921), 63.

48 Quoted in R. F. Foster, *W. B. Yeats: A Life* (New York: Oxford University Press, 1998), 80.

49 Quoted in Seymour, "Life," 205.

50 Ibid.

51 Letter from Swinburne to George Powell, June 6, 1873, Lang, *Swinburne*, 2:253.

52 Letter from D. G. Rossetti to Ford Madox Brown, April 19, 1873, in William Fredeman, ed., *The Correspondence of Dante Gabriel Rossetti*, 8 vols. (Cambridge, UK: Brewer, 2002–08), 6:125.

53 Letter from Swinburne to Theodore Watts, December 1, 1873, in Lang, *Swinburne*, 2:26.

54 Letter from Swinburne to Edmund Gosse, October 15, 1879, in Lang, *Swinburne*, 4:107.

55 Swinburne, "Simeon Solomon," 63.

56 Arthur Symons, *Studies on Modern Painters* (Freeport, N.Y.: Ayer, 1925), 8.

57 Quoted in *Solomon: A Family of Painters*, 30.

58 Quoted in Seymour, "Life," 221.

59 Quoted in Henry Arthur Sandberg, "The Androgynous Vision of a Victorian Outsider: The Life and Work of Simeon Solomon" (Ph.D. diss., Drew University, 2000), 188.

Chapter 7: The Science of Sex

1 Richard Burton, *Personal Narrative of a Pilgrimage to Al-Madinah and Meccah* (New York: Dover, 1964), 1:9.

2 Isabel Burton, *The Life of Captain Sir Richard Burton*, 2 vols. (London: Chapman and Hall, 1893), 2:59.

3 Kalyan Mall, *Ananga Ranga*, trans. Richard Burton and Frederick Arbuthnot (Cosmopoli: Privately printed for the Kama Shastra Society, 1885), 129.

4 Ibid., 93.

5 Ibid., 120.

6 Ibid.

7 Letter from Richard Burton to Richard Monckton Milnes, March 2, 1875, in David Young, ed., "The Selected Correspondence of Sir Richard Burton, 1848–1890" (Ph.D. diss., University of Nebraska at Lincoln, 1979), 212.

8 This is Mendes's speculation, based on his careful research of the rings of Victorian pornographers.

9 This material is also taken from Mendes's research.

10 From *Cythera's Hymnal*, quoted in Ronald Pearsall, *The Worm in the Bud: The World of Victorian Sexuality* (Gloucestershire: Sutton, 2003), 376–77.

11 Ibid., 375.

12 Quoted in Rikky Rooksby, *A. C. Swinburne: A Poet's Life* (Aldershot, UK: Scolar Press, 1997), 168.

13 *Times*, November 13, 1886.

14 Letter from Richard Burton to Richard Monckton Milnes, August 1859, quoted in James Pope-Hennessy, *Monckton Milnes*, vol. 2, *The Flight of Youth* (New York: Farrar, Straus and Cudahy, 1955), 125.

15 Quoted in Dane Kennedy, *The Highly Civilized Man: Richard Burton and the Victorian World* (Cambridge, Mass.: Harvard University Press, 2005), 217.

16 Quoted in Thomas Wright, *The Life of Sir Richard Burton*, vol. 2 (London: Everett, 1906), 66.

17 Richard Burton, "Terminal Essay," in *The Book of the Thousand Nights and a Night*, vol. 10 (Denver: Carson-Harper, 1900), 199–200.

18 William Acton, *The Functions and Disorders of the Reproductive Organs* (London: Churchill, 1865), 95.

19 *The Kama Sutra of Vatsayana*, trans. Sir Richard F. Burton (New York: Arkana, 1991), 252.

20 Ibid., 64.

21 Ibid., 242.

22 Burton, *Thousand Nights*, 4:32n.

23 *Kama Sutra*, 205.

24 Ibid., 219, 208.

25 Burton, *Pilgrimage*, 1:82–83.

26 Ibid., 88.

27 Ibid., 89.

28 Quoted in Fawn Brodie, *The Devil Drives: A Life of Sir Richard Burton* (Middlesex, UK: Penguin, 1971), 109.

29 Ibid., 107.

30 Burton, *Pilgrimage*, 1:9.

31 Burton, *Thousand Nights*, 1:xxv.

32 Burton, *Pilgrimage*, 1:59–60.

33 Ibid., 60.

34 Burton, *Thousand Nights*, 10:225.

35 The articles were then collected in the 4 vols. of *London Labour and the London Poor*.

36 Anonymous, *My Secret Life* (New York: Grove Press, 1966), 126.

37 Ibid., 127.

38 Ibid., 1940.

39 Richard Burton, *Anthropologia*, vol. 1 (London: Bailliere, Tindall, and Cox, 1875), 2–3.

Chapter 8: Burton's Exotica

1 Quoted in Mary S. Lovell, *A Rage to Live: A Biography of Richard and Isabel Burton* (New York: Norton, 1998), 688.

2 Isabel Burton, *The Life of Captain Sir Richard F. Burton*, vol. 2 (London: Chapman and Hall, 1893), 317.

3 Richard Burton, "Preface," *The Book of the Thousand Nights and a Night*, trans. Burton, vol. 1 (Denver: Carson-Harper, 1900), 1.

4 Ibid., 10:110–11.

5 Quoted in Fawn Brodie, *The Devil Drives: A Life of Sir Richard Burton* (Middlesex, UK: Penguin, 1971), 382.

6 Quoted in Lovell, *Rage*, 670.

7 Quoted in Brodie, *Devil*, 383.

8 Isabel Burton, *Life*, 2:298.

9 Ibid.

10 Quoted in Dane Kennedy, *The Highly Civilized Man: Richard Burton and the Victorian World* (Cambridge, Mass.: Harvard University Press, 2005), 227.

11 Ibid.

12 Quoted in Brodie, *Devil*, 391.

13 Isabel Burton, *Life*, 2:284.

14 Quoted in Rikky Rooksby, *A. C. Swinburne: A Poet's Life* (Aldershot, UK: Scolar Press, 1997), 218.

15 Charles Ashbee, *A Few Chapters in Workshop Reconstruction and Citizenship* (London: Guild and School of Handicraft, 1894), 160–61.

16 *My Secret Life*, 861.

17 C. R. Ashbee, *"Grannie": A Victorian Cameo* (London: Oxford, 1939), 50–53.

18 Burton, trans. and ed., "Tale of Nur al-Din Ali and His Son Badr al-Din Hasan," *The Arabian Nights* (New York: Modern Library, 2001), 148.

19 Ibid., 151.

20 Ibid., 151–52.

21 Ibid., 170.

22 Burton, "Preface," xxx.

23 Burton, trans. and ed., "How Abu Hasan Brake Wind," *Arabian Nights*, 327.

24 Ibid., 328.

25 Burton, "Preface," xxiv.

26 Burton, "Terminal Essay," *Thousand Nights*, 10:192.

27 Burton, *Thousand Nights*, 1:14.

28 Ibid.

29 J. S. Cotton obituary, in *Academy*, October 25, 1890, 365.

30 Burton, *Thousand Nights*, 10:21n.

31 Ibid., 5:76.

32 Ibid., 1:350n.

33 Ibid., 10:138.

34 Ibid., 239n.

35 Ibid., 203.

36 Quoted in James Nelson, *Publisher to the Decadents: Leonard Smithers in the Careers of Beardsley, Wilde, Dowson* (University Park: Pennsylvania State University Press, 2000), 14.

37 Quoted in Neil McKenna, *The Secret Life of Oscar Wilde* (New York: Basic Books, 2006), 260.

38 Burton, *Thousand Nights*, 10:205.

39 Ibid., 207.

40 Ibid., 209.

41 Ibid., 207.

42 Isabel Burton, *Life*, 2:262.

43 Ibid., 442.

44 Burton claimed that "scented" was a better translation than "perfumed," although it is possible he merely wanted to distinguish it from the first translation.

45 John Addington Symonds, *Vagabunduli Libellus* (London, 1884), 127.

46 John Addington Symonds, *A Problem in Modern Ethics, Being an Inquiry into the Phenomenon of Sexual Inversion* (London: Privately Printed, 1896), 8.

47 Ibid., 13.

48 *Priapeia*, trans. Richard Burton and Leonard Smithers (London: Privately Printed, 1890), Poem 9.

49 Ibid., Poem 6.

50 Ibid., Poem 10.

51 Ibid., Poem 68.

52 Quoted in Brodie, *Devil*, 416.

53 Letter from Oscar Wilde to Reggie Turner, August 10, 1897, *The Complete Letters of Oscar Wilde*, ed. Merlin Holland and Rupert Hart-Davis (New York: Henry Holt, 2000), 630–31.

54 Peter Mendes, *Clandestine Erotic Fiction in English, 1800–1930: A Bibliographical Study* (Hants, UK: Scolar Press, 1993), 16.

Chapter 9: Cabinets of Curiosity

1 Anonymous, *My Secret Life* (New York: Grove Press, 1966), 1815.

2 Ibid., 1816.

3 Ibid., 2074.

4 Ibid., 2075.

5 Ibid., 2078.

6 Ibid., 2078–80.

7 Ibid., 1504.

8 Ibid., 2043.

9 Ibid.

10 Letter from Swinburne to Alice Swinburne (his sister), August 10, 1869, in Cecil Lang, ed., *The Swinburne Letters*, 6 vols. (New Haven: Yale University Press, 1959–62), 2:22.

11 Ibid.

12 Ibid.

13 Letter from Swinburne to Lady Jane Henrietta Swinburne (his mother), August 13, 1869, in Lang, *Swinburne*, 2:24.

14 Swinburne, "Elegy."

15 Edmund Gosse, *The Life of Algernon Charles Swinburne* (London: Macmillan, 1917), 179.

16 Wilfred Scawen Blunt, *My Diaries*, vol. 2 (New York: Knopf, 1921), 129–31.

17 Burton, "Terminal Essay," *The Book of the Thousand Nights and a Night*, vol. 10 (Denver: Carson-Harper, 1900), 207.

18 Ibid.

19 Ibid., 206–7.

20 Ibid., 208–10.

21 Ibid., 248.

22 Ibid.

23 Ibid., 217.

24 Ibid.

25 George Augustus Sala, *Gaslight and Daylight* (London: Tinsley, 1872), 217.

26 Quoted in Linda Merrill, *The Peacock Room: A Cultural Biography* (New Haven: Yale University Press, 1998), 60.

27 Letter from Dante Gabriel Rossetti to Madox Brown, 1864, in William Michael Rossetti, ed., *The Rossetti Papers, 1862–70* (London: Sands, 1903), 49.

28 William Michael Rossetti, *Some Reminiscences of William Michael Rossetti*, vol. 1 (New York: Scribner's, 1906), 283.

29 Quoted in E. R. and J. Pennell, *The Whistler Journal* (Philadelphia: Lippincott, 1921), 170.

30 Henry Spencer Ashbee, *Index Librorum Prohibiorum* (London: Privately Printed, 1877), xxvi.

31 Ibid., lii.

32 Ibid., xxviii.

33 Henry Spencer Ashbee, *Catena Librorum Tacendorum* (London: Privately Printed, 1885), 189.

34 Ashbee, *Index Librorum Prohibiorum*, viii.

35 Ibid., xxvi, n29.

Credits

Illustrations with text

p. 21: Hulton Archive, Getty
p. 53: Hulton Archive, Getty
p. 62: Hulton Archive, Getty

Color insert

1. © Tate, London 2010
2. © Tate, London 2010
3. © Tate, London 2010
4. © Tate, London 2010
5. © Manchester Art Gallery, UK / The Bridgeman Art Library
6. © Walker Art Gallery, National Museums Liverpool / The Bridgeman Art Library
7. © The Barber Institute of Fine Arts, University of Birmingham / The Bridgeman Art Library
8. Hulton Archive, Getty
9. Popperfoto Collection, Getty

Index

Page numbers in *italics* refer to illustrations.